DATE DUE

JOSTEN'S 30 508

GLOSSARY OF ART,

ARCHITECTURE

AND DESIGN

SINCE 1945

TERMS AND LABELS DESCRIBING MOVEMENTS
STYLES AND GROUPS DERIVED FROM THE
VOCABULARY OF ARTISTS AND CRITICS

JOHN A WALKER
BA ALA

GLOSSARY OF ART,

ARCHITECTURE

AND DESIGN

SINCE 1945

TERMS AND LABELS DESCRIBING MOVEMENTS
STYLES AND GROUPS DERIVED FROM THE
VOCABULARY OF ARTISTS AND CRITICS

CLIVE BINGLEY *b* LONDON

FIRST PUBLISHED 1973 BY CLIVE BINGLEY LTD
16 PEMBRIDGE ROAD LONDON W11 · SET IN 10 ON
12 LINOTYPE PLANTIN WITH SPARTAN TITLING
AND PRINTED IN THE UK BY THE CENTRAL PRESS
(ABERDEEN) LTD · COPYRIGHT © JOHN A WALKER ·
ALL RIGHTS RESERVED · 0 85157 153 0

CONTENTS

ACKNOWLEDGEMENTS

My thanks to David Cheshire, librarian of Hornsey College of Art, for his constant supply of references, to Michael Hazzledine for the entry on Concrete Poetry, to Lynn Riggall for the loan of her thesis on Flash Art, and to Judy Hoffberg for information concerning certain American groups.

JOHN A WALKER

INTRODUCTION

I am for Kool-Art, 7-UPart, Pepsi-Art, Sunshine art, 39 cents art, 15 cents art, Vatronol art, Dro-bomb art, Vam art, Menthol art, L × M art, Ex-lax art, Venida art, Heaven Hill art, Pamrly art, San-o-med art, Rx art, 9·99 art, Now art, New art, How art, Fire sale art, Last chance art, Only art, Diamond art, Tomorrow art, Franks art, Ducks art, Meat-o-rama art. CLAES OLDENBURG 1967

It is a commonplace that the number and variety of art movements, styles, groups and techniques have increased rapidly since the beginnings of modern art; since 1945 the rate of increase seems to have been exponential. Part of this proliferation may be more apparent than real in that the means of recording and disseminating information about art has probably expanded at a greater rate than art activities themselves; thus we may be more aware of current art than our forebears were of the art of their time. Nevertheless the increase is substantial enough and has been accompanied by a matching growth in the number of art terms, or labels, to encompass new developments.

As Clement Greenberg remarks: ' There are Assemblage, Pop and Op; there are Hard Edge, Colour Field and Shaped Canvas; there are Neo-Figurative, Funky and Environmental; there are Minimal, Kinetic, and Luminous; there are Computer, Cybernetic, Systems, Participatory—and so on. (One of the really new things about art in the sixties is the rash of labels . . . most of them devised by artists themselves—which is likewise new; art-labelling used to be the affair of journalists.)'[1]

Even the most cursory examination of today's art books, journals, newspaper articles and exhibition catalogues will confirm that a considerable nomenclature exists and there is no adequate published guide, that I am aware of, to help the reader negotiate the intricacies of modern art criticism.

The complexity of the contemporary art scene begins with the individual artist: he may be born in one country, train in another, work in several others, produce art belonging to three or four internationally recognised styles in the course of his career, he may also

7

associate with a number of polemical groups. The development of new media extends the coverage given to art, and the international circulation of periodicals and exhibitions brings a knowledge of new art to the most obscure corners of the earth. These factors tend to accelerate the rate of turnover of styles and labels (a succession of styles is already inherent in the notion of avant garde art). An art critic may organise a large exhibition to illustrate a new tendency only to find he has conducted its burial service, the massive exposure of a particular mode of art can provoke, within months, a reaction among younger artists who will develop art forms extolling values antagonistic to those of the first mode. Global conditions prevail and it is extremely difficult to make a convincing case for nationalistic schools of art, though occasionally an art term reflects the existence of a local movement.

Education and affluence in the developed countries have created a considerable interest in the arts. The existence, on the one hand, of an avid public and, on the other, a medley of art styles has led to an unprecedented demand for interpretation. The art critic attempts to communicate his aesthetic response to living art by means of words; in the face of new art the existing vocabulary often proves inadequate, so, as the artist discovers new forms, the critic coins new labels: an inexorable process. It should also be kept in mind that art critics are primarily journalists and work under the pressure of deadlines and a chronic lack of column space; consequently they are compelled to adopt catchwords as a form of shorthand.[2] Such writing has been accused of being a secret language developed by art critics for private communication via art magazines. Each critic, like the artists he discusses, wants to be remembered for his contribution to art history, and therefore he generates labels in the hope that his will gain public acceptance while his rival's terms fail.

The most prolific centre for art since the second world war has been in the United States; their art has also been the most original (not withstanding Patrick Heron's vaunting of British art achievements) and the triumph of American art is matched by the triumph of American art criticism, for the most creative and influential art critics are American or live and work in the United States: Clement Greenberg, Harold Rosenberg, Michael Fried, Jack Burnham, Max Kozloff, Lucy Lippard, Robert Morris, John Coplans, Lawrence Alloway (English but resident in the USA), among others. England fares rather better in the field of architectural criticism, having pro-

8

duced a number of polemical writers—Reyner Banham, Peter Cook, Charles Jencks—who delight in labels, categories and classifications of current architecture and design.

Many commentators on art have expressed profound doubts about the practice of art labelling; generally they oppose it on the grounds that it puts an obstacle in the way of appreciation, distancing the spectator from the artwork, for example consider the following quotations:

' One of people's hang-ups is labelling and categorising.'[3]

' Classification has always bothered people interested in visual art . . . if one can know where a work of art " belongs " one can diminish its challenge to the imagination and emotions.'[4]

' People who intellectualise about art are devoted to the idea of art history and therefore everything must have its place, its category and its labels.'[5]

Some artists also resent being categorised. As Jaroslav Serpan remarks:' Strange situation! Assigned by the inevitable stickers on of labels to several successive movements, how is it that I have never felt completely at home in any one of them?'[6]

The architectural writer Peter Collins objects to the speed with which labels are applied: '. . . nothing but frustration can result from labelling nascent developments with catchwords, and categorising their (architects) first expressions as paradigms, before the creators themselves are clearly aware of what they are aiming at, and before it is certain that the forms produced are of any historic worth.'[7]

In reply one might ask how long a critic should wait before he coins a name, before he determines historical worth—six months? Six years? Sixty years? Explorers name unknown mountains and rivers as they discover them; similarly, critics name new art or architecture as it appears, or when existing works are suddenly perceived in a new light. Art labels survive, or die, according to the same laws of evolution and change as affect the art they refer to.

Though labels are heavily criticised, the precise reasons why they are considered evil are rarely made explicit; exceptionally, one writer claimed that the architectural label ' New Brutalism ' was a bad term because the idea of ' brutal ' architecture put off prospective clients.

The most cogent and trenchant attack on art labels was mounted by Dore Ashton in 1966, when she compared them to the brand names of commodities, and claimed that art critics were performing middle man, packaging and merchandising operations in the cultural sphere,

9

directly paralleling those found in the business world. Furthermore she complained that critics encouraged status obsolescence and contrived fashions in art to produce a rapid turnover: 'the consumption of cultural products is up, but independent experience is down, brand names and slogans proliferate, but deep comprehension dwindles.'[8]

Ashton's analysis is undoubtedly correct, but one wonders whether she objects to packaging in the supermarket as much as she does in the cultural sphere; presumably the sales techniques she deplores are the result of vast industrial production and expanding economies. It seems likely that the introduction of merchandising techniques in the promotion of culture is the inevitable consequence of a comparable increase in the production of art, an increase made possible by the surplus wealth resulting from industrialisation. No solution to this dilemma can be expected until a radical change has taken place in the economic and social structure of Western consumer societies.

Most adverse comments on art labels reveal, it seems to me, a lamentable ignorance of the role of language in human affairs. The coining of neologisms to describe new phenomena and concepts, in order to add to the existing total of cultural knowledge, is a basic activity of human perception, thought and communication. A plausible reason for the dislike of new terms is given by Stroud Cornock: 'any change in our vocabulary must—by disturbing our delicate superstructure of belief and assumptions—threaten our existing cultural modalities . . . an unfamiliar vocabulary is like an insurgent or guerrilla force . . .'[9]

The development of specialist vocabularies characterises all new fields of knowledge, whether scientific, technological, social or artistic, without exception. What seems to disturb art commentators is the disparity between the label and the art it denotes, but *this disparity occurs between all words and the objects they describe*. Ultimately to criticise art labelling is to criticise language for being what it is. Linguists confirm that our picture of reality is, to a large extent, conditioned by the language of the group to which we belong, but, as I have already stated, this is a general problem and is not restricted to the vocabulary of art criticism. It is absurd to believe that the visual arts could exist in human experience isolated from the context of language.[10]

In any event, the flow of new terms will not be stemmed by mere disapproval. Even if art critics could be silenced there would still remain many artists prepared to manufacture slogans and labels to publicise their own work. Furthermore art feeds on art and it can be argued that the essence of the art of the late 1960's and early 1970's is that it is a form of art criticism: Conceptual artists consciously usurp the role of art critics. Indeed one of the insights of Conceptual Art is the importance of language as supportive to art, as Charles Harrison points out:

'Any information which the artist provides will inevitably become a part of the spectator's area of consideration—and this includes titles, however flippantly added.'

'. . . the spectator's experience of the work of art will come to include work by writers and others. Mud does stick. Fried's criticism is now a part of Noland's art. No wonder the better artists tend to protect their art from indifferent exposure; ie to protect the idea from indiscriminate presentation of its presentation. The notion of " cubes " obscures the endeavour of Braque and Picasso and no critic's initiative will prize it loose.'[11]

Evidently Harrison disapproves of Michael Fried's critical writing, and of the label ' Cubism ', but he does not suggest that criticism and labels can be dispensed with. On the contrary, he is pointing out that artists, having realised their importance, are increasingly exercising control over them.

In my view the only viable approach to art labels is not to ignore them but to confront them head on, to discriminate between the useful and the obscurantist. After all, criticism is a creative activity and some practitioners are more skilful than others, so that terms vary markedly in their usefulness or appropriateness. Udo Kultermann condemns all art labels as ' imprecise, misleading ' and believes they are ' symptomatic of the helplessness of the majority of art critics in the face of the phenomena which now assail them ' (ie the multiplicity of trends).[12] However, let us consider the term ' Minimal Art ', which seems to me an example of helpful description in that the adjective ' minimal ' summarises (as far as one word ever can) the nature of this particular mode of art. On the other hand ' New Realism ' is much less useful: ' new ' will soon lose its currency, and ' realism ' already possesses a cluster of historical associations. J P Hodin points out that art criticism is historically orientated (always relating the new to the past[13]), hence the tendency to attach the prefixes ' new ', or ' neo ', ' post' to existing terms: for example ' Neo-Dada ', ' Post-Minimalism '. Some writers resort to absurd and clumsy combinations of existing terms in order to categorise new art; for example the Argentine critic

Aldo Pellegrini has devised phrases such as ' Surrealising Neo-Figuration ' and ' Post-Expressionistic-Neo-Figuration '; clearly in these situations a neologism would have been infinitely preferable.

Frequently, critics fail to define their terms or to indicate the context in which they first appeared, and terms quickly become debased or loose in meaning as a result.

Often the intention behind the use of a particular label is derogatory; ironically such labels frequently stick (this was the case with ' Impressionism '). Many critics dismiss a colleague's terms with derision but in the process they give the despised terms wider currency. Unquestionably, terms become obsolete extremely quickly and many in this glossary are already of historical, sociological, or mere curiosity value. Some art terms are fatuous and I may be accused of giving them a spurious authority by listing them in glossary form, but often, even apparently trivial labels reveal the existence of a widespread approach to art, or the influence of a particular philosophical idea, peculiar to a certain period—for example, the use of the word ' situation ' by several different groups of artists around 1960.

A striking characteristic of art since 1945, revealed by the terminology of art criticism, is its desperate eclecticism, as Janet Daley confirms: ' The use of jargon in fashionable art propaganda is beyond parody but what distinguishes it from other jargon-ridden fields . . . is the promiscuousness with which it raids wildly disparate and often mutually contradictory fields of intellectual endeavour for its vocabulary . . .'[14]

This borrowing of concepts from non-art disciplines has added to the difficulty of compiling this glossary, because I cannot claim more than slight acquaintanceship with philosophy, ecology, science, technology, structuralism, linguistics . . . Therefore I apologise in advance to any specialists in these areas who find my treatment of their field of knowledge cursory.

Another salient feature of art since 1945 that has emerged during the compilation of this glossary is the overwhelming influence of a single artist: Marcel Duchamp. As an ex-student of Richard Hamilton I have been aware of the importance of Duchamp for many years, but I had not grasped the extent to which his art and example had informed the development of post-war Western art; whole movements appear to have been founded on his smallest gestures.

As I stated at the beginning of this introduction, there is no convenient source of reference concerning art labels appearing in periodical articles, exhibition catalogue notes, or the texts of art books (but almost never in their indexes) since 1945. (The end of the second world war was chosen as a starting point because the pre-war period has been reasonably well documented, and in order to limit the scale of the enquiry. However, I have not adhered rigidly to the date limit: the term 'Art Deco' has been included even though it refers to a pre-war style; other terms concerning taste have been listed because they are ignored by most art dictionaries.) Existing art dictionaries pay little heed to recent developments. McGraw Hill's five volume work, published in 1969, defines 'Op', 'Pop' and 'Kinetic', but as it encompasses the whole history of art the contemporary scene cannot be covered in detail. Art dictionaries also tend to ignore design and architectural terms, such as 'Borax', 'Styling', 'Environmentalism'; concepts of taste, such as 'Kitsch', 'Camp' or 'Good Design', are particularly elusive.

Normally, art dictionaries consist of short essays written by a number of different authors produced under the direction of an editor who attempts to impose a consistent approach and to achieve a balance between contributions; all too frequently poor modulation between terms and inadequate cross referencing result from this method. Some prestigious works, like the *Oxford companion to art*, are not as useful as they might be because they fail to provide a separate name and subject index to their A-Z entries, thus making it difficult to trace information scattered by the alphabetical arrangement.

The art magazine *Leonardo* regularly includes glossaries of terms derived from articles published in each issue, but unfortunately the entries are usually too brief or partial to be generally useful; furthermore, they consist, in the main, of definitions of scientific and technical processes rather than of art movements, styles or groups.

All the terms in this glossary are derived from the published literature on art since 1945 (see bibliographical note) and were selected on a pragmatic basis: the well known terms—'Abstract Expressionism', 'Colour-Field Painting', etc—selected themselves, the less familiar terms were noted if they were used by several different writers, and occasionally a term was listed if it encapsulated a useful, but otherwise undifferentiated, notion. The selection process was not merely mechanical; at all times it was tempered by a practical knowledge of art gained through the activity of painting and by regular visits to exhibitions held in London since 1956.

Although the glossary lists the more important foreign terms, the bulk of the entries are Anglo-American. The topics covered include architecture, art—painting, sculpture, ceramics—some graphic and industrial design, and some town planning; excluded are films, theatre, music, literature and fashion. Terms relating to craft operations, tools and technical processes have been excluded because there are several existing dictionaries which list them; also it has been my intention to concentrate on the more conceptual and theoretical notions which are so often neglected by art dictionary compilers. A number of artist's groups and names of art organisations are included, but great selectivity has been exercised in this area, for a separate volume is required to cover groups adequately.

A favourite ploy of art journalists is to name a new form of art after the material employed by the artist, for example, 'Wool Art', 'Sand Art'. The majority of such terms are trivial and self explanatory, and therefore they have been excluded.

Although I have attempted to cover the period since 1945 systematically, most emphasis has been placed on recent art; firstly because of the ever increasing complexity and interconnection of art movements as one moves towards the 1970's, and secondly because the information relating to recent art tends to be scattered in many disparate periodicals and exhibition catalogues which may only be available in a specialist art, or architectural, library, whereas information concerning earlier art movements is generally summarised in books which can be purchased, or borrowed via the public library system.

The glossary is intended primarily as a work of reference, but it could also form the basis of a list of subject headings for the classification of periodical articles in an art library. Furthermore it could serve as an art historical tool: an analysis of terms according to common characteristics would reveal the major trends in art since 1945, for example, one could list terms reflecting the influence of science and technology, terms reflecting the influence of consumerism, terms reflecting formalist preoccupations, etc.

Alphabetical filing in the glossary is word by word. Where a term or phrase is italicised in the body of an entry this means that it is also defined elsewhere in the glossary.

REFERENCES

1 C Greenberg 'Avant garde attitudes: new art in the sixties ' *Studio international* 179 (921) April 1970 p 142.

2 E Lucie Smith ' Problems of the working critic of the modern visual arts ' *British journal of aesthetics* 11 (3) Summer 1971 237-246.

3 J Toche ' Guerrilla Art Action ' *Art and artists* 6 (11) issue No 71 February 1972 p 22.

4 M Kozloff ' The inert and the frenetic '—essay in—*Renderings* (Studio Vista, 1970) p 248.

5 A Mackintosh ' Larry Bell: an interview ' *Art and artists* 6 (10) issue No 70 January 1972 p 39.

6 J Serpan—quoted in—*Abstract art since 1945* by W Haftmann and others (Thames & Hudson, 1971) p 159.

7 P Collins ' Historicism ' *Architectural review* 127 (762) August 1960 101-103.

8 D Ashton ' New York commentary: marketing techniques in the promotion of art ' *Studio international* 172 (883) November 1966 270-273.

9 S Cornock ' Towards a general systems model of the artistic process ' *Control magazine* (6) 1972 3-6.

10 M Black *The labyrinth of language* (Penguin, 1972) 160-165.

11 C Harrison ' Notes towards art work ' *Studio international* 179 (919) February 1970 42-43.

12 U Kultermann *The new painting* (Pall Mall Press, 1969) p 9.

13 J P Hodin ' Modernism '—essay in—*Encyclopedia of world art*, vol 10 (NY, McGraw Hill, 1965) 201-209 columns.

14 J Daley 'Art scientificism ' *Art and artists* 7 (1) issue no 73 April 1972 12-13.

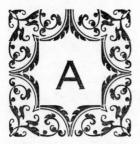

1 ABSOLUTE ARCHITECTURE: A proposal for a pure, non-objective and purposeless architecture made by Walter Pichler and Hans Hollein in 1962. Absolute Architecture can be regarded as the antithesis of functionalism, its form would be dictated by the individual architect's taste not by utilitarian requirements. See also Utopian Architecture.

V Conrads—editor—*Programmes and manifestoes on twentieth century architecture* (Lund Humphries, 1970).

2 ABSTRACT CLASSICISM: A form of *Hard-Edge Painting* practised by four American West Coast artists: Karl Benjamin, Lorser Feitelson, Frederick Hammersley, John McLaughlin. They used this phrase to emphasise their adherence to ' certain enduring principles of classicism '.

J Langster ' Four Abstract Classicists '—essay in—*West Coast Hard Edge* (catalogue) (ICA, 1960) 3-6.

3 ABSTRACT EXPRESSIONISM: A movement in American painting of the late 1940's and early 1950's acclaimed and imitated throughout the world. The dominance of American art dates from the success of the Abstract Expressionists, their formal innovations and new techniques were crucial to the subsequent development of Western art, and many artists today still make use of their ideas or react against them.

The phrase 'Abstract Expressionism' was first used consistently in 1929 to describe the works of Kandinsky, Robert Coates of the ' New Yorker ' applied it to American painting in 1945. The movement's name appears to indicate that it was a synthesis of two previous forms

of art—Abstraction and Expressionism—but this is an oversimplifica-
tion; Surrealism had a great influence on its development (exemplified
in the transitional work of Arshile Gorky), especially the automatic
writing techniques employed by the European artists. Certain Abstract Expressionists also had affinities with Oriental art (see Calligraphic Painting). The movement included a large number of painters
working in a wide variety of styles, consequently several other terms
have been coined—*Abstract Impressionism, Abstract Imagists, Abstract Sublime, Action Painting, Colour-Field Painting*—to draw attention to particular tendencies within Abstract Expressionism.

The main characteristics of Abstract Expressionist paintings: large
scale, generally abstract but with some figurative elements, deep involvement with subject content (see Intrasubjectives), romanticism,
loose painterly brushwork, asymmetrical composition, dramatic colour
or tonal contrasts. The artists laid great stress on the process of
painting, regarding it as a ritual act, they often used household paints
and developed unconventional methods of applying them to the canvas
(see Drip Painting). The major figures of the movement were Willem
De Kooning, Jackson Pollock, Franz Kline, Barnett Newman, Clyfford Still, Philip Guston, Mark Rothko and Robert Motherwell.

See also Tachisme, All Over Painting.

I Sandler *Abstract Expressionism: the triumph of American Painting*
(Pall Mall Press, 1970).

M Tuchman *The New York School: Abstract Expressionism in the
40's and 50's* (Thames & Hudson, 1970).

**4 ABSTRACT EXPRESSIONIST CERAMI-
CISTS:** A West Coast group of American artists producing experimental ceramics and polychrome sculpture, influenced by
Abstract Expressionism, who emerged in the mid 1950's. They were
given this rather clumsy label by John Coplans in 1967. The group
included Peter Voulkos, Kenneth Price, Billy Al Bengston, John
Mason, Mike Frinkens and Jim Melchert.

See also Funk Art.

5 ABSTRACT EXPRESSIONIST SCULPTURE:
During the late 1950's and early 1960's a number of American
sculptors produced work in the idiom of *Abstract Expressionism*.

Sculptors such as Richard Stankiewicz, John Chamberlain, Mark di Suvero and Claire Falkenstein tried to emulate those qualities of improvisation, spontaneity and loose structure characteristic of paintings by Willem De Kooning and Franz Kline. The traditional methods of sculpture, that is, the modelling and carving traditions, were considered antipathetic to such qualities; therefore the sculptors felt compelled to seek out new materials (see Junk Sculpture) and new techniques of composition (see Assemblage Art). The description 'Abstract Expressionist' has also been applied to certain works by the New York sculptress Eva Hesse, for example, the 1969 piece 'Contingent'.

N and E Calas 'Abstract Expressionist Sculpture'—chapter in—*Icons and images of the sixties* (NY, Dutton, 1971) 50-58.

6 ABSTRACT ILLUSIONISM: A tendency in American abstract painting of the middle 1960's, noted by Barbara Rose in October 1967, marked by a return to illusionism. The painters concerned—Darby Bannard, Ron Davis, Jules Olitski, Frank Stella, Larry Zox and others—used such pictorial devices as two point perspective, orthographic drawing, cool/warm colour contrasts to achieve depth effects. A few months earlier Lucy Lippard had described the same tendency, under the heading ' perverse perspectives ', as a new and incongruous illusionism ' incorporating the statement of the flat surface of a painting and counter statement of an inverse perspective that juts out into the spectator's space '.

The English critic Bryan Robertson, in his catalogue introduction to the Royal Academy ' British Sculptors ' exhibition of 1972, also used the expression 'Abstract Illusionism' to characterise the work of Kenneth Draper, Nigel Hall, Paul Huxley, Bridget Riley and William Tucker.

L Lippard ' Perverse perspectives ' *Art international* 11 (3) March 20 1967 28-33 and 44.

B Rose 'Abstract Illusionism ' *Artforum* 6 (2) October 1967 33-37.

7 ABSTRACT IMAGISTS: A name applied to certain artists of the Abstract Expressionist movement—Mark Rothko, Barnett Newman, Adolphe Gottlieb, Ad Reinhardt, Robert Motherwell and Clyfford Still—to distinguish them from gestural expres-

sionists such as Jackson Pollock or Franz Kline. The term derives from a 1961 Guggenheim Museum exhibition entitled 'American Abstract Expressionists and Imagists. These artists exploit large flatly painted coloured areas and sign-like elements to suggest a symbolic content. The term 'Quietistic' has also been proposed to describe this kind of painting.
See also Invisible painting.

8 ABSTRACT IMPRESSIONISM: Elaine De Kooning coined this term in 1951 to refer to paintings with a uniform pattern of brushstrokes, retaining the optical effects of Impressionism but without its representational content. (A consequence of the success of *Abstract Expressionism* was a revaluation of large scale *All-Over Painting*, such as the late works of Monet.) In 1956 Louis Finkelstein called Philip Guston's paintings 'Abstract Impressionist' in order to distinguish them from the more violent *Action Painting* created at the same time. Two years later the British Arts Council mounted an exhibition entitled 'Abstract Impressionism', organised by Lawrence Alloway; it included paintings by Bernard and Harold Cohen, Nicholas De Stael, Sam Francis, Patrick Heron, Joan Mitchell, Jean-Paul Riopelle and Pierre Tal Coat. The Argentine critic Aldo Pellegrini in his book 'New tendencies in art' also applies this label to a group of French Abstractionists—Jean Bazaine, Alfred Manessier and Gustave Singer whose work was popular in the immediate post-war period.

L Alloway 'Some notes on Abstract Impressionism'—essay in— *Abstract Impressionism* (Arts Council of Great Britain, 1958).

L Finkelstein 'New look: Abstract Impressionism' *Art news* 55 (1) March 1956 36-39, 66-68.

9 ABSTRACT LANDSCAPE: A mode of painting practised in the middle 1950's by a number of artists belonging to the School of Paris: Zao Wou-Ki, Pierre Tal Coat, Vieira da Silva, James Guitet, John F Koenig and others. Michael Ragon, the French art critic, coined the term 'Paysagisme abstrait' in 1956 in an attempt to characterise abstract paintings which by their naturalistic colours and atmospheric use of tones suggest natural landscape; Ragon himself admits that the term is absurd.

M Ragon *Vingt cinq ans d'art vivant* (Paris, Casterman, 1969).

10 ABSTRACT SUBLIME (or American Sublime): A phrase used by the American art critic Robert Rosenblum in 1961 to characterise paintings by Jackson Pollock, Barnett Newman, Mark Rothko and Clyfford Still. Newman had previously employed the word ' sublime ' about his own work in 1948, having been influenced by Edmund Burke's theory of the division between the beautiful—smoothness, gentle curves, polish, delicacy—and the sublime—terrible objects, obscurity, solitude, vastness. Rosenblum found a parallel between those qualities typical of the Romantic Movement and those characteristic of *Abstract Expressionism;* this relationship has also been discussed by Lawrence Alloway.

R Rosenblum ' The Abstract Sublime '—essay in—*New York painting and sculpture: 1940-1970* by H Geldzahler and others (Pall Mall Press, 1969) 350-359.

L Alloway 'American sublime ' *Living arts* (2) 1963 11-22.

11 ACTION ARCHITECTURE: A phrase coined by G M Kallmann in 1959. It refers to the work of a new generation of architects who seek ' fierce, direct and brutal action in design ', who use materials ' as found ' and who respond to particular situations. According to Peter Collins it refers to architecture created with the aid of sketches rather than precise working drawings, and by the personal supervision of the architect on the building site. The concept of Action Architecture is clearly derived from Harold Rosenberg's formulation *Action Painting.*

P Collins *Changing ideals in modern architecture* (Faber, 1965).

G M Kallmann ' The "Action" architecture of a new generation ' *Architectural forum* 111 (4) October 1959 132-137 and 244.

12 ACTION OFFICE: A flexible system of office furniture for individuals or groups capable of being arranged in a variety of different configurations. The Action Office was designed in 1964 by the American architect George Nelson, for the furniture manufacturers Herman Miller Inc, after a research study into the work pattern of American business executives conducted by Robert Propst.

See also Bürolandschaft.

R Cuddon ' Design review: office furniture ' *Architectural review* 140 (837) November 1966 369-370.

G Nelson 'Action office' *Architectural design* 36 (2) February 1966 p 101.

13 **ACTION PAINTING** (also called Gestural Painting): Harold Rosenberg, a critic on the staff of 'Art news', invented this term in 1952 to describe the loosely painted, gestural works of Jackson Pollock, Franz Kline, Willem De Kooning and Jack Tworkov. Such painting depended upon the unconscious as a source of inspiration; it extended into oil painting the automatic writing technique developed by the Surrealists. Rosenberg's use of the word ' action ' stressed the existentialist act of painting—the process of making was given greater emphasis than the finished work (the question of when a painting could be regarded as ' finished ' being a major talking point at that time). Rosenberg regarded the canvas as an arena in which the painter could act, the result being not so much a picture as an event. Mary MacCarthy riposted in a review ' you cannot hang an event on a wall, only a picture '.

See also Abstract Expressionism, Tachisme, Drip Painting, Process Art.

H Rosenberg ' The American Action Painters '—essay in—*The tradition of the new* (Thames and Hudson, 1962) 23-39.

H Rosenberg 'Action Painting: crisis and distortion '—essay in— *The anxious object: art today and its audience* (Thames and Hudson, 1965) 38-47.

H Rosenberg 'The premises of Action Painting ' *Encounter* 20 (5) May 1963 47-50.

14 **ACTION SPACE:** A community arts association established in 1968 by a group of artists who had been involved with Joan Littlewood's *Fun Palace* project, it is led by Ken Turner and is located in Gospel Oak, North London. Action Space has organised *Intermedia* events throughout Britain and uses pneumatic structures, tents, sound, light, movement, film and drama. Activities take place in open spaces and are aimed at the general public. The emphasis is on sensory awareness, fun and participation.

See also Participatory Art, Inter Action.

'Action Space ' *Catalyst* January 1971 p 2.

'Invisible London ' *Time out* (116) May 5 to 11 1972.

O Pritchett 'Action Space Man' *The guardian* August 17 1972 p 6.

1 5 ACTIONS (or Aktions): In Germany the word 'aktion' has recently become very popular; it means 'activity, process, undertaking, procedure'. In the context of recent art it refers to a form of event, somewhat similar to *Happenings*, developed primarily by German and Austrian avant garde artists (see Direct Art, Haus-Rucker Co, Fluxus). In Bern an art gallery is devoted to this form of art, the 'Aktiongalerie'. A number of Austrian artists, especially those who make up the Vienna Institute of Direct Art, belong to a movement called the 'Wiener Aktionismus', the essential concept of which is 'material action'. These artists have abandoned the use of a medium to depict or represent reality, in favour of the direct use of reality itself as a means of formal creation; thus Actions are not theatrical performances (pretended reality), they are literal events. They can be regarded as a determined attempt to end the art/life dichotomy.

Actions imply a developing social and political consciousness among artists: Joseph Beuys has formed a political party and a recent Action of his at the Tate Gallery in 1972 consisted of the artist, equipped with chalk and blackboard, discussing politics and education with visitors to the gallery for several hours; the event was recorded on video tape. One also finds the word 'action' employed by community art associations in Britain—*Inter-Action, Action Space*—and by radical groups in the United States—*Guerrilla Art Action*. According to Pierre Restany, the American architect and critic Gene Swenson has been instrumental in the creation of a new form of protest criticism—picketing cultural institutions such as *MOMA*—also described as 'Actions'.

See also Process Art, Video Art.

P Restany '1972—the American crisis and the great game of the establishment' *Domus* (507) February 1972 47-51.

P Weiermair 'New tendencies in Austrian art' *Studio international* 183 (944) May 1972 207-209.

W Vostell *Aktionen: Happenings und Demonstrationen seit 1965* (Hamburg, Rowohlt, 1970).

16 ACTIVIST ART (or the Arts of Activism): A term used by 'Arts in society' magazine in 1969 to characterise posters, drawings, poetry, guerrilla theatre, etc making a political protest against American involvement in the Vietnam war, against racial discrimination, against the regime in France in 1968. The expression 'Angry Arts' has also been used to describe this type of protesting art.

See also Polit Art, Prop Art.

'The Arts of Activism' *Arts in society* 6 (3) Fall/Winter 1969 special issue.

17 ACTUAL ART: A form of *Street Art* or *Happenings* performed in Prague in the middle 1960's by a number of Czechoslovakian artists called 'Art of the Actual Group' or 'Group Actual'. It is led by Milan Knizak and members include Sona Svecova, Vit Mach and Jan Trtilek.

A Kaprow *Assemblage, Environments and Happenings* (NY, Abrams, 1965) 299-310.

M Knizak 'Aktual in Czechoslovakia' *Art & artists* 7 (7) issue no 79 October 1972 40-43.

18 ACTUALISM: A term used by the French writer Alain Jouffrey to describe what happens to art in revolutionary situations such as those in France during May 1968. In such situations art as an independent entity distinct from social reality is abolished. Once works of art cease to be categorised as art then their real significance, or irrelevance, is revealed by their actual meaning and action. Jouffrey believes that art should no longer function as the armchair of the state, that artists should seek the 'death' of art in order to communicate directly with all sections of society.

See also Living Art.

A Jouffrey 'What's to be done about art?'—essay in—*Art and confrontation: France and the arts in an age of change* (Studio Vista, 1970) 175-201.

19 ADDITIVE ARCHITECTURE: Jorn Utzon's term for architecture and furniture consisting of standardised parts that can be added to as the need for expansion arises.

See also Kinetic Architecture.

20 ADHOCISM: A method of design in recent architecture, identified by Charles Jencks, in which each part of a building, or complex of buildings, is produced separately by a specialist or expert with little regard to the conception as a whole. Jencks claims that it is no longer necessary for an architect to invent new forms, he can select the best of what already exists from catalogues and collage the parts together. This process is also referred to as 'Bricolage' (Levi Strauss's term), meaning doing it yourself with whatever is at hand.

C Jencks 'Criticism: Adhocism on the South Bank' *Architectural review* 144(857) July 1968 27-30.

21 AERIAL ARCHITECTURE (or Immaterial Architecture or Invisible Architecture): A futuristic concept postulated in 1960 by the architect Werner Ruhnau and the painter Yves Klein for a city roofed by moving air. They proposed the air conditioning of large geographical areas and the replacement of buildings by walls of water and fire. Furniture would be superseded by air beds and air seats. Bernard Etkin and Pete Goering of the University of Toronto Institute for Aerospace studies have already conducted research into the use of jets of air instead of conventional building. Such 'Invisible Architecture' would represent an expenditure of energy instead of materials and allow for 'instant buildings'.

See also Utopian Architecture, Imaginary Architecture.

22 AESTHETIC RESEARCH CENTER (ARC): An organisation concerned with art and technology located in Venice, California.

23 AFFICHE LACERÉES torn posters): torn or lacerated posters obsessed a number of European artists in the post-war period and they were elevated to the realm of fine art by the polemics of Pierre Restany in 1960 (see Le Nouveau Réalisme). Raymond Hains, a French photographer, began collecting torn posters from hoardings in Paris in 1949; later he was assisted by J de La Villeglé. In 1959, another Frenchman, François Dufrêne became interested, especially in the reverse side of posters. Two

Italians, Mimmo Rotella and Alberti Moretti, also developed a preoccupation with torn posters independently of the French during the 1950's. The art of torn posters consists of three stages: (1) selection and presentation of posters as they are discovered in the streets, (2) the creation of torn posters by the unsticking process called *Décollage*, (3) the rubbing of the backs of posters to produce images. Many Affiche Lacerées resemble the paintings of *Abstract Expressionism* or *L'Art Informel* produced during the same period.

J de la Villeglé ' L'Affiche Lacerée; ses successives immixtions dans les arts ' *Leonardo* 2 (1) January 1969 33-44.

24 AIR ART:

A broad category encompassing a variety of different structures and activities which have in common the fact that they exploit the possibilities of compressed air, or the natural force of the wind, usually in association with plastic envelopes of various kinds. Alternative terms to describe Air Art include ' Gonflabe Art ', ' Inflatables ', ' Blow Up Art ', ' Sky Art '. In recent years many architects have designed pneumatic structures—Jean Paul Jungmann of the *Utopie Group*, Yutaka Murata, Cedric Price . . . At first such structures appeared as novelties at international expositions, but their technology is now well understood and they are commercially viable as offices or storage depots. According to one writer, Inflatables were the symbol of freedom, adventure, and radicalism among architectural students during the 1960's, because they represented the first practical manifestation of advanced technology available to students.

Blow Up furniture made of opaque or transparent plastic by designers such as Quasar Khanh, Verner Panton and Italians centred in Milan also became popular in the 1960's. Gernot Nalbach created a ' furniture carpet ' consisting of a series of plastic columns, whose height and internal air pressure could be adjusted to form different kinds of seating as required.

Fine artists who have made use of air include Andy Warhol (helium inflated cushions), David Medella (' Cloud Canyons ' of soap bubbles) and the *Haus-Rucker-Co*. The Los Angeles artist Michael Asher has produced a series of air works consisting of jets of air blown through small nozzles in different directions inside a room, in 1969 he entered a ' curtain of air ' project for the Whitney Museum 'Anti-illusion ' show.

Other artists such as Graham Stevens, and those comprising the 'Event Structure Research Group' devote their whole energy to the neglected aesthetic of air: they create airmobiles, hovertubes, air mattresses, atmosfields . . . their activities can be regarded as forms of *Environmental Art* and/or *Participatory Art* since they often envelop an audience and stimulate adult play. Those artists totally committed to Air Art tend, in their excitement at its future prospects, to make exaggerated claims for it; for example, they describe air structures as being a cultural expression of the energy continuum of the universe, or they claim that air structures have a revolutionary potential for social change.

See also Eventstructure.

G Stevens 'Blow Up' *Art & artists* 7 (2) issue no 74 May 1972 42-45.

25 ALL-OVER PAINTINGS: Works avoiding any kind of central composition or grouping of forms into areas of special interest to create a figure/ground effect. They are usually painted in a uniform manner or with accents distributed evenly across the surface of the canvas, filling it up to the framing edges. The phrase is frequently applied to the paintings of Jackson Pollock and also to the late works of Monet. C H Waddington finds a connection between all-overness in art and certain ideas in science, namely, the everywhere dense continuum of events concept that has replaced the 'billiard ball' atomic theory of matter.

See also Non-Relational Painting.

'Panel: All-over Painting' *It is* (2) Autumn 1958 72-77.

C H Waddington *Behind appearance* . . . (Edinburgh University Press, 1969).

26 ALTERNATIVE ARCHITECTURE: Makeshift structures erected by members of the alternative society at such venues as Pop Music Festivals. Also refers to geodesic domes constructed out of the debris of the consumer society by members of rural communes such as those living at Drop City, near Trinidad, Colorado, in the United States.

See also Ant Farm, Underground Art, Urban Guerrilla Architecture.

27 **AMERICANS IN PARIS:** A phrase used to describe American painters such as Sam Francis and Paul Jenkins, working in Paris at the time of the success of *Abstract Expressionism*.

28 **AMERICAN-TYPE PAINTING:** that is, painting characteristic of *Abstract Expressionism*: large scale, abstract but owing nothing to Cubism, colour replacing tonal values. This term derives from a major article by Clement Greenberg published in 1955.

29 **ANARCHITECTURE:** A word coined by Robin Evans from the Greek 'an' meaning 'non', and 'architecture'. An-architecture means non architecture, or Anarchi-tecture meaning the 'tectonics' of non control'.

R Evans 'Toward anarchitecture' AAQ 2 (1) January 1970 58-69.

30 **ANONIMA:** A group of American painters—Ernst Benkert, Francis Hewitt and Edwin Mieckowski—who operate as a research team. The group was established in Cleveland in 1964 and moved to New York in 1967. The members of Anonima set themselves rigorous programmes of research into perceptual problems relating to the art of painting. Their paintings are abstract and executed in a hard edge style (see Hard Edge Painting), their work is featured in their own journal 'Anonima' and in books on *Op Art*. The name 'Anonima' was selected from a book on Italian steamships; in Italian the word means 'incorporated'.

H P Raleigh 'Anonima Group' *Leonardo* 2 (4) October 1969 423-430.

31 **ANT FARM:** A group of American architects, designers and others from a variety of backgrounds formed in San Francisco in 1968 by Doug Michels and Chip Lord. Its strange name came from a remark that the only interesting things in architecture were happening underground, 'like an ant farm'. The group is concerned with architecture, educational reform, communication, graphic design, film, life-theatre, and high art. It sets no limit to the media it may use. The members of the group describe themselves as a family and attempt to create a common life style; they hope to transform existing social and economic systems by presenting alternatives. Their work is featured in Underground magazines, in 'Architectural design' and 'Progressive architecture', where they are described as 'architecture freaks' and 'environmental nomads'; projects include a portable snake plus media van with video equipment, an electronic oasis for nomadic tribes of the future; they also provide information on do-it-yourself domes and inflatable structures.

T Albright 'Ant Farm' *Rolling stone* (48) December 13 1969 p 36.
'Conceptual Architecture' *Design quarterly* (78/79) 1970 5-10.

32 ANTI-ART: A notion most critics regard as having originated with Dada, the European movement which totally repudiated bourgeois culture and art; artists such as Marcel Duchamp—dubbed 'the master of Anti-Art'—challenged the traditions of Western art by declaring that everything and anything could be art; later they were disgusted to find the objects, or replicas of them, selected on this basis had been assimilated by the art establishment and lovingly preserved in museums as examples of *Modern Art.*

After Dada, as Harold Rosenberg points out, art's denial of its own identity became a ritual gesture, a formality among avant garde movements.

Radically new works of art inevitably expand our notion of what art is (art is not a static concept, new art encroaches on areas of experience previously considered non art), and therefore laymen and critics who describe new work as 'Anti-Art' reveal by their reaction that an existing concept of art held by them has been changed, in their view for the worse. In this manner many new movements, for example *L'Art Brut, Pop Art,* were regarded as Anti-Art when they first emerged.

Herbert Marcuse's criteria for Anti-Art is work that is visual and involves drawing but is not deliberately intended as art, for example graffiti. Gregory Battcock suggests that works existing outside the accepted standards of morality, for example, Underground sex comics, are Anti-Art; he regards the term itself as unsatisfactory and proposes 'outlaw art' as a replacement.

Thus Anti-Art can be divided into four categories: (1) non-art

29

objects selected by artists with the intention of subverting established notions of art; (2) art objects produced by artists that pretend they are not art; (3) art objects produced by artists believed to be Anti-Art by the public and certain critics; (4) drawings not intended as art, drawings offensive to the current standards of morality.

G Battcock ' Marcuse and Anti-Art ' *Arts magazine* 43 (8) Summer 1969 17-19.

G Battcock ' Marcuse and Anti-Art 2 ' *Arts magazine* 44 (2) November 1969 20-22.

H Rosenberg *Artworks and packages* (NY, Dell 1964) 24, 26.

33 ANTI-FORM: A term used primarily by the American artist Robert Morris to describe sculptures of the late 1960's which focus on materials, the force of gravity, and the process of creation and by so doing react against the geometric, predominantly rectangular forms of previous abstract sculpture, in particular *Minimal Art*. Max Kozloff regards such works as an attack on the status of the object in art. Allan Kaprow insists that no sculpture can be against or without form, and suggests that 'Anti-Form' means ' anti-geometry '; he also points out that a similar approach to art was developed in *Happenings*. Morris has also defined Anti-Form as an ' attempt to contradict one's taste '.

See also Process Art.

A Kaprow ' The shape of the art environment: how anti-form is "Anti-form" ' *Artforum* 6 (10) Summer 1968 32-33.

M Kozloff ' 9 in a warehouse ' *Artforum* 7 (6) February 1969 38-42.

R Morris 'Anti-Form' *Artforum* 6 (8) April 1968 33-35.

G Muller ' Robert Morris presents Anti-Form: the Castelli Warehouse show ' *Arts magazine* 43 (4) February 1969 29-30.

34 ARCHIGRAM: An organisation of architects, designers and environmental researchers led by Peter Cook, based in London and the United States. Members include Warren Chalk, Ron Herron, Dennis Crompton, David Greene and Michael Webb. 'Archigram magazine ', or manifesto, has been published since 1961, but the group itself was formed two years later by young architects reacting against the boredom and sterility of post-war British architecture. Archigram delights in experimental projects; the group greatly admires the kind of advanced technology displayed in the American space programme. Their schemes are often consumer orientated and make use of combinations of services and appliances rather than traditional architectural structures. Projects include *Plug-in Architecture*, Clip-on architecture, capsule dwellings, mobile villages, instant cities. Archigram communicates its ideas largely via lively collages and graphics.

'Archigram Group, London: a chronological survey' *Architectural design* 35(11) November 1965 534-535.

P Cook—editor—*Archigram* (Studio Vista, 1972).

35 UNE ARCHITECTURE AUTRE: Reyner Banham coined this phrase in 1955 (it was derived from *Un Art Autre*) to describe a trend in the architectural thinking of the period subversive to the norms of traditional architecture. In his view this trend was characterised by vehemence, by new concepts of order, by an uninhibited attitude to materials, that were related to similar qualities found in the paintings of Jean Dubuffet, Jackson Pollock, and in Musique Concrete. Banham also suggested that 'Other Architecture' should consider alternative means of defining environments or solving functional needs besides the building of monumental structures. According to Banham the only designer whose approach approximated to his concept of Other Architecture was Buckminster Fuller.

R Banham *The New Brutalism: ethic or aesthetic* (Architectural Press, 1966) 68-69.

36 ARCHITECTURE WITHOUT ARCHITECTS: Title of an exhibition of photographs, collected over forty years by Bernard Rudofsky, held in New York in 1965. The photographs illustrated shelters and structures—caves, earthworks, tree houses, tents, villages . . . —used or built by people with no professional training in architecture: early man, ancient and primitive peoples, nomadic tribes, peasants . . . This type of architecture has also been called 'Non-pedigreed', 'Vernacular', 'Anonymous', 'Spontaneous', 'Indigenous', 'Rural', 'Rude' and 'Exotic'.

B Rudofsky *Architecture without architects* (NY, MOMA, 1965).

31

37 ARCHIZOOM (Studio Archizoom Associati): A group of six Florentine architects and designers—Andrea Branzi, Gilberto Corretti, Paolo Deganello, Massimo Morozzi, Dario and Lucia Bartolini—founded in 1966. The members of Archizoom are representative of the *Supersensualist* trend in Italian design, their approach is anti-functional, they revel in *Kitsch* decoration and stylisation especially in the creation of furniture: dream beds, dream wardrobes. They are also concerned with urban planning and have published a proposal for a No Stop City. Their work is featured in 'Architectural design', 'Domus' and in the Milanese magazine 'In'.

'Conceptual architecture' *Design quarterly* (78/79) 1970 17-21.

38 ARCOLOGY: A new conception of architecture proposed by Paolo Soleri, an Italian architect resident in the United States. According to Henryk Skolimowski, Arcology—the word was invented by Soleri—'is not architecture plus ecology; it is a fusion of the two; it is the result of the realisation that at a certain point in the historical development of society, architecture becomes inseparable from ecology'.

Arcology is Soleri's solution to the urban problems of the twentieth century; he proposes vast vertical *Megastructures* capable of housing up to three million inhabitants.

H Skolimowski 'Paolo Soleri: the philosophy of urban life' AAQ 3 (1) Winter 1971 34-42.

P Soleri *Arcology: the city in the image of man* (Cambridge, Mass, MIT Press, 1969).

D Wall *Visionary cities: the Arcology of Paolo Soleri* (Pall Mall Press, 1971).

39 UN ART AUTRE: Title of a book by the French writer Michel Tapié published in 1952. In the same year a Paris exhibition showing work by Karel Appel, Camille Bryen, Wols, Willem De Kooning, Mark Tobey, Jean-Paul Riopelle, Alberto Burri, Jean Dubuffet, Jean Fautrier and Georges Mathieu was organised with the same title. In his book Tapié also uses the phrase *L'Art Informel* and the literature is rather confused as to the usage of these two terms. Tapié claimed that post-war trends indicated a complete break with traditional modes and that the chief characteristic of this ' other art ' was the relinquishing of all forms of control. According to H H Arnason the term is so broad as to be almost meaningless.

M Tapié *Un art autre* . . . (Paris, Gabriel-Giraud, 1952).

40 **L'ART BRUT** (raw art): The French painter Jean Dubuffet tried consistently in his work and his statements to avoid the traps of traditional fine art or *Cultural Art,* and to rehabilitate discredited materials and values. For many years he collected work of a crude, unsophisticated nature—street graffiti, paintings and drawings by psychotics, prisoners, primitives, children, by any non-professional artist—which he called ' L'Art Brut '. In 1948 he founded a society to encourage the study of raw art and a year later he organised an exhibition of his collection at the Galerie René Drouin, Paris. Dubuffet admired raw art for its unprofessional qualities—innocent vision, direct technique, use of unconventional materials—and emulated them in his own painting; for example, he experimented with different materials such as sand, ashes, vegetable matter to produce rough textures in which he scrawled and scratched childlike imagery, and thus his work has also come to be known as L'Art Brut.

See also Matter Art.

J Dubuffet *L'Art Brut préféré aux arts culturels* (Paris, Compagnie de L'Art Brut, 1949).

P Selz *Dubuffet* (NY, MOMA, 1962).

41 **ART DECO:** This term derives from the title of a 1925 Paris exhibition: ' L'Exposition Internationale des Arts Décoratifs et Industriels Modernes '. It was used as early as 1935 but has only become fashionable in the late 1960's as a result of a spate of articles and books. Bevis Hillier defines Art Deco as ' an assertively modern style, developing in the 1920's and reaching high point in the thirties; it drew inspiration from . . . Art Nouveau, Cubism, the Russian Ballet, American Indian art and the Bauhaus . . . it ran to symmetry . . . and to the rectilinear.' It was the style of Odeon cinemas, ocean liners and hotel interiors, it tried to adapt design to the requirements of mass production and was expressed therefore in the applied rather than fine arts. Art Deco has also been called 'Aztec Airways ', ' Jazz Modern ', ' Modernistic ', ' Functional ' or named after its chief artists, ' Style Poiret ', ' Style Chanel ', ' Style

2

Puriforcat' or it was referred to by the date of the exhibition, 'Style 1925', 'La Mode 1925', 'Paris 25'.

Another authority on the period, Martin Battersby, claims that the term 'Art Deco' has been misused; he says that it was a curvilinear style, but more formalised than Art Nouveau, making use of vivid colours such as cerise, orange, violet, emerald . . . and that it ended in 1925, the simpler more geometric design appearing after that date Battersby calls 'Modernist'. A third writer, Peter Wollen, believes that the subject is still undefined; he attacks the cult of Art Deco and describes it as *Kitsch*, haute trend, second rate vanguardism. He regards the leading Art Deco artists as parasites on the genuine creators of *The Modern Movement*. The revival of 1920's and 1930's design in recent years has influenced the work of a number of fine artists, notably Roy Lichtenstein, Frank Stella and Colin Self.

M Battersby *The decorative twenties* (Studio Vista, 1969).

M Battersby *The decorative thirties* (Studio Vista, 1971).

Y Brunhammer *The nineteen twenties style* (Hamlyn, 1969).

B Hillier *Art Deco of the 20's and 30's* (Studio Vista, 1968).

B Hillier *The world of Art Deco* (Studio Vista, 1971).

B Nevil 'Fashions in living—Art Deco: the first modern style' *Vogue* (British) 126 (10) August 1969 92-97.

G Veronesi *Into the twenties: style and design 1909-1929* (Thames & Hudson, 1968).

P Wollen 'Decor Artif'—book review—*Studio international* 182 (938) November 1971 213-214.

42 L'ART ENGAGÉ (and l'Art Dirigé): In the immediate post-war years, totalitarian regimes condemned formalist abstract art and demanded that artists in Western Europe produce works that were socially and politically committed, Soviet Socialist Realism being the only acceptable style. In France the Communist party literary spokesman Louis Aragon echoed these demands, and painters such as André Fougeron and Boris Taslitzky fulfilled them. The Italian artist Renato Guttuso, a member of the Communist party since 1935, emerged as the leading Social Realist painter of Europe.

43 ART INFORMATION REGISTRY (AIR): A London organisation founded in 1967 by Peter Sedgley, Stuart Brisley and others to provide a channel between artists and their public, to act as an alternative to the present gallery system. The registry, or artists' index, consists of colour slides, photographs, press cuttings, catalogues and biographical details of approximately 350 artists, which are shown to public and private art collectors and to exhibition organisers. Any artist can submit documentation and there is no selection process. The service is free to artists but a small fee is charged to all other users. In 1972 the registry moved from the East End of London to premises in the Royal Academy of Arts, Piccadilly. AIR used to publish a compilation of artists statements, news and addresses called 'Catalyst' and contributions were reprinted in the form they were submitted. 'Catalyst' is now defunct and has been replaced by 'Air mail'.

See also Space Provision for Artists (Cultural and Educational) Ltd.

S Braden 'A.I.R. R.A. R.I.P.? S.P.A.C.E.D.' *Time out* (84) September 24-30 1971 20-21.

Report on Art Information Registry 1967-1971 (AIR, 1971).

44 **L'ART INFORMEL:** An extremely broad term devised by the French writer Michel Tapié in his book *Un Art Autre* to describe a trend in the art of the 1950's towards a mainly abstract, but non-geometric style characterised by the adjectives 'shapeless', 'intuitive', 'improvised'. L'Art Informel included such tendencies as *Tachisme, Matter Art, Lyrical Abstraction,* and American *Abstract Expressionism* (though it primarily refers to European art); it dominated Parisian taste for a decade until 1962 when, to the relief and satisfaction of Concrete and Kinetic artists, it suddenly became unfashionable.

English writers have invariably translated 'informel' as 'informal', thus 'L'Art Informel' becomes 'Informalism'. However, the words are not equivalent and 'informel' is not to be understood as the opposite of 'formal'. Exceptionally in 1970, the American critic Carter Ratcliff described several New York painters as *'The New Informalists'* because their work sidesteps the 'formalist' concerns of American painting of the previous decade.

45 **ART OF THE REAL:** Title of an exhibition of American art held at the Tate Gallery, London in 1969 to illustrate a tendency in recent American painting and sculpture: to make no appeal to emotion but to offer works in the form of simple irreducible, irrefutable objects. The exhibition contained many, disparate styles more precisely described as *Hard-Edge Painting, Minimal,* and *Op Art.* Among the artists represented were Sol Le Witt, Robert Morris, Ellsworth Kelly, Kenneth Noland, Frank Stella, Donald Judd, and Larry Poons.

46 ART POVERA (Poor Art or Impoverished Art): A term devised by the Italian critic Germano Celant in 1967. It describes certain works by artists such as Robert Smithson, Douglas Huebler, Richard Long, Eva Hesse, Joseph Beuys, Jan Dibbets, Joseph Kosuth, Dennis Oppenheim, Hans Haacke, Carl Andre, Robert Morris, Richard Serra and Walter De Maria. In a book he edited in 1969 Celant listed alternative terms—*Actual Art, Conceptual Art,* Earthworks, Impossible Art, Raw Materialist Art, Microemotive Art, *Anti-Form*—indicating that Art Povera is a broad category encompassing several international trends in the art of the 1960's (in my view Art *Povera* occupies the middle ground between the two extremes of *Minimal Art* and *Conceptual Art*). Celant's label stresses the poverty or unworthiness (*ie* non fine art) of the materials employed by these artists listed above: coal, sand, earth, wood, stones, twigs, cement, felt, rubber, rope, newspapers, etc. Art Povera is temporary by nature and its creation often takes place at remote sites; its occurrence is only made permanent and known to the public by means of documentation. Such works implicitly attack the precious object/art-gallery system or make it hard for this system to assimilate them. Art Povera seems to reflect a new romanticism or a new primitivism: the penchant for rural or wild country, the artist as magician or alchemist working with natural elements (water, snow, ice, grass) and making use of natural physical forces (gravity, wind, growth). A hostile reviewer described Art Povera as ' poor art, of poor materials, in exultation of a poor life '.

See also Earth Art, Ecological Art, Matter Art.

G Celant *Art Povera* (Studio Vista, 1969).

47 ART WORKERS' COALITION (AWC): A group of art workers with a steady membership of about 100 founded in New York in 1969. One of its key figures, Carl Andre, explains that the term 'art worker' is preferred to 'artist' not for its Marxist overtones but because it includes everyone who 'makes a productive contribution to Art'.

The coalition is opposed to the capitalist gallery/dealer establishment and the 'star' system of promoting artists. It supports social and political protest in the field of art, specifically it demands reform of museum administration, equal rights for black and Puerto Rican artists, and it is opposed to the war in Vietnam. Members of AWC are prepared to remove 'their' works from the public galleries that own them as a form of protest, to organise strikes, sit-ins, demonstrations and picketing. (In England a related group called the 'International Coalition for the Abolition of Art' disrupted the opening of the 1970 'Young Contemporaries Exhibition'.) A larger grouping called the 'New York Strike' consists of former AWC members plus museum and gallery workers, and two smaller but more militant American groups are called '*Guerrilla Art Action*' and 'Art Workers United'.

See also Cultural Art, Artists' Union, Black Art.

L Picard 'Protest and rebellion: the function of the Art Workers Coalition' *Arts magazine* 44(7) May 1970 18-24.

T Schwartz 'The politicalisation of the avant garde II' *Art in America* 60(2) March/April 1972 70-79.

C Tisdall 'Any old iron' *The guardian* June 1 1972 p 10.

48 ARTHROPODS: are invertebrate animals with articulate, segmented bodies and limbs, a term applied by Jim Burns to a number of experimental design groups because 'their members are articulated or interconnected for singular purposes of environmental creation, while still being segmented into their individual personae as artists, architects, designers, planners or performers'. The groups in question include *Haus-Rucker-Co*, God & Co, Missing Link Productions, 9999, *Superstudio*, Coop Himmelblau, Eventstructure Research Group, Onyx, and others.

J Burns *Arthropods: new designs futures* (NY, Praeger, 1972).

49 ARTIST PLACEMENT GROUP (APG): A British organisation founded by John and Barbara Latham in 1966. Its purpose is to place artists within industrial companies, not primarily to produce art objects, but as a radical cultural alternative to the production/profit structure of industry. APG maintain that the artist should have autonomous professional status within the companies and be paid a retaining fee for his services. The theory of artist placement makes use of a concept of creativity called 'the Delta principle'. Artists who have been involved with industry via APG include Gareth Evans, Stuart Brisley, Leonard Hessing and Andrew Dipper. An exhibition of their work was held at the Hayward Gallery, London in December 1971. APG has been sharply criticised in numerous articles on the grounds of muddled thinking, false claims, misuse of language and amateurism.

See also Technological Art.

S Braden 'Exhibitions: APG' *Time out* (91) November 12-18 1971 p 21 (Part I).

'Exhibitions: APG' *Time out* (92) November 19-25 1971 p 18 (Part II).

G Metzger 'A critical look at Artist Placement Group' *Studio international* 183(940) January 1972 4-5.

50 THE ARTISTS' UNION (initially called Art Workers' Union or Artists' Association): In 1971 a small number of British artists, calling themselves 'the Policy Group', initiated a scheme for the establishment of an Artists' Union to be affiliated to the Trades Union Congress (TUC). It is proposed that the union becomes a branch of the militant 'Association of Scientific, Technical and Managerial Staffs' (ASTMS) once it has the minimum of 100 members. The aims of the Artists' Union are to influence the decision making processes that affect artists and thereby gain benefits for members, to foster the living arts, to encourage a closer relationship between art and the needs of the people.

'The Artists' Union' *Studio international* 183 (944) May 1972 p 192.

'The artists' union—a statement' *Art & artists* 7(5) issue no 77 August 1972 12-13.

S Braden 'Exhibitions: dispute in the art industry' *Time out* (132) August 25-31 1972 p 37.

P Fuller 'United artists . . .?' *Art & artists* 7(4) issue no 76 July 1972 12-14.

'Union now!' *Art & artists* 7(6) issue no 78 September 1972 10-13.

51 **ARTS LAB:** Jim Haynes, an American resident in Britain since 1956, established the first Arts Laboratory in Drury Lane, Covent Garden, London in 1967. It contained a theatre, cinema, art gallery and bookshop, all housed in an abandoned scrap-metal warehouse. To raise money and to overcome censorship problems Haynes ran the Arts Lab on the lines of a private club.

By the end of 1969 over 150 other Arts Labs had been founded throughout the United Kingdom. Their purpose was to provide an alternative to the commercial art-as-commodity systems; to provide artists with workshop facilities; to develop avant garde, Underground or experimental art projects and to provide the public with—in the words of Richard Neville—'centres for fun, new culture and madness'.

Because of their lack of permanent funds and their experimental character, Arts Labs tended to be ephemeral organisations: the original Arts Lab closed in October 1969 and its successor the New Arts Lab, located in Roberts Street, London was equally shortlived. Many artists found it impossible to work in the presence of a constant stream of inquisitive visitors, and consequently a separate organisation—the *Institute for Research in Art and Technology*—was set up to concentrate on creative activities.

J Allen 'The Arts Lab explosion' *New society* November 21 1968 749-750.

N De Jongh 'Lights out for the Arts Lab' *The guardian* October 21 1969 p 11.

P Fryer 'The Arts Laboratory' *New society* October 26 1967 p. 557.

J Haynes 'Arts Lab: a fortress and haven for adult games' *Ark* (45) Winter 1969 22-28.

H Judson 'The Arts Laboratory: swinging smorgasbord' *Life* May 13 1968.

R Neville *Playpower* (Cape, 1970).

52 **ASSEMBLAGE ART:** The word 'assemblage' was first used by Jean Dubuffet to describe his own work in 1953; he preferred it to 'collage' because he thought the latter word should be restricted to the works of Cubism. Assemblage is a generic concept designating all forms of composite art—three dimensional collage or collage sculpture—which are usually made up of pre-formed natural or manufactured non-art materials, though no theoretical limit is set as to what materials may be used. In contrast, traditional sculpture tends to be pure in its attitude to materials. Allan Kaprow maintains that Assemblage developed out of advanced painting and marks a stage in the evolution towards *Environmental Art*.

Assemblage Art was extremely fashionable in the late 1950's and early 1960's: a large exhibition called 'Art of Assemblage' was held in New York at the Museum of Modern Art in 1961. The best artists associated with the movement during that period were American and included Allan Kaprow, Jim Dine and Robert Rauschenberg.

See also Combine Painting, Junk Sculpture, No Art, Object Art.

A Kaprow *Assemblage, Environments, Happenings* (NY, Abrams, 1965).

W C Seitz *The Art of Assemblage* (NY, MOMA, 1961).

53 ATELIER POPULAIRE (People's Studio): Students of the 'Ecole de Beaux Arts', Paris involved in the May 1968 revolutionary events set up a workshop in their college to issue political posters produced by means of the silk screen process. Before the riot police closed down the workshop in June the students had designed approximately 350 different posters and distributed 120,000 copies. The art students were determined to avoid the errors of *Cultural Art*, therefore designs were approved by comrades committees and were issued anonymously. The posters attacked the French government and police brutality, their style was completely determined by their political function, and visually they achieved the kind of direct statement found in road signs.

J Berger 'Arts in society: marking the road' *New society* March 5 1970 404-405.

Texts and posters by Atelier Populaire: posters from the revolution, Paris, May (Dobson, 1969).

54 AUTO-DESTRUCTIVE ART: A term invented by Gustav Metzger to describe his own work during the early 1960's. Influenced by the self-destroying machines of Jean Tinguely, Metzger developed an equally public form of *Destructive Art*: at a demonstration on London's South Bank on July 3 1961, he used acid as a medium and sprayed it on to sheets of nylon cloth. The acid immediately attacked the nylon, creating rapidly changing shapes until the sheet was completely consumed. Thus the work was simultaneously auto-creative and auto-destructive. Metzger maintained that his use of destruction was a protest against the massive arms expenditure of modern states; he also believed the Auto-Destructive Art could provide a socially acceptable outlet for human aggression.

See also Expendable Art.

G Metzger ' Machine, Auto-creative and Auto-destructive Art ' *Ark* (32) Summer 1962 7-8.

5 5 **AUTOMATIC ART** (or Automatism): Paintings, drawings, or writing produced while under the influence of the subconscious. ' Doodles ' are an everyday example of this phenomenon. Many examples of this type of art were produced in the nineteenth century and in the twentieth century. Automatism has been used as a painting technique: in Europe by the Surrealists and practitioners of *L'Art Informel*, in the United States by painters associated with *Abstract Expressionism* and in Canada by the group called *Les Automatistes*.

A Gauld 'Automatic Art ' *Man, myth & magic* (7) 1970 189-193.

5 6 **LES AUTOMATISTES:** A Canadian group of painters active between 1946 and 1951, whose work has been variously described as Surrealist, *Action Painting*, or *Lyrical Abstraction*. The group was formed by Paul Emile Borduas and its members included Jean-Paul Riopelle, Fernand Leduc, Albert Dumouchel and Jean Paul Mousseau. They called themselves ' Les Automistes ' because their technique of painting was based on the automatic writing method employed before the war by the Surrealists. In 1958 the group caused a scandal by publishing a manifesto attacking Canadian life. Works by the group were shown in Paris exhibitions during the second half of the 1940's; Borduas and Riopelle both moved to Paris in the early 1950's.

G Robert ' Ecole de Montreal ' *Cimaise* (75) February/April 1966 24-36.

57 AVANT-GARDE ART (or Vanguard Art): The French phrase 'avant-garde' means the advance guard of an army—Nigel Gosling detests the phrase because of its 'bellicose overtones of warriors pushing forward fearlessly into unfriendly territory' —and this military metaphor was first applied to art and literature by political writers in France during the nineteenth century.

Therefore Avant-Garde Art is that art of the current moment in history that is more advanced, more up to date, more radical, or extreme, than all other art of present times. Renato Poggioli claims that this concept of art originated in Romanticism and that it is inseparable from the development of *Modern Art*. He stresses the link between the Avant-Garde and the phenomena of movements so typical of *Modern Art*: Impressionism, Symbolism, Fauvism, Cubism, Futurism, Dada, Surrealism, Expressionism, etc. He lists the characteristics of Avant-Garde Art as Activism (the taste for action, dynamism, marching forward, exploration), Antagonism (opposition to the historic and social order, anti-tradition), Nihilism (destructiveness, infantilism, extreme behaviour), Agonism (Romantic agony, pathos, tension, sacrifice, spiritual defeatism), Futurism (pre-vision, prophesying the art of the future.

Paradoxically, Avant-Garde Art has its conventions and many writers speak of the 'tradition of the Avant-Garde'. Poggioli sees Avant-Garde Art as a manifestation of the alienation of the modern artist, and he believes such art is here to stay: 'avant-gardism has now become the typical chronic condition of contemporary art'.

N Gosling 'Art: straggling onwards' *The observer* September 3 1972 p 30.

R Poggioli *The theory of the Avant-Garde* (Cambridge, Mass, Belknap/Harvard, 1968).

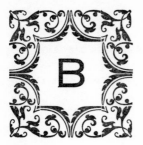

58 BASIC DESIGN: In England during the 1950's a number of fine artists—Victor Pasmore, Richard Hamilton, Harry Thrubron, Tom Hudson and Maurice De Sausmarez—lectured at art schools such as the Central School of Arts and Crafts, London and at the art departments of universities such as Leeds and Durham (the latter located in Newcastle upon Tyne). These artists established a series of Basic Design courses modelled on the Bauhaus preliminary course run by Johannes Itten. The aim of these courses was to provide students, no matter what their individual speciality, with a grounding in the fundamental characteristics of visual design. Practical exercises were set on themes such as the relationships of colour, shape and three dimensional structures, exercises which tended to the abstract, but observation of natural forms, patterns and processes was also encouraged.

Pasmore claimed that Basic Design provided, for the first time, a scientific basis for art training. Such training attempted to develop the intellectual, analytical powers of the student, but intuition and the use of devices for harnessing the subconscious were not neglected. The concept of a unified basic training persists today in British art schools in the form of the foundation year studies applicable to all students, and Pasmore's scientific analogy is continued by 'Visual Research' departments.

Some critics have claimed that Basic Design courses in the United States have influenced the development of *Minimal Art*.

R Banham 'The Bauhaus Gospel' *The listener* September 26 1968 390-392.

M De Sausmarez *Basic Design: the dynamics of visual form* (Studio Vista, 1964).

The developing process (Newcastle upon Tyne, Durham University, 1959).

W S Huff 'An argument for basic design' *Architectural design* 36(5) May 1966 252-256.

P L Jones ' The failure of basic design' *Leonardo* 2(2) April 1969 155-160.

E Sonntag 'Foundation studies in art' *Leonardo* 2(4) October 1969 387-397.

59 BAY AREA FIGURATION: A description applied to the work of a number of West Coast American painters —David Park, Elmer Bischoff and Richard Diebenkorn—who had studied or taught at the 'California School of Fine Arts' (where Clyfford Still and Mark Rothko had also taught in the late 1940's). These artists produced figurative work, but their style of painting was strongly influenced by the brush work of *Abstract Expressionism.* Clement Greenberg applied the term *Homeless Representation* to this kind of painting.

60 BEHAVIOURAL ART: The British artist Steve Willats, editor of ' Control magazine ', advocates a new form of art based on the concepts and techniques of cybernetics and behavioural social sciences. He believes that all art is concerned with altering the behaviour of an audience, therefore he maintains that the modern artist must take note of this fact and operate in the social environment. Willats has organised several projects involving members of the general public, who belonged to different social groups, he used market research and social survey methods as artistic strategies, the projects are designed to increase the participants awareness of their social environment so that they can make better use of it. In 1972 Willats founded the ' Centre for Behavioural Art ' at Gallery House, London.

See also Cybernetic Art.

S Willats 'Cognition and control' ' *Control magazine* ' (6) 1972 10-13.

S Willats 'West London Social Resource Project '—in—*A survey of the Avant-Garde in Britain I* (Gallery House, 1972) 3-7.

61 BIOTECTURE: A term combining 'biology and 'architecture' coined by Rudolf Doernach. It means architecture
as an 'artificial super system' as 'live, dynamic, mobile, fantastic,
environment systems'.

R Doernach 'Biotecture' *Architectural design* 36(2) February 1966
95-96.

62 BLACK ART (also called Afro-American Art, Neo-
African Art, Negro Art): According to Barbara Rose 'Black
Art' has three connotations (1) art containing 'specific subject matter
relating to the Black experience', (2) art which rejects 'the forms of
European art in favour of primitive African forms', (3) in its broadest
sense, paintings and sculpture produced by American negro artists.
Black art, in this last sense, is a variety of *Ethnic Art* and reflects the
new consciousness of racial pride and separatism associated with Civil
Rights and the Black Power movements of the 1960's.

In an effort to appease the demands of minority groups, American
museums and galleries have mounted a plethora of Black Art shows
since 1968, including a large scale show at the Whitney·Gallery in
New York in 1971. A showplace for Black Art, called 'Studio
Museum' was established in Harlem in 1968.

Washington DC is a city with a predominantly negro population and
a number of black artists who reside there have become internationally
known, notably Sam Gilliam, Alma Thomas and Carroll Sockwell.

Self-help groups and militant promotional organisations have been
established to assist black artists. For example, 'Studio Watts' in
Los Angeles and a subgroup of the 'New York Art Strike' called
'Women Students and Artists for the Black Art Liberation' (WSABAL).

The major issue confronting American black artists is whether to
address themselves purely to aesthetic problems and to compete with
white artists for recognition from the white, art establishment, or to
subsume their art to the political struggle of black liberation and to
develop alternatives to the gallery system.

J W Chase *Afro-American Art* (NY, Nostrand Reinhold, 1972).

H Ghent 'Notes to the young black artist: revolution or evolution'
Art international 15 (6) June 20 1971 33-35.

B Rose 'Black Art in America' *Art in America* 58(5) September/
October 1970 54-67.

A Werner 'Black is not a colour' *Art & artists* 4(2) May 1969
14-17.

63 **BODY ART** (or Body Sculpture, Body Works, Corporal
Art): An international trend in art, dating roughly from
1967, associated with sculptors who had previously worked in the
mode of *Earth Art*. Amongst the arts sculpture in particular has a
special relationship with the human body: sculptors are acutely
conscious of 'body ego' and the appreciation of sculpture depends to
a large extent on a physiological empathy between spectator and
artwork; hence it was a logical step for sculptors to turn to their own
bodies as material for creating art, to treat their bodies as both object
and subject.

In the name of art sculptors such as Vito Acconci, Terry Fox,
Bruce Mclean, Barry Le Va, Bruce Nauman, Dennis Oppenheim,
Larry Smith, Keith Sonnier and William Wegman have subjected
their bodies to a host of indignities: parts of the body have been cast
in plaster, marks and incisions have been made on the skin, the flesh
has been scorched by the sun, hair has been burnt off, concrete blocks
have been dropped on toes, tooth picks have been thrust into gums,
transformation of bodily processes and expressions have been produced by breathing exercises or by violent activities such as hurling
oneself against a stone wall until exhausted. Sexuality has not been
ignored—a work by Acconci called 'Seed bed' performed in a New
York Gallery in 1972 consisted of the artist masturbating beneath a
ramp.

Since the activities of Body Art are transitory they are recorded for
publicity and exhibition purposes in photographs, or on film or video
tape (see Video Art).

Precedents for Body Art have been found in the work of Yves
Klein and Marcel Duchamp, and according to Peter Weiermair it was
also anticipated by Gunther Brus and Arnulf Rainer of the 'Wiener
Aktionismus' (see Actions). In many instances Body artists combine
ideas discussed under the headings of *Process Art, Conceptual Art* and
Performance Art. The emergence of Body Art in recent years is contemporaneous with a widespread upsurge of interest in the human
body: encounter groups, body painting and tattooing, nudity in the
theatre, 'Hair', the sexual revolution; in terms of art it marks a
reaction to the aseptic quality of *Minimal Art* and the dry, cerebral

nature of most *Conceptual Art*. As Germano Celant points out, 'the body has a language that is crude, violent and vulgar', the official, computerised language of much recent art is 'challenged by the slang of the body', a slang that is popular and primitive, expressing itself in terms of sweat, hair, the penis and the nude.

In the autumn of 1972 the *Institute of Contempory Arts,* London organised a programme of lectures and events dealing with the body as a medium of expression, a group called BAAL—Body Arts at Large—assisted with the programme.

See also Soft Sculpture, Living Sculpture.

J Benthall 'The body as a medium of expression: a manifesto' *Studio international* 184 (946) July/August 1972 6-8.

'Body Works' *Interfunktionen* (6) September 1971 2-33.

G Celant 'Vito Acconci' *Domus* (509) April 1972 54-56 and 60.

R Pincus-Witten 'Vito Acconci and the conceptual performance' *Artforum* 10(8) April 1972 47-49.

W Sharp 'Body Works' *Avalanche* (1) Fall 1970 14-17.

64 BOMBERG SCHOOL (also called Neo or Post-Bomberg School): David Bomberg, a British avant garde artist was well-known during the 1920's, but the remainder of his life, up to his death in 1957, was spent in obscurity. He taught at the 'Borough Polytechnic', London and influenced a number of his students who formed two groups, 'The Borough Group' (1947) and 'The Borough Bottega' (1953). Leon Kossoff and Frank Auerbach are the best known of Bomberg's followers. They produce figurative paintings, based on nudes or landscapes, using thick impasto applied with impassioned, if rather turgid brush strokes, which reflect the influence of Bomberg's late style.

65 BORAX (or the Borax look): An American slang term dating from the 1920's, referring to cheap, showy merchandise, applied especially to shoddily built furniture, so called because of the premiums offered by the Borax soap company. It has also been used in England since 1945 by writers such as Michael Farr and critics in 'Design' magazine to describe a characteristic mannerism of the design of the 1940's and 1950's: a bogus streamlining, blubbery inflations or curves, often accompanied by parallel stripes or bands acting as decorative features on the surface of mass produced items such as juke boxes.

See also Styling.

E Kaufmann ' Design review: Borax, or the chromium plated calf ' *Architectural review* 104 (620) August 1948 88-93.

E Kaufmann—letter—*Architectural review* 104 (624) December 1968 p 314.

66 **BOWELLISM:** The work of Michael Webb and other students at the 'Regent Street Polytechnic School of Architecture ', London during the years 1956 to 1959. They were influenced by Le Corbusier, Antonio Gaudi and the appearance of the human bowels. According to Peter Cook, Bowellism represented a lost movement, nothing was actually built.

P Cook *Experimental architecture* (Studio Vista, 1970).

67 **BRITAIN CAN MAKE IT:** Title of an important exhibition of British design, organised by the ' Council of Industrial Design ', held at the Victoria and Albert Museum in 1946. After the austerity of the war years long queues of visitors formed outside the V&A to see consumer goods that were not at that time generally available; consequently the exhibition was renamed by visitors ' Britain can't have it '.

68 **BÜROLANDSCHAFT:** A sophisticated form of office planning developed in Germany by the specialists in office organisation, Eberhard & Wolfgang Schnelle, during the late 1950's and early 1960's, since copied by businesses throughout the world. Bürolandschaft—literally office landscape—exploits the possibilities of open plan office (cellular offices were replaced by open plan offices in some firms in the United States before the second world war, but furniture in such offices tended to be arranged in a regimented fashion); the departments of a business and their furniture are disposed according to the flow of paperwork, communications and the movement of staff. The result looks casual, it seems to echo the soft lines of a landscape, an impression heightened by the use of potted plants; thick carpets, canteen units and a community atmosphere creates a domestic type environment.

The advantages of Bürolandschaft are claimed to be increased business efficiency, better communications, better staff conditions, greater flexibility—the furniture can easily be re-arranged, departments can easily be re-organised.

See also Action Office.

A Boje *Open Plan Offices* (Business Books, 1972).

'Chaos as system' *Progressive architecture* (10) October 1968 160-169.

F Duffy 'Skill: Bürolandschaft' *Architectural review* 135(804) February 1964 148-154.

69 **THE BUTTERY HATCH AESTHETIC:** A characteristic of buildings designed by the American architect Louis Kahn is that services are sharply differentiated from the areas they serve. Kahn usually houses services in vertical box-like structures built alongside the blocks used by humans (see for example his 1961 Medical Research Building, Pennsylvania). In some critics' eyes this approach to services is analogous to the storage of food in larders, hence ' Buttery Hatch Aesthetic '.

R Banham ' On trial 2: Louis Kahn, the Buttery Hatch Aesthetic ' *Architectural review* 131(781) March 1962 203-206.

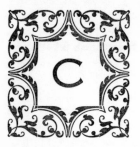

70 CALLIGRAPHIC PAINTING: This description has been applied to the work of a number of American and European artists who fall into two categories: (a) those whose brush technique and painting process was directly influenced by the Oriental tradition of calligraphy; and (b) those artists associated with *Abstract Expressionism, Action Painting* and *Tachisme,* who arrived independently at an approach to painting which seemed to observers comparable to the calligraphy of the East. In category (a) we can place the West Coast painter Mark Tobey, who learnt about Chinese calligraphy through a friend Teng Kuei in the 1920's, who visited Japan and later developed a form of miniature calligraphy which he called 'White Writing'. Also in this group we can include Ulfert Wilke, Morris Graves, Julius Bissier and Henri Michaux. In category (b) we can list Franz Kline, Robert Motherwell, Bradley Walker Tomlin and Hans Hartung.

G Nordland 'Calligraphy and the art of Ulfert Wilke' *Art international* 15 (4) April 20, 1971 21-24.

71 CAMP: According to Susan Sontag, Camp is a taste or sensibility characteristic of certain groups in twentieth century society, a private code among urban cliques—historically homosexual—a form of dandyism in an age of mass culture. It is also a quality discoverable in objects just before they become fashionable. Camp taste delights in artifice, theatricality, exaggeration, extravagance, playfulness, a love of the unnatural. Certain kinds of *Kitsch* can also be Camp if they are in extremely bad taste; this attitude is summed up in the phrase 'it's so bad it's good'. Camp Art emphasises elegance, texture and style rather than content or function: Baroque art is described as being 'Camp about religion'. Camp taste is said to have begun with

the eighteenth century passion for Gothic novels, Chinoiserie, carica-
ture and fake ruins. Examples of visual art regarded as Camp include
drawings by Aubrey Beardsley and Erté, paintings by Carlo Crivelli,
David Hockney, Marie Laurencin and the Pre-Raphaelites, architecture by Antonio Gaudi and comics such as ' Old Flash Gordon ' and
' Batman '. Sontag regards Art Nouveau as the most typical and fully
developed Camp style (presumably this opinion is now out of date,
Art Nouveau's popularity is no longer restricted to a small number of
cognoscenti).

The origins of the word ' Camp ' are uncertain, Roger Baker thinks
it derives from the Italian ' campeggiare ' (to stand out from a background), Alan Brien prefers the French verb ' se camper ' (to posture
boldly); both have theatrical associations.

R Baker 'Anatomy of Camp ' *Queen* February 19th 1969 48-51.

A Brien ' Campers courageous ' *Harpers Bazaar* 64(1) April 1961
p 138.

A Brien ' Private view: camper's guide ' *New statesman* June 23
1967 873-874.

' Camp ' *The listener* October 20th 1966 572-573.

C Isherwood *The world in the evening* (Penguin, 1966).

' Playboy after hours: Camp ' *Playboy* September 1965 27-28.

S Sontag ' Notes on Camp '—essay in—*Against interpretation*
(Eyre & Spottiswoode, 1967) 275-289.

72 CAPITALIST REALISM: Paintings by three
German artists—Gerd Richter, Konrad Fischer-Lueg and
Sigmar Polke—based on photographs of contemporary personalities
and events. Capitalist Realism developed in the early 1960's and can
be regarded as a German variant of *Pop Art*. The term itself is an
ironic comment, that is ' Capitalist Realism ' is West Germany's
answer to the ' Socialist Realism ' of East Germany.

H Ohff ' Poetry in contemporary German art ' *Studio international*
168(860) December 1964 262-267.

73 CASSA: An acronym for ' Centre for Advanced Study of
Science in Art '. The idea for CASSA was originated by
Marcello Salvadori in 1961, and workshop facilities were established

in North London in the middle 1960's. The centre is largely concerned with *Kinetic Art*.

' CASSA' *ICA bulletin* (160) July 1966 p 9.

74 CENTRE FOR ADVANCED VISUAL STUDIES (CAVS): This centre is part of the ' Massachusetts Institute of Technology ', Cambridge, Mass, USA, and is directed by Gyorgy Kepes. CAVS is concerned with research and experiment into all aspects of art and creativity in relation to science/technology, the environment, and communications media.

75 CENTRE 42: A project for an arts centre, to bring art and culture into the lives of workers, canvassed by the English playwright Arnold Wesker in the 1960's. The centre was to be located in a disused railway engine house, called ' The Roundhouse ', in Chalk Farm, North London. The name of the project derived from a 1960 Trades Union Congress resolution—number 42—which recommended trade union involvement in the arts. Because of lack of funds and ideological difficulties Centre 42 never materialised, but the Roundhouse building has become noted as an arts and entertainments centre. It is run on a commercial basis by George Hoskins.

M Foster ' The Roundhouse ' *AAQ* 3(1) Winter 1971 43-55.

N Lyndon ' The Roundhouse, Chalk Farm Rd NW1 ' *Time out* (129) August 4-10 1972 12-15.

A Wesker ' Brief for an architect ' *London magazine* 5(5) August 1965 78-83.

76 CENTRE NATIONAL D'ART CONTEMPORAIN (CNAC): In 1967, a centre to document current art and artists on an international scale was established in Paris by the ' Ministry of Cultural Affaires '.

B Hunnisett ' Centre National d'Art Contemporain, Paris ' *ARLIS Newsletter* (9) October 1971 2-3.

77 CENTRO DE ARTE Y COMMUNICACION (CAYC): The ' Centre of Art and Communication ' was established in 1968 in Buenos Aires, its director is Jorge Glusberg. The organisation is composed of artists, sociologists, psychologists,

mathematicians and art critics; exhibitions are mounted that are relevant to its interests, which are the relationship of art to science/technology and of art to its social setting.

78 **CHEMICAL ARCHITECTURE:** A proposal for a new kind of organic architecture made by the American philosopher and industrial designer, William Katavolos in 1960. Chemical powders and liquids can be activated by the addition of agents to expand into pre-determined shapes.

79 **CINETISATIONS:** Pictures of contorted and shattered buildings created by the French sculptor Pol Bury in 1966. These images are produced by the simple device of cutting or stamping out a series of concentric circles at key points in photographs, engravings, or reproductions of architectural subjects. The resulting rings are then remounted slightly askew. This utterly destroys the stability of the buildings. Bury enlarges his pictures and transfers them onto canvas or lithographic plates.

S Watson Taylor 'Pol Bury Cinetisations' *Art & artists* 1 (10) January 1967 8-13.

80 **CITY WALLS:** An artists' co-operative established in New York in 1969, with the encouragement of the urban planner David Bromberg, for the purpose of improving the environment of the city by decorating walls with murals and colourful abstract designs. Members of City Walls include Jason Cram, Robert Wiegard, Tania, and Allan D'Arcangelo; the last named artist is internationally known for his *Pop Art* roadscapes.

'Painting for City Walls: the Museum of Modern Art, New York' *L'architecture d'aujourdhui* (145) September 1969 91-94.

81 **CIVILIA:** A plan proposed by a development corporation, the 'North Nuneaton Consortium' in 1971 for a new, high density city with a population of one million to be sited in the West Midlands region of England. The concept of Civilia is an attempt to reverse the present decay of city life, caused by dispersal, to provide an alternative to the suburban sprawl. A special issue of

53

'Architectural review' was devoted to Civilia, and illustrated with elaborate collages made up of clips from photographs of existing cities.

'Civilia: the end of suburban man' *Architectural review* 149 (892) June 1971.

- I De Wolfe—editor—*Civilia: the end of suburban man* (Architectural Press, 1971).

82 CLASTIC ART: The American artist Carl Andre invented this term to describe those of his sculptures consisting of ready made units such as pebbles, bricks, steel slabs, bales of hay, plastic or wooden blocks and iron rods. 'Clastic' derives from a Greek word meaning to break—in English something that can be taken to pieces and re-assembled if required. Andre offers Clastic Art as an alternative to plastic art: 'whereas plastic art is a repeated record or process, clastic art provides the particles for an ongoing process'.

Andre believes it is not necessary to cut material in order to make sculpture, because the material itself is 'a cut in space'. He arranges the found elements for a certain period and if they are not purchased they return to their original non-art condition. He is also concerned with the idea of re-cycling materials unwanted by society.

See also Modular Art.

L R Lippard *Changing: essays in art criticism* (NY, Dutton, 1971) p 274.

C Tisdall 'Any old iron' *The guardian* June 1 1972 p 10.

'Carl Andre' *Avalanche* (1) Fall 1970 19-27.

83 THE CLUB (or Artists' Club): An artists' meeting place and discussion forum at thirty nine East Eighth Street, New York, founded in 1948 by Barnett Newman, Mark Rothko, Robert Motherwell and William Baziotes, and frequented by the Abstract Expressionists during the 1950's.

See also Subjects of the Artist.

I H Sandler 'The Club' *Artforum* 4(1) September 1965 27-31.

84 CLUSTER: An architectural and planning term much in vogue during the 1950's. The urbanist Kevin Lynch first discussed the Cluster concept in an article in the *Scientific American* in 1954. It refers to a form of city layout that has many small centres instead of a nodal point surrounded by concentric rings and a radial road pattern.

In 1957 Alison and Peter Smithson defined a Cluster, rather obscurely, as 'a close knit, complicated, often moving aggregation, but an aggregation with a distinct structure'. Denys Lasdun's residential towers designed from 1953 onwards were also called 'cluster blocks'.

Sibyl Moholy-Nagy uses Cluster to mean groups of houses scattered haphazardly in the twilight zone between cities and the open countryside.

'Cluster blocks . . .' *Architectural design* 28(2) February 1958 62-65.

K Lynch 'The form of cities' *Scientific American* 190(4) 1954 54-63.

S Moholy-Nagy *Matrix of man: an illustrated history of the urban environment* (Pall Mall Press, 1968) 241-282.

A & P Smithson 'Cluster city: a new shape for the community' *Architectural review* 122 (730) November 1957 333-336.

A & P Smithson 'Cluster patterns' *Architecture and building* 31 1956 271-272.

85 COBRA: Founded in Paris in 1948 by the Belgian poet and essayist Christian Dotremont. It was a group of European artists who regarded themselves as representing an International of experimental art, opposed to *Geometric Abstraction* and strongly influenced by Expressionism and Surrealism. The name of the group derives from the initial letters of the three capital cities where key members lived: COpenhagen, BRussels and Amsterdam. The best known artists associated with Cobra were Karel Appel, Asger Jorn, Corneille, Karl H Pederson, Pierre Alechinsky, Egill Jacobsen and Lucebert. The group had strong literary connections and published their ideas in a review called 'Cobra' issued in Denmark. Certain members of Cobra were also associated with the *Situationists*. Exhibitions were held at the Stedelijk Museum, Amsterdam in 1949, at Liege and Paris in 1951. Cobra artists produced works superficially resembling *Abstract Expressionism*; like the Americans, they attempted to blend abstraction and figuration, their brushwork was as vehement as De Kooning's, but despite its violence the results seem more decorative than the American's painting. Unlike the Abstract Expressionists, Cobra painters employed thick impasto combined with crude childlike drawing; their imagery was often drawn from primitive or folk art sources. Cobra only existed for three years but in spite of its brief life critics now claim that it was one of the most influential artistic movements of post-war European Art.

See also the Experimental Group.

E Langui 'Expressionism since 1945 and the Cobra movement '— essay in—J P Hodin and others *Figurative art since 1945* (Thames & Hudson, 1971) 59-90.

M Ragon 'The Cobra Group and lyrical expressionism' *Cimaise* (59) May/June 1962 26-45.

86 COLOUR-FIELD PAINTING: A description most commonly applied to the work of a generation of American painters—Morris Louis, Kenneth Noland, Jules Olitski and Gene Davis—exhibiting in the late 1950's and early 1960's. Exponents of *Hard-Edge Painting*, for example, Ellsworth Kelly, are sometimes included in the Colour-Field category. The term is also applied retrospectively to paintings produced in the late 1940's by three Abstract Expressionists: Barnett Newman, Clyfford Still and Mark Rothko; Newman is usually considered the originator and chief exponent of the Colour-Field concept.

The meaning of the term itself is complicated by the fact that art critics talk about 'Colour Painting', or 'Chromatic Abstraction', and also 'Field Painting'; 'Colour-Field' is clearly a combination of the two. Field painting began with Jackson Pollock. Field painters treat the picture surface as a continuous or extended plane, the whole picture is regarded as a single unit so that figure and ground tend to be given equal value. Colour-field painters replace tonal contrasts and brushwork by solid areas of colour (or in the case of the acrylic *Stain Painting* of Morris Louis and others with thin washes of colour) which extend, in most cases, across the canvas from edge to edge. These areas of colour seem as though they are, in Thomas B Hess's phrase, 'stamped out' of a larger sheet; thus it is implied that the fields of colour extend beyond the confines of the canvas to infinity. Colour is liberated, in this type of painting, from any limitation imposed by internal forms or structure.

In no longer treating the picture space as a box-like cavity Colour-Field Painting departs radically from the depth/illusionistic tradition of Western oil painting. (According to Peter Plagens, a colour field does have a shallow depth, in contrast to a spot of colour which appears to reside on the surface of the canvas). However what Colour-Field painting lacks in depth it makes up for in breadth: most Colour-Field painters work on a monumental horizontal scale and their canvases are intended to be viewed at close quarters (Newman's idea) so that the whole <u>field</u> of vision of the spectator is engulfed, and then the intensity of the colour creates dramatic optical effects and great emotional impact. Because this type of painting 'envelopes' the spectator it is often described as 'environmental'.

E B Henning 'Colour and Field' *Art international* 15 (5) May 20 1971 46-50.

T B Hess *Barnett Newman* (Tate Gallery, 1972).

I Sandler 'Colour-Field Painters'—chapter in—*Abstract Expressionism: the triumph of American painting* (Pall Mall Press, 1970) 148-157.

87 COMBINE PAINTING (or Stand up Painting):
Robert Rauschenberg's term for those of his easel pictures incorporating non-art objects: coke bottles, pillows, a stuffed ram, radios . . . plus traditional pigments. John Cage has remarked that these combinations of disparate objects are, from the subject point of view, non-relational—that is, they have as much or as little in common as the different stories in a newspaper layout. Rauschenberg's Combines carry the Cubist collage principle to extreme conclusions; they stretch the accepted convention of the easel picture to breaking point.

See also Assemblage Art.

88 COMPUTER ART: More accurately described as 'computer aided art' or 'computer generated art'. It has been produced internationally since about 1956 by a wide range of people belonging to a wide variety of professions—poets, artists, composers, engineers, industrial designers, mathematicians—in fact, anyone with access to computer time. Although computers have been used in the production of *Concrete Poetry* and electronic music for many years, their importance to the visual arts did not emerge fully until the 'Cybernetic Serendipity' exhibition held in London in 1968, as a result of which a 'Computer Arts Society' was founded in England.

The ' art ' produced by computers is mostly drawings and graphics: computers have been programmed to print out specified geometric shapes in random combinations or to transform images by a series of discreet steps—for example, the image of a man into the shape of a bottle and then into a map of Africa. Sculpture has also been produced via computer, punched tape and milling machines. The creative process is greatly assisted by the sketching facility of a light pen and cathode ray tube attached to a computer. The Korean artist Nam June Paik believes that such devices will in due course totally replace painting. Artistic improvisation and intuition are simulated in computer programming by the use of random numbers.

Even enthusiasts for Computer Art admit that aesthetically the results achieved so far are disappointing, and the limiting factor is clearly the creativity of human programmers. Nevetheless some progress has been claimed: (1) scientists and technicians with no previous interest in art have been involved; (2) the high speed of computer processing telescopes the time required to run through the possible permutations of a visual idea, which is especially useful in architectural design. Jasia Reichardt believes that Computer Art is the last stance of abstraction because of the impersonality of computing procedures. Up until now computers have acted as sophisticated tools; if and when they achieve the status of independent artificial intelligences comparable in complexity to the human brain, then we may expect a radically new and authentic Computer Art.

See also Cybernetic Art.

J Burnham ' The aesthetics of intelligent systems '—essay in—*On the future of art* edited by E Fry (NY, Viking Press, 1970) 95-122.

' Computer Arts Society ' *Leonardo* 2 (3) July 1969 319-320.

H W Franke *Computer graphics—computer art* (Phaidon, 1971).

J Reichardt *The computer in art* (Studio Vista, 1971).

J Reichardt—editor—*Cybernetic serendipity: the computer and the arts* (Studio International, 1968).

89 **CONCEPTUAL ARCHITECTURE**: In 1970 a special issue of 'Design quarterly ' edited by J S Margolies, was devoted to this theme. Contributors were asked to take account of the communications/psychological/entertainment environments. The issue contained a number of projects and statements—some serious, some humorous; it included plans for futuristic cities, a menu for 'Eatable Architecture' and featured groups such as *Ant Farm, Archigram, Archizoom, Haus-Rucker-Co* and *Superstudio,* also artists such as Les Levine and Ed Ruscha. The words 'conceptual' and 'architecture' were employed in a cavalier fashion: they were 'defined' in an 'essay' by Peter D Eisenman which contained no text, only footnotes.

'Conceptual Architecture' *Design quarterly* (78/79) 1970.

90 CONCEPTUAL ART (also called Con Art, Concept Art, Idea Art, Impossible Art, Documentary Art, Post-Object Art, Non-Object Art, Dematerialised Art, Blind Man's Art, Head Art, Meta-Art, Project Art, Analytical Art): An international —though largely Anglo-American—idiom of *Avant-Garde Art* dating from the middle 1960's, emerging in part from the emphasis placed on artistic decision making in *Minimal Art* and *Process Art,* and reflecting also the influence of Marcel Duchamp (his ready mades and critical statements), Ad Reinhardt (his writings) and the *Neo-Dada* artists, all of whom raised questions about the ontological status of the art object. While these influences are acknowledged they are not revered, and English Conceptualists in particular have examined them very critically.

The term 'Conceptual Art' has been credited by some writers to Sol Le Witt (he, Donald Judd, and Robert Morris are the Minimal artists most respected by the Conceptualists), but Henry Flynt, an American member of the international movement called *Fluxus,* has consistently advocated the notion of 'Concept Art' since 1961; Yoko Ono, another one time member of *Fluxus,* has also described her work, over the years, as 'Con Art'.

The major Conceptual artists include Joseph Kosuth, Lawrence Weiner, Douglas Huebler, On Kawara, Victor Burgin, Christine Kozlov, Bernar Venet, Terry Atkinson, David Bainbridge, Michael Baldwin and Harold Hurrell. The last four named British artists publish 'Art language', subtitled the 'journal of conceptual art', and are often referred to as 'Analytical Artists' or as the 'Art-Language Group'. They have also influenced a number of younger British artists, based in Coventry, who published another journal called 'Analytical Art' (now defunct). The notion of 'Analytical Art' crops up again in the name of a New York group 'The Society for Theoretical Art and Analyses', consisting of Ian Burn, Mel Ramsden and Roger

Cutforth. In San Francisco Thomas Marioni Founded in 1970 'The Museum of Conceptual Art' (MOCA), and in Tokyo, Tatsuo Yamamoto established 'The Conceptual Art Research Association' (CARA). The English critic Charles Harrison is a leading apologist for Conceptual Art, and is now editor of 'Art language'. Previously he was on the editorial staff of 'Studio international', a periodical which has published many articles on and examples of Conceptual Art in recent years.

It is difficult to provide a concise and exact definition of 'Conceptual Art', because, as Donald Brook points out, 'no single use of the phrase . . . has secured de facto general acceptance '; in an attempt to define it he distinguishes at least four different senses in which the phrase can be used. In view of this problem it is only possible here to indicate, empirically, the salient characteristics of the art form :

(1) Conceptual Art rejects out of hand the physical art object, it is concerned with software not hardware. Minimal and Process artists showed the extent to which the making of art is dependent on a series of rules (to a motorist the rules of the road are just as important as the road itself), which can be used to generate objects if required; as Le Witt observed 'an idea is a machine that makes art'. Conceptual artists came to regard the rules not the physical objects as the essential feature of art. They despise the art object because (a) it is too closely tied to the use of particular materials and craft skills, emphasising the artist's hand rather than his mind, and (b) it appeals to sensory experience—what Duchamp called 'visual thrill '—at the expense of conceptual experience. Initially, in pursuit of a dematerialised art, conceptual artists created works composed of inert gases or invisible to the human senses, works composed of inert gases or electromagnetic waves (see Natural Sculpture), whose existence could only be detected by readings on instruments.

Nevertheless ideas have to be communicated through some physical means, hence the use of documentation: photographs, videotape, texts or speech (the artist Ian Wilson uses oral communication—conversation—as his art form). However the physical form is not crucial to the expression of concepts, as an early work by Kosuth illustrated: the concept of 'chair' was expressed by means of a real chair, a photograph of the chair, and a photostat of the dictionary definition of the word 'chair' exhibited in a gallery. In this case the different physical objects were merely forms of presentation of an idea.

In view of the above remarks the reader can appreciate why exhibitions of Conceptual Art are few and far between. The only major show to date, called 'Conceptual Art and Conceptual Aspects', was held at the New York Cultural Centre in 1970.

(2) Conceptual Art annexes the function of art criticism and art theory. In doing so it has drawn attention to those support languages that surround art objects. Kosuth notes that a scientist's theoretical writings are considered just as much 'science' as his experimental laboratory work, whereas an artist's theories were regarded, in the past, as merely extras. In this way what was once secondary material —art criticism, art history, art theory—now becomes primary. Art critics, especially those in the United States, have countered the usurpation of their role by themselves producing examples of Conceptual Art.

(3) Although Conceptual Art encompasses a wide variety of artistic behaviour, including examples of what I prefer to call *Performance Art*, in its extreme form—known as 'acute' or 'ultra-conceptualism' —it is a philosophical enquiry into the concept 'art'. Hence Conceptual Art is concerned with abstraction, not in the sense of abstracting from nature by reduction, but in the sense of dealing with general ideas such as are embodied in words. Kosuth, author of the expression 'Art as idea, as idea', maintains that art is a language, that art works are propositions 'presented within the context of art as a comment on art' and that each genuinely new art-work must extend our concept of art; thus he believes art is a tautological system: 'art is the definition of art'. The 'Art-Language Group' share Kosuth's belief in the essentially linguistic structure of art (some Conceptualists have been called 'Folk Linguists'). To them the reference to language is no mere analogy, since they use the English language as the material for their art; their texts rely heavily on the methods and terminology of philosophy.

The development of Conceptual Art can be accounted for in several ways: on the one hand it can be seen as a reaction to the hedonism of *Pop Art* and the easy visual appeal of *Op Art* and similar movements in painting, as an attempt to re-introduce intellectual stringency into art, to restore the academic tradition of fine art; on the other hand it can be interpreted as a manifesation of despair on the part of artists with no public and no market, since it is a fact that modern society trains a large number of art students but only supports a minute number of practising artists. Thus in disposing of the physical art object the Conceptual Artist solves a number of practical problems.

Conceptual Art has aroused much adverse criticism: it has been called ' a reactionary gimmick' and ' verbiage art'; the language of the Conceptualists has been called ' gibberish'; their art has been described as ' cerebral wanking' because of the mental labour it involves; its advocates agree that it is ' private', ' cryptic', ' baffling', since Conceptualists believe that today art exists for artists and an informed minority (like higher mathematics and other specialities), and they deny any general communicative responsibility. In my view Conceptual Art has performed a valuable service in highlighting the conceptual element in all works of art; however, I suspect that future art historians will regard it as the *Tachisme* of our time.

L Borden ' Three modes of Conceptual Art' *Artforum* 10(10) June 1972 68-71.

D Brook ' Toward a definition of Conceptual Art' *Leonardo* 5 (1) Winter 1972 49-50.

K Friedman ' Notes on Concept Art' *Schmuck* March 1972 6-16.

C Harrison ' "A very abstract context"' *Studio international* 180 (927) November 1970 194-198.

J Kosuth 'Art after philosophy' I *Studio international* 178 (915) October 1969 134-137.

J Kosuth 'Art after philosophy' II *Studio international* 178 (916) November 1969 160-161.

J Kosuth 'Art after philosophy' III *Studio international* 178 (917) December 1969 212-213.

L Lippard ' The dematerialisation of art'—essay in—*Changing: essays in art criticism* (NY, Dutton, 1971) 255-276.

P Manz & G de Vries—editors—*Art & language* (Cologne, Dumont, 1972).

V Meyer *Conceptual Art* (NY, Dutton, 1972).

E Migliorini *Conceptual Art* (Florence, Edizioni d'Arte Il Fiorino, 1972).

91 CONCRETE ART (In French: Art Concret, in German: Konkrete Kunst): A form of art propounded by a group of artists established in Paris in 1930, led by Theo Van Doesburg, who also edited a review/manifesto entitled 'Art Concret'. The word ' concrete' was introduced to replace ' abstract': the latter was regarded as unsatisfactory because it suggested a separation from reality; ' concrete' on the other hand is, according to the dictionary,

' concerned with realities or actual instances rather than abstractions ',
exemplified by the expression ' give me a concrete example '; the
noun ' concretion ', meaning ' the act or process of becoming solid
or calcified ', is also relevant. Thus the Concrete artist does not
abstract from nature. He constructs from the given elements of
natural phenomena (colour, form, space, light, etc) objects which are,
according to their originators, ' the concretion of the creative spirit '.

Many artists have exploited the notions of Concrete Art, the best
known of whom is Max Bill. It was one of the major tendencies of
European art to survive the second world war because its practitioners
lived in neutral countries such as Switzerland and Argentina. In the
immediate post-war period, major exhibitions of Concrete Art were
organised and a number of groups were formed. In Italy, for example,
Gillo Dorfles founded in 1948 the ' Movimento Arte Concreta ' (MAC).
The word ' concrete ' gained wider currency when it was adopted by
a new generation of artists concerned with *Concrete Poetry*.

However the mainstreams of European and American art soon
moved away from pure construction, and since 1950 the term
' Concrete Art ' has been little used.

A Pellegrini *New tendencies in art* (NY, Crown, 1966) 17-20.

92 CONCRETE EXPRESSIONISM: Irving Sandler's name for the work of a group of American painters, including Al Held, exhibiting in New York in 1965.

93 CONCRETE POETRY: (Including: Audiovisual Texts, Constellations, Evident Poetry, Kinetic Poetry, Machine Poetry, Objective Poetry, Optical Poetry, Poem-Paintings, Poetry of Surface, Popcrete, Process Texts, Publit, Semiotic Poetry, Typestracts, Typewriter Poems, Visual Texts, Word Art).

In its visual form Concrete Poetry has been placed ' between poetry
and painting ' (the title of an exhibition at the *Institute of Contemporary Arts*, London, in 1965). The Concrete poet organises language
spatially like a painter, relying on the juxtaposition of words etc, on
the page to convey meaning, rather than on linear syntax. Like any
visual image, his work must be reproduced exactly: the particular
typeface(s) chosen and every other visual feature are essential to its
identity. The movement took its definitive form in the early 1950's in

the work of Eugen Gomringer and a Brazilian group called the
'Noigandres', and although the term 'Concrete' is now used to
describe the activities of many kinds of poet-artist, they all share a
primary concern with the actual, concrete material of language, as
opposed to its 'secondary' use as a vehicle for the expression of a
subjective feeling or idea.

Their forerunners in the nineteenth century were Lewis Carroll (' The
mouse's tale ') and Mallarmé (' Un coup de dés '), and in this century,
Pound, Joyce, and E E Cummings. Perhaps more radical influences
were the poetry and manifestos of the Futurists, Dadaists and Russian
Constructivists; Marinetti, for instance, called for the liberation of
words from syntax, and a poetry made of nouns only, left standing in
their 'naked purity' and 'essential colour'. In 1943 Carlo Belloli
realised these ideals in the poster-poems that he called ' wall text-
poems '. Later in the same decade the Lettrists used hieroglyphics and
letter-forms in their paintings and graphics, and in 1953 Oyvind
Fahlstrom published in Sweden a 'Manifesto for Concrete Poetry'
that related his poetry to Concrete music.

When Gomringer and the Brazilian Decio Pignatari agreed, in 1955,
on the name 'Concrete' for their poetry, they were taking as their
model the *Concrete Art* of Max Bill, which was a non-figurative and
autonomous art that aimed at clarity and mathematical perfection. To
make self-sufficing works of this nature in the medium of language,
the poets' most typical strategy was to create self-referring verbal
ideograms, in which verbal and non-verbal communication coincided.
This was effected, preferably, not by shaping words into a picture,
but by exemplifying in the poem's structure some quality or process.
Another method was to bring words together into what Gomringer
called 'Constellations', which defined a limited yet complete world
of meaning, and which allowed the reader to make his own connections
within a 'play area of fixed dimensions'. They saw their work as
clarifying, and improving the efficiency of, language: a kind of meta-
language parallel to linguistics and information theory. The influence
of scientific disciplines such as these can be seen in the common
Concrete practices of repetition and permutation of verbal material.

Concrete Poetry is an international movement. The 'Noigrandes'
group of Brazil has already been mentioned; in addition, work in the
pure Concrete manner has been done in Germany by Bremer, in
Austria by Rühm and Achleitner, in Mexico by Goeritz, in Scotland
by Edwin Morgan, in the USA by Emmett Williams, and in Czecho-

slovakia by Barborka, whose 'Process Texts' have expanded the style to book-length.

Gomringer restricted himself to one typeface and one colour—black, on white paper—while the 'Noigandres' used a wider range of colours and typefaces, but retained the same classical balance between visual and semantic content. During the 1960's the movement developed into a multitude of forms and labels, some employing a much wider range of techniques and a looser, more expressionist structure. Ian Hamilton Finlay has used stone, metal and other materials, all closely related to the sense of his poems. Pignatari has moved on to the invented sign-systems of 'Semiotic Poetry', and Augusto De Campos to the sequences of photographic images that he calls 'Popcrete'. Belloli has kept his distance from the Concrete poets, preferring to call his later work, however similar, 'Audiovisual Texts'. The visual qualities of word and letter forms have been explored in the 'Poetry of Surface' of Franz Mon, the 'Poem-Paintings' and 'Publit' of Kriwet, the 'Evident Poetry' of Kolář and 'the Optical' poems of Valoch.

The typewriter has been used frequently as a medium, particularly by the 'Kinetic' poet, Don Sylevester Houédard, who uses the term 'Typestracts' for his finished work. Another typewriter poet, Pierre Garnier, who calls his work 'Machine Poetry', published a manifesto in 1963 in which he used the word 'Spatialism' (also used by Lucio Fontana in the 1940's) to cover all the current trends in experimental poetry whose common aim, he says, is to transmit and liberate energy. In recent years all labels have fallen out of favour, except perhaps 'Visual Texts' and 'Concrete Poetry' in its most general sense.

See also Lettrism, Spatialism, Calligraphic Painting.

S Bann—editor—*Concrete poetry, an international anthology* (London Magazine, 1967).

'The changing guard 1' *Times literary supplement* (3258) August 6 1964.

'The changing guard 2' *Times literary supplement* (3262) September 3 1964.

(Concrete Poetry) *Akros* 6(8) March 1972. Special issue.

J Reichardt 'The whereabouts of concrete poetry' *Studio international* 171 (874) February 1966 56-59.

Schuldt 'Word Art' *Arts magazine* 43(8) Summer 1969.

J Sharkey—editor—*Mindplay, an anthology of British Concrete poetry* (Lorrimer, 1971).

3

M E Solt—editor—*Concrete poetry, a world view* (Bloomington, Indiana University Press, 1968).

Sound texts/?Concrete Poetry/Visual texts (Amsterdam, Stedelijk Museum, 1971).

M Weaver 'And what is Concrete Poetry' *Art international* 12(5) May 15 1968 30-33.

E Williams—editor—*An anthology of Concrete Poetry* (NY, Something Else Press, 1967).

94 **CONSTRUCTIONISM**: The American artist Charles Biederman coined this term in 1938 to describe his own work—a form of relief deriving from painting but sharing some of the three dimensional qualities of sculpture—and a method of creation. The French artist Jean Gorin produced similar works at the same time but the artists were unaware of each other's art until the late 1940's. Since then a number of American and European artists have adopted the Constructionist label (some indiscriminately—in 1952 Biederman felt constrained to introduce a new term *Structurism*).

During the 1950's a generation of British artists—John Ernest, Adrian Heath, Anthony Hill, Kenneth and Mary Martin, Victor Pasmore, Peter Stroud and Gillian Wise—were influenced by Biederman's ideas; Pasmore in particular was deeply impressed by Biederman's monumental history of art as the evolution of visual knowledge, which he read in 1951.

C Biederman *Art as the evolution of visual knowledge*. (Red Wing, Minnesota, Biederman, 1958).

95 **CONSTRUCTIVISM**: The origins of Constructivism date back to 1914 and the work of Tatlin; however the term has been employed—perhaps unwisely—since 1945, by writers such as George Rickey, to encompass such diverse movements as *Op Art, Kinetic Art, Hard-Edge Painting, Minimal Art* and *Post-Painterly Abstraction*.

However, the continued vitality of the Constructivist tradition is illustrated by the establishment in 1969 of the CO-MO Centre, Paris. 'Le Centre d'Art Constructif et Mouvement' welcomes artists working in the modes of *Serial Art, Modular Art*, Geometrical Art and Neo-Constructivism.

G Rickey *Constructivism: origins and evolution* (Studio Vista, 1967).

96 CONTEMPORARY STYLE: During the period 1945 to 1956 the word 'contemporary' was used by many British writers to describe the art, architecture and design of their era; for example, the *Institute of Contemporary Arts* was founded in 1947, Herbert Read's book 'Contemporary British Art' was published in 1951. Characteristics of the Contemporary Style were most clearly seen in the applied arts, but they were also manifested to some extent in *Action Painting*: lightness, gaiety, a spiky, spindly look. In furniture this appearance resulted from the use of thin metal rods and pale timber instead of dark, of wooden legs which were often splayed out and tapered, metal fittings which had brightly coloured plastic blobs at their extremities. Magazine racks were constructed of wire covered with plastic, the gaps between metal supports were bridged by decorative lacing made of plastic, a mannerism that derived from the sculpture of Naum Gabo, Alexander Calder and Barabara Hepworth. Wallpaper and textile design favoured geometrical patterns: snow crystals, coffin shapes or elongated hexagons.

The Contemporary Style was popularised by the Festival of Britain exposition of 1951, giving rise to another term 'Festival Style' or 'South Bank Style'; 'Design' magazine also calls it the 'New English Style'. Authorities on design disagree as to whether a Festival Style really existed, but they do admit that the phrase has been used; Richard Hamilton regards it as a sub-classification of Contemporary Style. Peter Cook says that 1952 design 'contained a mixture of post-war spinoff (the technology of laminates, alloys and micromechanics) and latter-day thirties styling'.

In the context of an exhibition, experimental design was appropriate, but the mannerisms of 1951 quickly became clichés disfiguring the interior decor of coffee bars, public houses and exterior features such as street furniture. Many Contemporary style products were eccentric in design and poorly constructed. Their look is antipathetic to today's taste, but a revival in the near future seems an historical inevitability if the progression apparent in the Art Nouveau and *Art Deco* revivals continues.

'FoB + 10' *Design* (149) May 1961 40-51.

P Cook *Experimental Architecture* (Studio Vista, 1971) p 17.

M Frayn 'Festival'—essay in—*Age of austerity 1945-51* edited by M Sissons and P French (Penguin, 1964) 330-353.

97 CONTINUUM: A group formed by three artists, Bob Janz, Mike MacKinnon and Dante Leonelli, exhibiting light and motion works at the Axiom gallery, London in 1968. The name 'Continuum' refers to transformations through time—multiple form —achieved by artworks capable of change, as opposed to the sculptural qualities of static works. Although their works resemble *Kinetic Art*, the members of the group claim to have more in common with the work of American artists such as Kenneth Noland and George Rickey. Continuum believes in the close co-operation of its members, but not anonymous group activity. It exploits modern materials such as neon light and plastics and maintains close contact with industry.

C L Morgan 'Continuum light and motion systems' *Art & artists* 5(3) June 1970 60-63.

98 CONTRACT FURNITURE: Large quantities of furniture produced as a result of an agreement, or contract, between an architect, or a corporation, and a furniture manufacturer, or supplier. During the post-war building boom large-scale office blocks and institutions were constructed and required complete ranges of furniture to equip them; as a result Contract Furniture became an important and profitable part of the furnishing trade. As one writer noted, because architects order large quantities of such furniture they are in a position to demand improvements in design and quality.

S Southin 'Furniture—subject to contract' *Design* (182) February 1964 22-29.

99 COOL ART: In jazz circles 'cool' has been used since the late 1940's to refer to an intellectual, emotionally restrained musical style; more recently in colloquial speech the word means 'smart', 'up to date', 'fashionable'. In 1964 Philip Leider applied it to a group of Los Angeles artists—Robert Irwin, Kenneth Price, Joe Goode, Ed Ruscha, Larry Bell and others—who manifested 'a hatred of the superfluous, a drive toward compression, a precision of execution . . . impeccability of surface' (see also Finish Fetish), and whose work marked 'a new distance between artist and work of art, between artist and viewer': a 'hands off' quality, coldness, austerity.

Since 1964 other critics have employed the phrase 'Cool Art' (derogatorily) to refer to a detached, impersonal anti-expressionistic tendency in American and English art of the middle 1960's, a tendency they detected in movements as various as *Pop Art*, *Hard-Edge Painting* and *Minimal Art*.

P Leider 'The Cool School' *Artforum* 2(12) Summer 1964 p 47.

I Sandler 'The new Cool Art' *Art in America* 53(1) February 1965 99-101.

100 COP ART: According to Paul Gerhard, Cop Art—short for 'Copulation Art'—is a new concept in erotic or pornographic art, a style practised by artists such as Allen Jones, Heimrod Prem and Lothar Fischer. The expression 'Cop Art' is also used by the group, known as *NE Thing Company*, to mean the use, exploitation or annexation of another artist's works.

P Gerhard *Pornography or art?* (Words & Pictures, 1971).

101 CORRESPONDENCE ART (also called Mail Art, Envois): In recent years an increasing number of individuals—poets, designers, photographers, architects, painters, typographers—and small groups of artists, mostly residing in the United States and Canada, have made use of the postal system as a means of creating art. The postal service enables information to be recycled, it enables artists to form communication networks, it acts as an interface between artists and the world outside art.

The originator of Correspondence Art was probably Ray Johnson, an American painter who in the late 1950's presided over the creation of a series of seminal collages; they were produced with the help of friends and strangers who posted them to each other for alterations and additions. Johnson describes these activities under the heading 'the New York Correspondance School'. Hundreds of people are now involved in Johnson's network, which Thomas Albright describes as 'a continuous happening by mail'. Currently such 'schools' are legion: 'Airpress', 'Fat City School of Finds Art', the 'North West Mounted Valise', 'Ace Space Company', 'a space', 'Image Bank', 'Mail Order Art', 'Sam's Cafe', *Ant Farm* and also the international art federation known as *Fluxus*. Individual artists exploiting the postal system include Robert Watts and John Dowd. The growth of Correspondence Art can be accounted for in various ways:

(1) it marks a response by artists to the information explosion and the massive output of printed ephemera and images associated with it;

(2) the availability of cheap offset printing machines and xerox machines;

(3) it reflects a desire on the part of many artists to collaborate in the creation of artworks, especially to collaborate in ways which make use of the element of chance;

(4) its popularity in North America may be due to a feeling of isolation experienced by artists who are separated by vast geographical distances;

(5) it provides an outlet for subversive artists who hope to undermine the art establishment and other social institutions by an anti-functional use of communication systems, by means of humour, crank letters, and misinformation (this attitude has given rise to the expression ' Guerrilla Art ').

Thomas Albright claims that Correspondence artists form an underground whose work is intended as an alternative to the museum/gallery system; however, the movement is now documented, anthologies of Correspondence Art are being published, and large scale exhibitions have already been mounted, for example at the Whitney Museum, New York in 1970. Therefore Correspondence Art seems fated to become overground, established art.

See also Media Art, Underground Art.

T Albright ' New Art School: Correspondence ' *Rolling stone* (106) April 13, 1972 p 20.

T Albright ' Correspondence Art ' *Rolling stone* (107) April 27, 1972 20-21.

D Bourdon ' Notes on a letter head ' *Art international* 13(9) November 1969 78-80.

J G Bowles ' Out of the gallery into the mailbox ' *Art in America* 60 (2) March/April 1972 p 23.

' The New York Correspondance School ' *Artforum* 6(2) October 1967 50-55.

J M Poinsot *Mail Art* (Paris, Cedic, 1972).

102 **CRITICAL REALISTS:** A group of German montage artists, including Hans-Jurgen Diehl, Wolfgang Petrick, Peter Sorge, Klaus Vogelgensang, Bettina von Arnim and Gerd Winner, who make use of photographs and headlines drawn from magazines and newspapers to mount critical attacks on contemporary culture.

103 CULTURAL ART: A pejorative term employed by European critics, such as Jean Clay, since the abortive French revolution of May 1968. Cultural Art is roughly equivalent to Fine Art, in the sense of art as pure investigation for its own sake. Such art is 'Tame Art'. The cultural artist plays at freedom instead of living it, he is harmless, his art is a safety valve for the discontents of society; in return society accords him a privileged status—in reality an invisible prison. Any attempt to escape from the cultural ghetto by means of group activities or by the production of *Multiples* is doomed to failure; the artist must inevitably fall back upon the bourgeois gallery system and its exploitation of art for money. The alternative to Cultural Art is called 'Wild Art'—the artist is urged to intervene in social life, to take direct political action, to develop the concept of *Street Art*, in order to break away from the normal art venues and modes of expression.

See also Atelier Populaire.

J Clay 'Art tamed and wild' *Studio international* 177 (912) June 1969 261-265.

104 CUSTOM PAINTING: Mass produced goods, in particular motorcycles and automobiles, have been personalised by means of painted decoration since the late 1940's. This art form emerged in Southern California and its originator is claimed to be Van Dutch Holland. Nowadays production model vehicles are little used, customising has become a cult of the fantastic—the Kustom car cult—involving the total fabrication of an automobile or motorcycle from special parts.

The expression 'Custom Painting' was also used in the 1960's by the British Pop artist Peter Phillips to describe a series of his own works. Phillips selected images from particular sub-cultures, such as that of the leather jacketed rockers, as a step towards a custom made art. For the further development of this concept see Hybrid Enterprises and Fine Artz.

G Card 'Custom Painting'—letter in—*Studio international* 174 (891) July/August 1967 p 7.

T Wolfe *The kandy kolored tangerine flake streamlined baby* (Cape, 1966) title essay 76-107.

105 **CYBERNETIC ART** (also called Cyborg Art, Cyberart, Post-Kinetic Art): Norbert Weiner, the principal founder of the scientific theory of cybernetics described it as 'control and communication in the animal and the machine', and also as the study of messages as a means of controlling machinery and society. Fundamental to cybernetics is the concept of feedback, that is the return of part of the energy output of a system, in the form of information, for correcting or controlling the future behaviour of the system.

During the 1960's a number of artists, predominantly European Kineticists, began to apply these scientific ideas in their work; cybernetics seemed to provide a means of overcoming the limitations of *Kinetic Art* in respect of spectator participation. Several Cybernetic sculptures were built capable of responding to environmental stimuli, including the proximity of the spectator or any sounds that he might make. Nicholas Schoffer created such a work as early as 1954. Other artists who have produced similar sculpture or environments include Enrique Castro-Cid, Nam June Paik, Charles Mattox, Robert Breer and the American art and technology group *Pulsa*. Jack Burnham believes that the aim of what he calls Cyborg Art (the cybernetic organism as an art form) is to achieve the degree of communicative interaction of two humans conversing together. Such art attempts to simulate the structure of life rather than imitating its appearance, and its ultimate goal is total integration with intelligent life forms; at this level artifacts are replaced by systems, Cybernetic Art is superseded by *Systems Art*.

The English artist Roy Ascott has been influenced by Cybernetics in his work and in his theories. He maintains that the trend towards a fusion of the arts can be accounted for by a 'cybernetic vision' in which art is regarded as a behaviour within society. Several other English artists who are cybernetics orientated contribute to a journal published in London, edited by Steve Willats, called 'Control magazine' (see Behavioural Art).

A note of warning: artists, critics and exhibition organisers often use the term 'cybernetics' and 'computers' interchangeably, but while the two are related and frequently occur together in practice, they are not identical fields of knowledge; Cybernetic Art and *Computer Art* are not one and the same.

M J Apter 'Cybernetics and art' *Leonardo* 2(3) July 1969 257-265.

R Ascott 'Behaviourist art and the cybernetic vision' (Part 1)

Cybernetica 9(4) 1966 247-264; (Part II) *Cybernetica* 10(1) 1967 25-56.

R Ascott 'The cybernetic stance: my process and purpose' *Leonardo* 1(2) April 1968 105-112.

J Burnham 'Robot and Cyborg Art'—chapter in—*Beyond modern sculpture* . . . (Allen Lane, Penguin Press, 1968) 312-376.

J Reichhardt—editor—*Cybernetics, art and ideas* (Studio Vista, 1971).

J Reichardt—editor—*Cybernetic serendipity: the computer and the arts* (Studio International, 1968).

106 **CYMATICS** (or Kymatic): This word, deriving from the Greek 'Kyma' meaning the wave, is used by the artist/scientist Hans Jenny to describe his research into the structure and dynamics of waves, vibrations, and periodic phenomena. Strictly speaking Cymatics is not an art term, but many of Jenny's experiments relate to *Kinetic Art* and his photographs and books interest many artists; consequently Cymatics is often featured in art journals and in exhibitions taking place in art galleries.

H Jenny *Cymatics: the structure and dynamics of waves and vibrations* (Basle, Basilius, 1967).

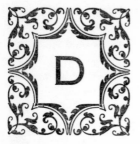

107 **DÉCOLLAGE:** The opposite of collage. It means ungluing, unsticking, taking off. The art of décollage occurs naturally in cities when poster hoardings are torn and defaced revealing several layers of imagery. Décollage was discovered by the Surrealist Leo Malet in 1934 and became extremely popular as a method of producing art in Europe during the 1950's. Artists associated with this latter development included Raymond Hains, Jacques de la Villeglé, François Dufrêne, Mimmo Rotella, Austin Cooper and Gwyther Irwin.

A magazine called ' Décollage ' was issued in Germany by the avant garde group known as *Fluxus*; to Wolf Vostell, one of its leading artists, the word ' décollage ' had a much more profound meaning than merely a technique for producing decorative artifacts such as torn posters, to him it signified the destruction, dissolution and change inherent in human existence: 'Life is dé - coll - age in that the body in one process builds up and deteriorates as it grows older—a continuous destruction '; as a result he developed a series of destructive events or *Happenings* reflecting this insight.

See also Affiche Lacerées, Veriwischung, Auto-Destructive Art.

L Malet 'A new art medium (1) how poetry devours walls ' *Leonardo* 2(4) October 1969 419-420.

W Vostell ' Dé-coll-age ' *Art and artists* 1(5) August 1966 9-10.

108 **DEDUCTIVE STRUCTURE:** A theory of pictorial construction expounded by the American art critic Michael Fried in numerous articles since 1965. Fried makes a useful distinction between the actual shape of the support which he calls ' literal shape ', and the internal patterning of a painting which he calls ' depicted shape '. According to Fried the vertical bands (depicted shape) in Barnett Newman's canvases are deduced from the two side-framing edges (literal shape) and this explicit acknowledgement of the shape of support marks a significant step in the development of *Modernist Painting*. This theory has also been applied to the paintings of Kenneth Noland, but in particular to the work of Frank Stella, to explain the phenomenon of the *Shaped Canvas*. A fuller discussion of the theory can be found in W S Rubin's book 'Frank Stella' (NY, Museum of Modern Art, 1970) 54-60.

109 DESIGN COUNCIL: A British organisation established by the Board of Trade in 1944 and known until 1972 as 'The Council of Industrial Design'. Its purpose was 'to promote ... the improvement of design in the products of British industry'. This aim was to be achieved by awards, publicity, and exhibitions. In 1949, the council began publication of 'Design' magazine, and in 1956 a permanent display centre—the 'Design Centre' located in the Haymarket, London—was opened to the public. The director of COID during the years 1947 to 1959 was the British furniture designer Gordon Russell.

See also 'Good Design'.

M Farr *Design in British industry: a mid century survey* (Cambridge, University Press, 1955) 208-222.

F MacCarthy *All things bright and beautiful: design in Britain 1830 to today* (Allen & Unwin, 1972).

110 DESIGN RESEARCH UNIT (DRU): A British industrial design office established in January 1943 by the Ministry of Information. The idea for DRU was originated by Marcus Brumwell, Milner Gray, Misha Black and Herbert Read; the last mentioned became its first director. The purpose of DRU was to provide a practical service to industry in the form of advice, research and consultancy, to improve the quality of design in British products so that they could compete in post-war world markets. It was thought that only a team of designers pooling their specialist knowledge could offer a service sophisticated enough to tackle large-scale design commissions. The DRU has worked successfully in the areas of exhibition design, interior design and corporate design for national bodies and large British industrial organisations.

J & A Blake *The practical idealists: twenty five years of designing for industry* (Lund Humphries, 1969).

111 DESTRUCTIVE ART: The twin phenomena of violence and destruction so characteristic of the history of the twentieth century have featured as subject matter in modern art, but during the first half of the 1960's a number of artists from different countries, conscious of the unprecedented potential for destruction created by mankind since 1945, developed a new form of art in which violence and destruction were used as methods of creation, and Destructive Art emerged as an aesthetic in its own right. Such art usually took place in public, so that an audience could witness the transformations of objects by successive acts of destruction, the process of change being regarded as art not the resultant debris. Jean Tinguely exhibited self-destroying machines, Jean Toche smashed typewriters, John Latham built and exploded Skoob towers (' Skoob ' equals ' books ' spelt backwards), Werner Schreib drew images with fire : a technique he called ' Pyrogravure ', Gustav Metzger used acid to destroy nylon sheets (see Auto-Destructive Art). Tosun Bayrak, a Turkish/American artist working in New Rork, is noted for a kind of *Street Art* : orgies of destruction involving blood and animal corpses. In fact most *Actions* and *Happenings* contain a high proportion of aggression and destructive activity, especially in Austria (see Direct Art).

In 1966 a ' Destruction in Arts Symposium ' (DIAS) was held in London, organised by Gustav Metzger and John Sharkey. More than twenty artists from ten countries attended, and examples of their Destructive Art presented during the course of the symposium created a furore in the press and led to prosecutions for indecent exhibitions. DIAS claimed that destructive techniques in art were a worldwide activity, and that there was a close relationship between the new art form and social reality. They maintained that human aggression could be sublimated through art, and that violence would be socially acceptable in the form of art, but the critics did not agree—in their view violence breeds violence, and they condemned Destructive Art as ' perverse, ugly and anti-social '. A second DIAS was held in the United States in 1968.

Art & artists 1(5) August 1966 (A special issue on violence and destruction in art).

Happening and Fluxus (Cologne, Kölnischer Kunstverein, 1970).

J Reichardt 'Gallery: destruction in art' *Architectural review* 140(838) December 1966 441-444.

C Willard 'Violence and art' *Art in America* 57(1) January/February 1969 36-43.

112 **DIMENSIONAL PAINTING**: Three-dimensional forms with painted surfaces, a term devised by the English abstract painter Justin Knowles.

See also Shaped Canvas.

P Overy 'Justin Knowles: dimensional paintings' *Studio international* 173(885) January 1967 32-33.

113 **DIRECT ART**: A group of Austrian artists—Otto Muhl, Hermann Nitsch and Gunther Brus, calling themselves the 'Vienna Institute for Direct Art'—have organised since 1965 a series of *Actions* which are somewhat similar to the American *Happenings*. Their events include brutal sexual and sado-masochistic behaviour; food stuffed into bags which are then burst, the dead carcass of a lamb crucified in an eight hour ceremony, blood and flesh smeared over participants. These artists belong to an Austrian movement known as the 'Wiener Aktionismus', the central idea of which is 'material action'. They believe that the representation of reality via a medium —painting, sculpture, theatrical performance—is no longer meaningful, that the only relevant art is one which employs reality itself as a means of formal creation. Thus their art consists not of performances but of direct literal events.

Because this form of art accentuates the horrific and macabre aspects of daily life in the twentieth century, in order to act as a social irritant, it has been called 'Irritart' by the Italian critic Lea Vergine.

P Weiermair 'New tendencies in Austrian Art' *Studio international* 183(944) May 1972 207-209.

114 **DIRECTED ARCHITECTURE** (or Programmed Architecture): A concept developed by the Italians Leonardo and Laura Mossi: architecture or structural planning generated by the creativity of masses of individuals—like language—with the help of computer systems.

L & L Mosso ' Self generation of form and the new ecology ' *AAQ* 3(1) Winter 1971 8-24.

L & L Mosso ' Manifesto of Directed Architecture ' *AAQ* 3(1) Winter 1971 25-28.

115 DRIP PAINTING: A technique used in gestural or *Action Painting and Tachisme*, made famous by Jackson Pollock in the late 1940's and early 1950's. Pollock laid unstretched canvas on the floor of his studio and dripped and poured liquid house-paint (Duco) onto it; the paint was flung across the surface with the aid of a stick or allowed to dribble from holes punched in the bottom of paint cans. Several critics have pointed out that the formal significance of this technique is that it compresses the problems of drawing and painting into a single action. American artists have demonstrated a remarkable ability to find solutions that ' telescope ' traditional problems of painting.

See also Stain Painting, Process Art.

116 DÜSSELDORF SCHOOL: In the years since 1960 Düsseldorf has emerged as an important international art centre, where German and other European artists continue the tradition of experimentation established by *Group Zero*; the best known of these artists are perhaps Dieter Rot and Joseph Beuys. A large scale exhibition of work by the Düsseldorf School, organised by the ' Richard Demarco Gallery ', called ' Strategy: get arts ' was held at the ' Edinburgh School of Art ' in 1970.

117 DYMAXION: This word, a combination of ' dynamism ', ' maximum ' and ' ion ', was coined in 1929 by two public relations men, employees of ' Marshal Fields ', a Chicago department store, to describe a futuristic house designed by Buckmister Fuller displayed in the store as a setting for new furniture. They invented the term after a close study of Fuller's writings and vocabulary. Since 1929 Fuller has often used the word: ' Dymaxion Car ', ' Dymaxion Bathroom ', ' Dymaxion chronofile'. He means by it maximum efficiency and performance in terms of the available technology.

R W Marks *The Dymaxion world of Buckminster Fuller* (Carbondale & Edwardsville, Southern Illinois University Press, 1960).

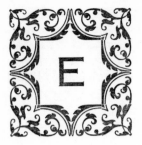

118 EARTH ART and Land Art (also called Earthworks, Dirt Art, Site Art, Topological Art, Field Art): An international movement which emerged in the middle 1960's, developing out of *Minimal Art* and closely related to *Art Povera* and *Conceptual Art*. Earth artists rejected the traditional materials of sculpture in favour of 'actual' materials such as rocks, soil, turf and snow. They began by dumping quantities of earth onto the floors of art galleries and allowing it to form its own shape, then they dug into the earth's surface creating holes and trenches (Carl Andre called the resulting cavities 'negative sculptures'). Recently earth-moving equipment has been used to create large-scale monuments reminiscent of pre-historic earthworks.

The introduction of the term 'Land Art' suggests a shift away from the sculptural emphasis on material towards a more pictorial attitude: land artists create lines by walking through grass, often large patterns are produced which are only visible, in total, from the air (Land art has been criticised on the grounds that it is exclusive to owners of aircraft). Field Art refers to works located in farming areas, where the artist harvests crops or controls the layout of crop seeding. In other works man-made constructions are juxtaposed with landscape backgrounds and recorded photographically; walking or cycling tours are recorded by routes marked on maps (as in *Conceptual Art* documentation is all important; ironically, such documentation is displayed in art galleries in very conventional ways).

According to Richard Cork, the advantages of this mode are: a release from the precious-object/art-gallery system, a greater freedom for the artist (if he likes the outdoor life), a return to the pre-historic function of art as a private act of faith. Earth Art has also been called the 'New Picturesque' because of its affinity with the eighteenth century vogue for landscape gardening. The French critic Jean Clay disapproves of the Land artist's traditionalism, his back-to-nature ideology, and claims that real aesthetics have been replaced by aestheticised reality. Artists who have produced Earth or Land Art include Walter De Maria, Sol Le Witt, Carl Andre, Robert Morris, Dennis Oppenheim, Neil Jenny, Robert Smithson, Richard Long, Michael Heizer and Jan Dibbets.

See also Landscape Sculpture, SITE.

D Hickey, ' Earthscapes, landworks and Oz ' *Art in America* 59(5) September/October 1971 40-49.

' Land Art/Earth works ' *Interfunktionen* (7) September 1971 46-59.

R Smithson 'A sedimentation of the mind ': Earth projects ' *Artforum* 7(1) September 1968 44-50.

S Tillim ' Earthworks and the new picturesque ' *Artforum* 7(4) December 1968 42-45.

119 EARTHWORK ARCHITECTURE: The German architect Engelbert Kremser proposes to construct buildings by applying concrete to mounds of soil acting as formworks; once the concrete has set the earth can be removed; cave-like structures will result. Kremser claims that his proposal would ' reinstate the almost forgotten relationship between architecture and sculpture '.

' Earthwork Architecture ' *Architectural review* 145(866) April 1969 241-243.

120 ECCENTRIC ABSTRACTION: Title of an exhibition of American sculpture organised by Lucy R Lippard, held at the Fischbach Gallery, New York in the Autumn of 1966; the show included work by artists such as Eva Hesse, Bruce Nauman, Keith Sonnier, Don Potts and Gary Kuehn. The adjective ' eccentric ' was applied to this sculpture because its forms, unlike the geometric tradition, were perverse, bizarre.

The Eccentric Abstractionists had evolved a style which combined characteristics of *Minimal Art*, and paradoxically, Surrealism. They shared with Pop artists an acceptance of ugly or vulgar synthetic materials, often with qualities of flexibility and limpness (see Soft Sculpture). Lippard also included in her category ' Eccentric Abstraction ', the West Coast *Funk Art* movement.

D Antin, 'Another category: Eccentric Abstraction' *Artforum* 5(3) November 1966 56-57.

L Lippard ' Eccentric Abstraction '—chapter in—*Changing: essays in art criticism* (NY Dutton, 1971) 98-111.

121 ECOLOGICAL ART (also called Environment Art, Eco Art, Force Art, *Systems Art*, Thermostat Art, Bio-Kinetic Art): The environment and ecology are two subjects that received a massive amount of critical attention during the 1960's. Therefore, given the eclecticism of modern art, it was inevitable that towards the end of the decade a number of artists—Alan Sonfist, David Medella, Charles Ross, Hans Haacke, Robert Irwin, Dennis Oppenheim, John Van Saun, Takis, Gordon Matta, Newton Harrison, Luis F Benedit and Peter Hutchinson should have attempted to relate art and ecology. The critic, Herb Aach claims to have been the first person to use the term ' Ecological Art ' in 1968.

Ecological Art makes use of natural physical forces and chemical or biological cyclical processes; it involves such disparate elements as fire, the wind, water, humidity, crystals, worms, locusts, bees, snails, fungus, and activities such as the planting of crops, the farming of fish. Such art ' works ' in a literal sense, since Eco artists create open systems that engage in a dialogue with nature. Formal restraints are: a minimum of human interference and economy of materials. The intention of such art is to enhance our appreciation of the processes of nature by presenting microcosmic models of natural phenomena.

Some artists have been intrigued by the possibility of creating art in unusual environments. For example in 1969 Hutchinson and Oppenheim devised artworks in the sea off the coast of Tobago in the West Indies. These have been variously labelled ' Underwater sculpture ', ' Scuba sculpture ' or ' Oceanographic Art '.

Precedents for Eco Art have been found in certain works by Marcel Duchamp and Yves Klein, namely those using, as a means of creation, the action of the weather.

The occult and alchemy are two further topics that have become fashionable in recent years, and art historians have only lately discovered the extent of Duchamp's interest in alchemy; hence it is no surprise to find the artists Haacke, Van Saun, Takis, and Ross dubbed ' The New Alchemists ' because they isolate or make ' visible some of the elements, systems and forces around which the phenomenal world coheres'.

Eco Art has been criticised by a reviewer in the 'New Scientist' on the grounds that it is scientifically elementary—'O' level biology—and also that it glories in 'technomania' instead of attacking it.

Architects have also expressed interest in ecology: Graham Caine has designed an ecological house, due to be constructed in London in 1972, relying on solar energy and rainwater to generate a life-sustaining biological cycle, in an attempt to make it independent of existing mains power supplies.

See also Arcology, Environmental Art, Robot Art.

F Arnold 'Art: Alan Sonfist' *New scientist* August 5 1971 336-337.

'Art and ecology' *Arts Canada* 27(4) issue no 146/147 August 1970 (special issue).

J Benthall 'Art and ecology'—chapter in—*Science and technology in art today* (Thames & Hudson, 1972) 126-141.

J Benthall 'Sonfist's Art'—letter in—*New scientist* August 12 1971 p 389.

G Leach 'Living off the sun in South London' *The observer* August 27 1972 1-2.

C Nemser 'The alchemist and the phenomenologist' *Art in America* 59(2) March/April 1971 100-103.

A Robbin 'Peter Hutchinson's Ecological Art' *Art international* 14(2) February 1970 52-55.

D Young 'The New Alchemists' *Art & artists* 5(11) February 1971 46-49.

122 EKISTICS: A neologism coined from several Greek words meaning 'home', 'settlement' and 'settling down'. It was devised by the Greek architect and planner Constantinos A Doxiadis towards the end of the second world war, to designate a new field of knowledge: the science of human settlements. Ekistics collates information relevant to human settlements from many separate disciplines—economics, social sciences, political science, history, anthropology, technology, city and regional planning; it also attempts to provide systematic scientific and mathematical techniques for using this knowledge. Doxiadis is president of the 'Athens Centre for Ekistics', founded in 1963, which issues a journal with the title 'Ekistics'. In 1965 a 'World Society for Ekistics' was established in London.

C A Doxiadis *Ekistics: an introduction to the science of human settlements* (Hutchinson, 1968).

123 THE ELECTRIC GYPSY ROAD SHOW

(EGRS): A British 'alternative environmental agency and energy network' run by Idris Walters and Richard Scott, two ex-students of the 'Oxford School of Architecture'. The EGRS is particularly interested in environmental and urban problems. They mounted a show devoted to this theme at the *Institute of Contemporary Arts,* London in 1972 called 'Magikal Connexions', because it was based on *Correspondence Art* techniques.

Carol Dix 'The Electric Gypsy Road Show' *The guardian* March 22 1972.

124 ELECTROGRAPHIC ARCHITECTURE:

A phrase coined by the American writer Tom Wolfe to describe large scale, electric light, advertising signs found in the United States, especially in towns like Las Vegas and Los Angeles. Electrographics are not merely lettering, but the 'whole structures designed primarily as pictures or representational sculpture'. They are intended to be 'read' from moving automobiles. Wolfe claims that the commercial artists who design Electrographics are 'at least ten years ahead of serious artists in almost every field', and that their work is 'wild', 'baroque' and expresses 'the new age of motion and mass wealth'.

T Wolfe 'Electrographic Architecture' *Architectural design* 39(7) July 1969 379-382.

125 ELECTRONIC ART:

A variety of *Kinetic Art,* exploiting the abstract patterns appearing in the screens of cathode ray tubes or oscilloscopes. The American artist Ben F Laposky has worked with such devices since 1950, and he calls the results 'oscillons' or 'electronic abstractions'. A better known Electronic artist is the Korean Nam June Paik, who is particularly interested in the use of multiple television sets, often in association with human performers. He subjects the images appearing on the screens of the televisions to a series of extreme distortions.

B F Laposky 'Electronic Abstractions'—letter in—*Studio international* 174(893) October 1967 p 131.

126 **EMBLEMATIC ART** (or Emblemism, Sign Painting, Signal Art): A number of American painters, notably Frank Stella, Kenneth Noland, Jasper Johns and Robert Indiana have employed common emblems as motifs for paintings, that is flags, chevrons, stripes, targets, signs, numbers and maps. The appeal of these devices is that they provide a flat image for a flat surface; their imagery is 'given', and thus it releases the artist from the problem of subject matter, so that he is then free to tackle the 'real' subject matter of painting—the process of applying pigment to canvas. Emblems operate as a unifying factor over a series of paintings in which variations of colour, tone, scale, or brushwork have been played; lastly, they raise questions in the spectator's mind about the identity of the object he confronts.

127 **ENDLESS ARCHITECTURE**: A new approach to architecture identified by Richard Llewelyn-Davies in 1951, a method of design making use of identical units repeated in a building to suggest infinite extension. Llewelyn-Davies derived his ideas from paintings by Piet Mondrian and buildings by Mies van der Rohe (the notion also seems identical to Brancusi's 'Endless Column' sculptures; see also Colour-Field Painting and Serial Art). The English architect John Weeks, who had collaborated with Llewelyn-Davies, later extended the concept of Endless Architecture into what he called *Indeterminate Architecture*.

R Llewelyn-Davies, 'Endless Architecture' *Architectural Association journal* 67(755) September/October 1951 106-113.

128 **ENVIRONMENTAL ART**: A description that has been applied to a wide variety of structures—created by a number of fine artists, with different formal approaches—having in common the fact that they totally enclose the spectator and are large enough to allow him to move about within the work (of course architecture, interior design, museum and exhibition display and certain booths at fun fairs have always provided environments to delight and divert the senses, but these have usually served other functions besides the purely aesthetic). This form of art was prefigured by Kurt Schwitter's ' Merzbauten ' and the elaborate decor of Surrealist exhibitions in the 1930's, but recent Environmental Art developed out of post-war painting, via collage, *Assemblage* and *Tableau*, rather than out of pre-war Dada and Surrealism. *Colour-Field Painting* can be cited as an influence: the huge scale of American painting of this type dominated the spectator's vision, the use of fields of colour suggested an extension of pictorial space beyond the edge of the canvas, and thus the space of these works was called ' environmental '.

The emergence of Environmental Art reflects a desire on the part of many artists to escape the limitations of the single art object, which has to compete for our attention with all the other objects of the world, to escape the role of such objects as commodities in the gallery system; artists wanted to extend their control of spatial experience beyond the confines of painting or sculpture, in order to provide a spectator with a more comprehensive sensory experience; in Environmental Art the space of the art work coalesces with the space of the spectator.

The earliest post-war environments were constructed in the late 1950's by American artists such as Allan Kaprow, George Segal and Jim Dine; their works contained lots of rubbish, lights and recorded noises reflecting the improvised quality of *Abstract Expressionism*. Often the routes through such environments were made deliberately tortuous for spectators to negotiate. American environments of this period merge imperceptibly with *Happenings,* and they have been described as the passive and active sides of the same coin. Later, during the 1960's, environments tended to be more restrained in accordance with the cooler approach of *Minimal Art*.

However, once the genre was established, artists of all types produced examples: the English artist Victor Pasmore, working in the Constructivist tradition, created with others *Exhibit I and II* in 1957 and 1959; the assembler Ed Kienholz created ' Roxy's ', a complete replica of a brothel, in 1961, and ' The Beanery ' in 1965; the Kineticist Jesus Rafael Soto created environments called ' Penetrables ' in 1969; in 1970 at the *Institute of Contemporary Arts,* London ten young British artists, influenced primarily by *Pop Art,* designed fanciful domestic environments based on the theme of a sitting room; also in 1970, at the Tate Gallery, London three Los Angeles artists—Larry Bell, Robert Irwin and Doug Wheeler—created three separate environments precisely designed to control a spectator's perceptual experience. Artists associated with *Air Art* and *Psychedelic Art* are also concerned to structure environments for their respective purposes; groups who specialise in environments include *USCO* and *Space Structure Workshop*. Environmental Art need not consist of bulky physical structures of wood or stone: spatial experience can be delimited by means of light beams or sounds, see for example *Pulsa* and *Laser Art*.

The word ' environment ' has become extremely fashionable in recent years as a result of man's increasing efforts to produce totally controlled surroundings, from town planning and the design of office interiors, to the ultimate artificial environment, the space capsule. As a consequence of R Buckminster Fuller's advocacy, the whole earth is now seen as a spaceship, and the ecological crisis caused by pollution has created a new consciousness of the importance of our total environment. As a result there has been a shift of meaning in the use of the word ' environmental ' in the art context. It no longer refers exclusively to indoor structures, but also to a form of art making direct use of natural systems responsive to the environments in which they are placed (see Ecological Art), or to the work of artists who programme the man-made environment (see Media Art).

S Bann 'Environmental Art' *Studio international* 173(886) February 1967 78-82.

H Rosenberg 'Light! Lights!'—essay in—*Artworks and packages* (NY, Dell Publishing Co, 1971) 132-143.

129 ENVIRONMENTAL DESIGN: A relatively new discipline taught in many art schools, defined by Maurice Jay as 'the scientific design and control of the man-made environment'. Such design is concerned with the total environment, and covers such diverse topics as architecture, urban planning, interior design, engineering, lighting, acoustics, heating and ergonomics.

M Jay 'Environmental design: an introduction' *Design* (218) February 1967 44-49.

130 ENVIRONMENTALISM: According to Lance Wright, an approach to building design in which the architect relinquishing the will to structure space, attempts to blend his architecture into its setting to such an extent that it becomes almost invisible. The exterior walls of an ideal environmentalist building—

such as the IBM offices at Corsham, designed by 'Norman Foster Associates'—consist of glass surfaces that mirror the surrounding landscape, the interior is open plan to give the impression of infinite space, its inhabitants are not conscious of enclosure or structure. This approach to building design has emerged as a result of the development of internal services, for example air conditioning, which have become more important than external structures.

Other writers use the term 'Environmentalism' in a broader sense to describe the use made by many modern architects of bollards and trees in an effort to humanise the brutal appearance of their buildings.

In fine art criticism the word 'Environmentalism' has been employed to refer to art making use of natural systems responsive to the environments in which they are placed (see Ecological Art).

L Wright 'Offices: Corsham Hants' *Architectural review* 151 (899) January 1972 15-24.

131 ETHNIC ART: An expression that has been used increasingly in recent years, especially in the United States, to refer to art produced by distinct population groups, such as Puerto Ricans, and particularly racial groups such as negros (see Black Art). Its use reflects the importance now being given to the rights of minority groups in society.

132 EUSTON ROAD SCHOOL: A group of British painters—Claude Rogers, Victor Pasmore, Graham Bell, William Coldstream and Lawrence Gowing—whose work during the late 1930's and immediate post-war years shared a common aesthetic. These artists rejected the abstraction and Surrealism associated with the School of Paris, in favour of naturalistic painting in a style derived from Degas, Sickert, Cézanne and Bonnard. Their subject matter was banal: jellied eel stalls, railway stations, public house interiors.

Their work somewhat resembles Social Realism but they were not in fact politically committed. Their attitude to style was similarly luke-warm; their sources were anachronistic and the results of their eclecticism were mediocre because they showed an excess of refinement and good taste. Often their paintings are constructed of vertical strokes of paint blurred together as if the canvas had been rained on (unkind critics called them the 'fog brigade'). Nevertheless, this style of painting influenced several generations of British art students, because members of the Euston Road Group held influential positions in art education establishments after the war. The group were called after a London thoroughfare because they were all associated with a school of painting and drawing founded by Rogers and Pasmore in 1937 and located first in Fitzroy Street and later in Euston Road; the teaching school closed in 1939 at the outbreak of war.

F Whitford ' Of Pasmore and recent sculpture ' *Art gallery magazine* 15(5) February 1972 68-69.

133 EVENTSTRUCTURE: A concept of art devised by the British artist John Latham in the years since 1954, concerned with the structuring of events in time rather than the making of objects. Latham's ideas have been adopted by the ' Eventstructure Research Group ' (ERG) formed in Amsterdam in 1967 by three artists: Theo Botschiver, Jeffrey Shaw, and Sean Wellesley-Miller. ERG organises events or *Happenings* at public festivals in Holland and England. They also stage surprise events in the streets. The group's intention is to encourage public participation and adult play; their method is to provide a variety of PVC inflatables, such as tubes for walking on water. ERG hopes to create an alternative to ' museum art ' and to challenge the traditional concepts of art, architecture and sculpture. Their work has been described as ' operational art ' and it is claimed to be ' an art of real consequences '.

See also Air Art, Participatory Art, Street Art.

' Concepts for an operational art . . .' *Art & Artists* 3(10) January 1969 46-49.

J Latham ' Eventstructure ' *Studio international* 174 (892) September 1967 p 82.

134 EXHIBIT I & II: Two abstract environmental constructions devised by Victor Pasmore and Richard Hamilton. Exhibit I was shown at the *Institute of Contemporary Arts*, London and at Newcastle Upon Tyne in 1957, and Exhibit II at Newcastle in 1959. The construction consisted of variously coloured acrylic sheets, with differing degrees of transparency, placed at right angles to each other in metal frameworks or suspended from the ceiling. The result was a maze like spatial structure within which spectators could move, though this was not encouraged in the case of Exhibit II, where variations of transparency alone created an impression of penetration.

135 EXPENDABLE ART (or Disposable Art, Throwaway Art, Perishable Art, Ephemeral Art): All art objects are subject to decay. Most traditional artists attempted to defer the inevitable dissolution of their work by the use of durable materials and careful craftsmanship. In contrast, many modern artists are indifferent to permanence and perpetuity, and while there is no school of 'Expendable Art', the notion of expendability permeates a great deal of art activity since 1945.

This development is clearly related to the deliberate manufacture of disposable products, and goods with planned obsolescence, typical of today's consumer society. Expendability was in fact one of the characteristics of the products of popular culture admired by Richard Hamilton, at the time he was a member of the *Independent Group,* and listed by him in an inventory of qualities of pop culture to be emulated by fine artists (Hamilton himself has not adopted it).

Expendability manifests itself in recent art in varying degrees: (1) there are poorly constructed artifacts made of cheap materials which the artist knows will decay rapidly but is indifferent to the fact; most *Assemblage Art,* and paintings by Andy Warhol, fall into this category; (2) there are artworks using materials on a once-only basis, *Happenings* and some types of *Environmental Art, Art Povera* and Carl Andre's *Clastic Art* (in the last mentioned materials can be recycled); (3) there are artforms which incorporate expendability as an essential part of their aesthetic, *Auto-Destructive Art, Destructive Art* and *Food Art belong* to this group, also some examples of *Process Art.*

Authorities such as Douglas Cooper have criticised recent art on the grounds of poor workmanship, but such criticism fails to take into account the changed attitude which has now culminated in total rejection of the physical art object (see Conceptual Art).

J Reichardt 'Expendable Art' *Architectural design* 30(10) October 1960 421-422.

H Rosenberg 'The art object and the aesthetics of impermanence'—essay in—*The anxious object: art today and its audience* (Thames & Hudson, 1965) 88-96.

136 **THE EXPERIMENTAL GROUP**: Founded in Holland in 1948 by Karel Appel, Corneille and Constant; they produced primitive figurative paintings in a loose improvised style. They also issued a review called ' Reflex '. The group did not exist for very long, but its ideas were continued in the broader international organisation known as *Cobra*.

137 **EXPERIMENTAL PAINTING**: According to Stephen Bann it has been customary to use the word ' experimental ' to define ' the particular quality which distinguishes the art of the twentieth century from that of previous times ', that is modernity/novelty. He regards this usage as too loose, and proposes as a definition of an experimental painter, an artist ' committed to a particular path of controlled activity, of which the works he produces remain as evidence '. This definition makes explicit the scientific procedures suggested by the word ' experimental '.

S Bann *Experimental Painting* ... (Studio Vista, 1970).

R Wedewer ' Experimental Painting ' *Cimaise* (53) May/June 1961 28-43.

138 **EXPERIMENTS IN ART AND TECHNO-LOGY INC.** (EAT): A New York organisation founded in 1966, directed by Billy Kluver of Bell Telephone Laboratories and including among its members Robert Rauschenberg, Gyorgy Kepes, John Cage and Buckminster Fuller. EAT foster co-operation between artists and technologists by matching their interests and specialities. An exhibition of work by members of EAT called ' Some more beginnings ' was held at the Brooklyn Museum in 1969. It included computer generated films, *Kinetic Art,* Liquid Sculpture, psychedelic environments.

See also Technological Art.

' Experiments in Art and Technology (EAT) New York ' *Leonardo* 1 (4) October 1968 487-488.

B Kluver ' EAT ' *Metro* (14) June 1968 55-58.

J Reichardt ' EAT and after ' *Studio international* 175 (900) May 1968 236-237.

139 **EXPO ART**: The architecture of national pavilions, the graphic and product design displayed at international fairs and expositions and also works of art exhibited at such fairs.

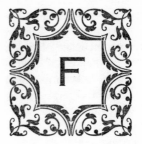

140 FANTASTIC REALISM: A number of Austrian painters—Ernest Fuchs, Rudolf Hausner, Wolfgang Hutter, Eric Brauer and Anton Lehmden—are known collectively as the 'Vienna School of Fantastic Realists'. They are mostly ex-students of A P Gutersloh, a teacher at the Vienna Academy, whose classes they attended in the late 1940's; they also studied paintings by the Mannerists and old masters such as Breughel and Van Eyck in the collection of the Museum of the History of Art, Vienna. The Fantastic Realists share a taste for literature and combine magical subject matter with academic techniques; in some respects their work continues the pre-war traditions of Surrealism.

The Fantastic Realists have achieved popular and official recognition but Peter Weiermair has criticised their work on the grounds of 'bland virtuosity' and 'erotic voyeurism'.

W Schmeid 'The imaginary and the fantastic'—essay in—J P Hodin and others *Figurative art since 1945* (Thames & Hudson, 1971) 123-147.

A Werner 'New Stirrings in Austria' *Art & artists* 4(2) March 1969 32-35.

141 FANTASY FURNITURE: Title of an exhibition held at the Museum of Contemporary Crafts, New York in 1966. Most modern furniture is designed within a narrow utilitarian concept of function, but the history of furniture design reveals examples of highly ornamented, elaborately carved and coloured pieces, often part sculpture, which fulfil man's emotional and psychological needs in addition to his practical requirements.

T Simpson *Fantasy furniture: design and decoration* (NY, Reinhold, 1968).

142 **FEMINIST ART:** The late 1960's saw the development of Women's Liberation movements in Western countries, especially in the United States, one consequence of which has been female militancy in the sphere of art. A number of exhibitions for women artists only, selected by women, have been mounted and designated 'Feminist Art'. Women's Liberation Groups (one is called WAR 'Women Artists in Revolution') have made protests against institutions, such as museums and galleries, which they regard as organisations run by male chauvinists who discriminate against women artists. A 'Feminist Art journal' is published in New York and a 'Feminist Art Programme' has been established at the California Institute of Art, Valencia.

In spite of alleged discrimination in favour of male artists, a number of women artists have achieved critical acclaim since the last world war, because of the quality of their work: Helen Frankenthaler, Grace Hartigan, Eva Hesse, Louise Nevelson, Joan Mitchell, Bridget Riley, Jann Haworth and Yoko Ono.

A R Krasilovsky 'Feminism in the arts: an interim bibliography' *Artforum* 10(10) June 1972 72-75.

L R Lippard 'Sexual politics, art style' *Art in America* 59(5) September/October 1971 19-20.

143 **FINE ARTZ:** In 1964 a group of ex-Slade School students—Terry Atkinson, John Bowstead, Roger Jeffs and Bernard Jennings—advocated a new role for art in a leisure-orientated consumer society. They rejected the traditional individuality of art creation in favour of teamwork; they admired the customising approach to design of teenage sub-cultures, and believed that a study of the needs of the younger generation would provide a blueprint for the future. They designed objects in modern materials using techniques such as motivation research and concepts such as *Styling*.

See also Custom Painting, Hybrid Enterprises, Programme Partnership.

Fine Artz Associates 'Visualising . . .' *Ark* (35) Spring 1964 38-41.

144 **FINISH FETISH** (also called the LA Look, California Finish Fetish, the Venice Surface): Some American artists, in particular those working in Los Angeles—Larry Bell, John McCracken, John Eversley and Ed Ruscha—are fanatically concerned to give their paintings, sculpture and environmental constructions a smooth, high gloss surface equal to those found on highly polished automobiles. Peter Plagens describes Finish Fetish as 'extra spit and polish in Pop and *Minimal Art* plus space age materials' and calls the artists 'effete craftsmen'. Complicated procedures and expensive technology are often required to produce a perfect sheen. The cult of impeccable finish is part of a wider Los Angeles aesthetic shared by craftsmen such as those who make surfboards. It also reflects the influence of Hollywood and its emphasis on the surface of things, the façade.

145 **FLASH ART:** The noun 'flash' and its adjective 'flashy' mean, among other things, 'glint, sparkle or gleam', 'superficial brilliance', 'ostentatious showy display'. In the opinion of some British art students these attributes are to be found in a whole range of artifacts and cultural behaviour—in popular entertainment, in fashion, in the custom car cult, in home decoration and in the fine arts—and while these attributes are manifested in the products of other periods, they are thought to be most typical of the late 1950's and early 1960's. The students consider that these characteristics are sufficiently distinct to warrant the creation of a new aesthetic category: Flash Art.

Flash in the entertainment world is epitomised by performers such as Liberace and pop music stars such as Elvis Presley, who dazzle their audience with gold lamé suits, jewels and shimmering, glittery fabrics. Such figures appear larger than life and present a cool image without content. The practise of customising is also considered Flash, as in the way ordinary people titivate their prize possessions—homes, cars, motor cycles, clothes—with excessive decoration in an attempt to make them appear glamorous. In the fine arts, artists who are labelled Flash include Allen Jones (for his exploitation of gaudy fashions), Peter Phillips (for his *Custom Painting*), Andy Warhol (for his use of silver and his cool, star image), Frank Stella (for his use of very large canvases and reflective metallic paints), Richard Hamilton (for his 'Guggenheim Museum' series of fibre glass reliefs sprayed with cellulose paints to give a highly polished surface), and sculptors such as Eduardo Paolozzi, Clive Barker and Lucas Samaras (for their use of chromium plate and mirror glass), Claes Oldenburg (for his exploitation of *Kitsch* decoration in his 'Bedroom ensemble').

Flash Art would appear from these examples to be a sub category of *Pop Art* or a blend of *Kitsch* and Pop.

Flash Art is also the title of an Italian periodical devoted to *Avant-Garde Art*.

L Riggall *Flash* (Hornsey College of Art, 1972). Unpublished thesis.

146 **FLOOR ART** (or Ground Art): Modern sculpture which eschews the traditional plinth and spreads itself across gallery floors or across patches of ground. Examples include open metalwork structures by Anthony Caro, *Clastic Art* works by Carl Andre, cut out shapes by Timothy Drever, pieces of rope by Barry Flanagan, lines of flour by Barry Le Va. Many modern sculptors use the floor in a painterly fashion, that is, as a ' ground ' against which to display their forms (Flanagan's rope pieces resemble the compositions of middle period Mondrians).

According to the French critic M J M Ricou, fragmentation followed *Minimal Art* and what was left were ' crumbs ', ' gestures ', ' leavings ', that is, cloth in shreds, piles of mud and sand scattered across the gallery floor. It is a short step from such works to the idea of creating sculpture directly out of the surface of the earth (see Earth Art).

Another writer claims that the use of the floor was the major sculptural innovation of the 1960's, and that the rejection of the vertical dimension in favour of the horizontal reflected the aerial viewpoint associated with jet travel.

147 **FLUXUS:** An international avant-garde movement born officially in 1962 and active throughout the 1960's. The word ' fluxus ' is Latin for ' flowing ', in English ' flux ' means ' a gushing forth ', ' an abnormal discharge of fluid or blood from a body ', ' a fusion ', ' a state of continuous change '; all these shades of meaning apply to the art movement Fluxus. According to Joseph Beuys, its purpose was to ' purge the world of bourgeois sickness . . . of dead art ', to ' promote a revolutionary flood and tide in art, promote living art, anti-art, promote non art reality . . .' and to ' fuse the cadres of cultural, social and political revolutionaries into united front and action '. The movement was centered initially in Germany; later Fluxus ' festivals ' were held in Paris, Copenhagen, Amsterdam, London and

New York. Fluxus overlaps to some extent with the *Happenings* of the United States and staged similar events, plus *Décollage,* situations, *Actions,* concerts of electronic music, anti-theatre, visual poetry, *Intermedia,* street performances. The rollcall of participants in Fluxus includes almost every major avant-garde artist of the past decade : Joseph Beuys, Wolf Vostell, Robert Filliou, George Brecht, Dick Higgins, La Monte Young, Ben Vautrier, Yoko Ono, Emmett Williams, Henry Flynt, Robert Watts and others too numerous to mention. The movement has been co-ordinated, and its many publications, edited by George Macuinas. Robert Filliou describes Fluxus as a ' non group ' because it was composed of individualists with divergent ideas and work, but they did share a revolutionary, Dadaist spirit, a desire to introduce spontaneity, joy and humour into art and avoiding at all costs any limiting theory or programme.

Ken Friedman claims that Fluxus originated the notion of *Conceptual Art* and that Fluxus is still a thriving, expanding movement.

' Free Fluxus now ' *Art & artists* 7(7) issue no 79. October 1972, special issue of Fluxus.

K Friedman ' Notes on Concept art ' *Schmuck* March 1972 6-16.

Happening and Fluxus (Cologne, Kölnischer Kunstverein, 1970).

148 **FOOD ART:** Cooking has long been described as an ' art ', and the decoration of food, especially the icing of cakes, is a minor folk art in its own right. However, the label ' Food Art ', popular in recent years, refers not to cooking but to at least three different kinds of work produced by fine artists: (1) alterations of shape and colour of existing foodstuffs and the creation of new objects composed of edible materials; (2) paintings and sculpture depicting or representing food; (3) art works composed of edible materials, depicting food.

(1) The Swiss artist Daniel Spoerri ran, for a number of years in Düsseldorf, a restaurant/gallery called ' Eat Art ' where invited artists exploited different foodstuffs. The American painter Richard Lindner has issued a series of ginger-bread *Multiples;* the German artist Tim Schroder has altered the shape of food and given it bizarre colours by the use of vegetable dyes; he calls the results ' Gourmet Art '. Food thus treated often forms the theme of festivals or *Happenings* involving up to 300 people; two Paris based artists, Antoni Miralda and Dorotheé Selz have organised such events.

(2) The American West Coast artist, Wayne Thiebaud, delights in painting items of food such as fancy cakes, which he renders in thick, succulent impasto to simulate the actual quality of cream and icing sugar coatings; these paintings have been described by one critic as 'edibles'. Another American Pop artist, Claes Oldenburg, often employs food as subject matter, producing sculptural facsimiles of popular snacks—hamburgers, ice cream cones—generally he enlarges their scale many times and constructs his pieces out of incongruous materials. In 1964 an exhibition called 'The Supermarket' was held at the Bianchini Gallery, New York in which Pop artists displayed images and three dimensional replicas of many varieties of vegetables, fruit and canned food; the whole *Installation* was arranged and signposted in faithful imitation of a supermarket.

(3) Peter Kuttner (another artist who enjoys altering the normal colouration of food) submitted to the John Moores exhibition in Liverpool in 1972, a picture of an iced cake 'painted' with icing sugar (it was not accepted).

M Deserti 'Cucina: a tavola con l'arte' *Cast vogue* (14) May/June 1972 126-129.

'Events by Miralda and Selz' *Studio international* 181 (932) April 1972 p 167.

P Kuttner 'Coloured food' *Studio international* 181(932) April 1972 p 166.

149 FORMALIST CRITICISM (also called The New Criticism): In the United States from 1960 onwards, the formalist tradition of art criticism received new impetus under the influence of Clement Greenberg and British linguistic philosophy. Writers such as Michael Fried, Rosalind Krauss, Sidney Tillim and others, mostly associated with 'Artforum' magazine, excluded lyrical description and literary generalisations from their writings. Instead they derived conclusions from close analysis of actual art works; as W Seitz remarks, they 'carried the verbalised observation and examination of art objects to questionable extremes of phenomenological and syntactical nuance and sometimes opaque rhetoric which did a disservice by ignoring content'. Subject content in the form of narration or symbolism was regarded as extraneous to the essential purpose of painting, which was reduced to a single concept: formal organisation (thus *Pop Art was* scorned by formalist critics because of its 'inessential' subject matter). The New Criticism also ignored the intentions, opinions and beliefs of the artist. Leo Steinberg describes such an attitude as interdictory—it tells the artist what he ought not to do—and he calls it 'preventive aesthetics'.

See also Modernist Painting, Objecthood, Prescence.

B M Reise 'Greenberg and the group: a retrospective view' *Studio international* 175 (901) June 1968 314-316.

W Seitz 'Mondrian and the issue of relationships' *Artforum* 10(6) February 1972, p 74.

L Steinberg 'Reflections on the state of criticism' *Artforum* 10(7) March 1972 37-49.

150 FREE ABSTRACTION:
A broad term used to describe paintings by Serge Poliakoff, Nicolas de Stael, Jean Atlan, Julius Bissier, Willi Baumeister and others, whose style occupies an intermediate position between *Geometric Abstraction* and the improvised abstraction typical of *L'Art Informel*.

151 FREE FORMS:
Organic, biomorphic forms or shapes produced by free hand drawing, as opposed to rectangular or circular shapes produced by rulers and compasses. This term was applied to the kind of forms featured in paintings by Arshile Gorky, William Baziotes and Mark Rothko, created during the 1940's; these artists had been influenced by the forms used by the Dada sculptor Hans Arp and by Joan Miró and other Surrealist painters.

In the following decade Free Forms, or 'quartics' as they are called in co-ordinate geometry, became extremely popular in the applied arts; for example, kidney shapes, boomerang shapes, egg shapes and rounded squares all appeared in the design of furniture, fabrics and tableware.

J Manser 'Free form furniture' *Design* (240) December 1968 28-33.

J A D Wedd 'Quartics' *Design* (49) January 1953 15-17.

J A D Wedd 'Two familiar quartics' *Design* (59) November 1953 25-27.

152 FREEDOM FURNITURE:
English furniture produced after 1948, the year in which state controls relating to the manufacture of furniture established during the second world war were lifted. Government-supervised furniture manufactured between 1942 and 1948 was called 'Utility'.

4

153 FRIENDS OF THE ARTS COUNCIL OPERATIVE (FACOP):

In 1969 500 artists and sympathisers met at St Katherine's Dock, London to discuss common problems and to consider the need for an *Artists Union*. They formed a short-lived pressure group, called FACOP, to lobby the 'Arts Council of Great Britain' because in their view it was not meeting the real needs of the majority of British artists.

D Bieda 'The need for an Artists Council' *Art & artists* 4(5) August 1969 p 64.

R Dodd 'Exhibitions: I remember FACOP' *Time out* (88) October 22-28 1971 p 18.

154 FRONTE NUOVO DELLE ARTI (New Front of the Arts):

A broad post-war Italian art movement sponsored by the critic Giuseppe Marchiori in 1947. A number of artists working in a variety of styles contributed to group exhibitions to draw the attention of the public to the achievements of avant-garde Italian art. The best known of these artists were Renato Guttoso, Guiseppe Santomaso, Emilio Vedova and Ennio Morlotti.

155 FUN PALACE:

A scheme devised by the theatrical director Joan Littlewood in 1961 for an entertainments and community arts centre to be established in London. The British architect Cedric Price produced designs for a construction whose only permanent fixtures were gantries, cranes and mechanical services. The purpose of the cranes was to erect, from a stock of components, different structures for a variety of activities; these structures could easily be dismantled, and therefore the system provided complete flexibility. Reyner Banham in his treatise on *The New Brutalism* called Price's concept an 'anti-building', because it avoided the solid, long lasting forms of traditional architecture; another critic has called it 'Aleatory Architecture'.

Littlewood's vision has never been realised, but the name 'Fun Palace' has been applied to other structures, such as one designed by Keith Albarn and displayed at the seaside resort of Girvan, Ayrshire. His 'palace' consisted of a series of plastic domes inside which spectators were diverted by sound and light patterns, wall textures and moving floors. After one year of operation the interior was re-designed by John Ballantyne and Denis Barns, and equipped with sound and light feedback systems capable of responding to the noise and movement of spectators (see Cybernetic Art). The term 'Fun Palace' has also been applied to recreation centres such as the vast structure called 'Summerland' created by the Japanese architects Kinji Fumada, Minoru Murakami and Toshio Sato.

A Best 'Funny business at the seaside' *Design* (251) November 1969 58-61.

'Fun Palace, Camden, London' *Architectural design* 37(11) November 1967 522-525.

'Summerland: a serviced space frame for changing fantasy and fun' *Architectural design* 38(7) July 1968 318-321.

156 FUNK ART

156 FUNK ART (also spelt Funck, Phunck, or called Grotesque Art, Sick Art): The adjective 'funky' was first applied to visual artworks by artists living in the Bay Area of San Francisco in the late 1950's. They borrowed the word from Blues or Jazz terminology where 'funky' means a heavy beat, an earthy sensual sound. Orthodox dictionaries reveal that the word has several meanings, one of which is 'strong smell or stink' and Jeff Nuttall has defined it as a 'thick pungent odour given off by sexually aroused female' (at least one artist's work has been described as 'funky as a whore's drawers'). In 1967, funky became a four letter word when the first exhibition with the title 'funk' was held at the University of California.

Funk Art is usually three-dimensional, but it does not resemble traditional sculpture. Rather is it an uneasy hybrid of painting and sculpture. Materials such as leather, clay, steel, fibre-glass, nylon, vinyl are employed in bizarre combinations; the resulting objects are eccentric in appearance and this imagery is visceral, organic or biomorphic, often with ribald, sexual or scatological connotations. Funk artists draw their inspiration from outside Fine Art; they delight in the vulgar and *Kitsch* elements of their surroundings. Their attitude to materials is anti-functional, anti-Bauhaus; their aesthetic is anti-intellectual, anti-formal; Nuttall describes it as the 'aesthetic of obscenity'. Precedents for Funk have been found in the sculpture of Joan Miró, in some of Marcel Duchamp's objects, in the architecture of Antonio Gaudi and in the *Pop Art* of Claes Oldenburg. Many Funk artists are ceramicists (their work is often called Pop Ceramics), and this medium seems peculiarly appropriate to the needs of the style.

Major artists included Kenneth Price, Bruce Connor, Robert Hudson, James Melchert, David Gilhooly, Robert Arneson, Peter Vandenberge, Clayton Bailey, Chris Unterscher, Joseph A Pugliese, Richard Shaw and Mel Henderson. The French critic Jean Clay regards the German Joseph Beuys as a Funk artist, because of his emphasis on materials, and also Richard Long, an English exponent of *Land Art* (see Earth Art and Land Art), defining their work as the ' embodiment of nostalgia '. See also Eccentric Abstraction.

J Nuttall *Bomb Culture* (Paladin, 1970) p 173.

J Pierre ' Funk Art ' *L'Oeil* (190) October 1970 18-27 and 68.

P Selz *Funk* (Berkeley, University of California, 1967).

D Zack ' California myth making ' *Art & artists* 4(4) July 1969 26-31.

D Zack ' Funk Art ' *Art & artists* 2(1) April 1967 36-39.

D Zack ' Funk 2 : the Grotesque show at Berkeley, California ' *Art & artists* 2(7) October 1967 20-21.

157 **FURNITURISATION:** This word, coined by Reyner Banham, refers to the way designers always tend to solve human requirements—for seating, for domestic services such as heating and cold food storage—in terms of elaborate, monumental objects, that is furniture. It also describes the way these objects are arted-up, that is, their visual form and appearance are given precedence over performance and function.

R Banham ' The chair as art '—essay in—*Modern chairs 1918-1970* (Whitechapel Gallery, 1970) 19-23.

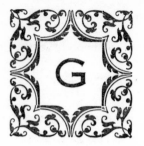

158 GAME ART:

158 GAME ART: The expressions 'Game Art', 'Toy Art', 'Play Art' refer, in most instances, simply to games, toys, or playthings made by artists. A large-scale exhibition of such works, entitled 'Play Orbit', was held in 1969 at the *Institute of Contemporary Arts, London.* However, in other instances the expressions refer to a more sophisticated notion of art. Since 1945 many artists have become convinced that play, for adults as well as children, serves important cultural functions (as outlined by Johan Huizinga in his book *Homo ludens*), and that play will become more vital as time passes, assuming that the leisure society becomes a reality. Consequently they have created works with variable elements (see Option Art), which encourage spectator involvement (see also Participatory Art) and adult play.

As a result perhaps of the uncertain political climate since the second world war, some scientists have developed a keen interest in the theory of games, in particular the theory of war games, and an artist who has exploited war games as subject matter is Oyvind Fahlstrom.

Wittgenstein used the analogy of the game in his linguistic philosophy, and on occasion some art critics are tempted to apply the same analogy to art, but, to my knowledge, no writer has yet made a systematic study of the relationship between game theory and art. Many critics have noted Marcel Duchamp's penchant for games of all kinds; no doubt his work would feature prominently in such a study.

N Calas 'Games'—essay in—*Icons and images of the sixties* by N & E Calas (NY, Dutton, 1971) 316-323.

'Fun & Games' *Art & artists* 2(9) December 1967 (special issue on games).

'Games & Toys'—entry in—*Encyclopedia of world art* vol 6 (NY, McGraw Hill, 1962) 1-18 columns.

J Huizinga *Homo ludens: a study of the play element in culture* (Routledge, 1949).

G Ortman 'Artists games' *Art in America* 57 (6) November/December 1969 69-77.

J Reichardt—editor—*Play Orbit* (Studio International, 1969).

159 **GAMES OF ART FOR SPECTATOR PARTICIPATION** (GASP): A British group formed in 1970 by Rob Con, Julian Dunn and Harry Henderson while they were students at Wolverhampton Polytechnic. The group supervises participatory games for children, and gives stylized ritual performances for adults in public houses.

A Everitt 'Four exhibitions in the midlands' *Studio international* 183 (941) February 1972 76-78.

160 **GENERATION:** A word art critics have used a great deal since 1945, in expressions such as ' new generation ', ' first generation ', ' second generation ', ' middle generation ', to describe waves of artists who emerge into public view at roughly the same time and who are generally of similar age. In America ' first generation ' invariably refers to *Abstract Expressionism*. Robert Hughes points out that it is a mistaken notion to expect, as some exhibition organisers and critics appear to do, a fresh generation of talent to emerge annually; he regards this expectation as a parody of the accelerated turnover in the avant-garde.

R Hughes 'Arts in society: stop wasting time' *New society* February 2 1967 170-171.

161 **GEOMETRIC ABSTRACTION:** A broad category of art, encompassing both sculpture and painting, which finds in geometric forms universal symbols for rational, idealist concepts. Geometric Abstraction makes use of shapes such as circles, rectangles and triangles, its colours are usually primary and its forms are sharply defined; all its elements are carefully composed and related one to another (*cf* Non-Relational Art). Because of its cool rationality, Geometric Abstraction has also been termed ' Cold Abstraction ' and described as ' hygienic '. This kind of art developed largely in Europe in the years between the two world wars and was associated with the

Bauhaus, De Stijl and *Constructivism*. In the immediate post-war years art entered a post-geometric phase: artists in Europe and the United States, linked with *L'Art Informel* and *Abstract Expressionism*, rejected Geometric Abstraction in favour of looser, more intuitive styles. However, in the 1960's geometric forms re-appeared, for example, in the *Minimal Art* movement (and also to some extent in *Op Art* and *Hard-Edge Painting*). Consequently some critics describe sculpture by artists such as Carl Andre, Sol Le Witt and Richard Artschwager as Geometric Abstraction.

H L C Jaffé, 'Geometrical Abstraction: its origin, principles and evolution'—essay in—*Abstract art since 1945* by W Haftmann and others (Thames & Hudson, 1971) 163-190.

162 THE GEOMETRY OF FEAR: A phrase used by Herbert Read to characterise the work of a number of British sculptors—Lynn Chadwick, Reg Butler, Kenneth Armitage, F E MacWilliam and Bernard Meadows—who achieved international recognition in the early 1950's. Their sculpture was influenced by the work of Alberto Giacometti and Germaine Richier; it had an angst-ridden look which reflected the post-war mood of tension and uncertainty. Their work was figurative, often combining human and animal forms; they made use of welded metal to construct cage-like structures enclosing or piercing modelled forms with tortured surface textures.

D Thompson, 'A decade of British sculpture' *Cambridge opinion* (37) January 1964 24-36.

163 GESTURAL ABSTRACTION: Painting that emphasises brushwork and the movement of the artist's hand and arm. It is a broad term used by many critics in relation to *Abstract Expressionism*, *Action Painting* and *L'Art Informel* in order to distinguish them from the other major tradition of abstract painting, *Geometric Abstraction*.

164 GILBERT AND GEORGE: The Christian names of two English artists [they have renounced the use of their surnames] trained as sculptors at 'Saint Martin's School of Art', London, who have attracted a good deal of publicity in the late 1960's

and early 1970's. They maintain that art is for all, that anyone can be an artist, and that anything one can do or say can be regarded as art if presented as such. Most of their work challenges the accepted notion of sculpture: they give deadpan performances, dressed in business suits, with hands and faces painted gold, singing banal songs and repeating dance routines, performances which last several hours; these are called *Living Sculpture*. Feature articles on their ideas are called 'magazine sculpture', etc.

See also Conceptual Art, Performance Art.

B Reise 'Presenting Gilbert & George, the living sculptures' *Art news* 70(7) November 1971 62-65, 91-92.

Gilbert & George, the sculptors *Side by side* (Art for All, 1972).

165 GLASS BOX ARCHITECTURE: Box like office blocks encased by glass curtain walls. John Jacobus describes Glass Box Architecture as 'a trend in commercial architecture which reached fever peak in the mid 1950's' and 'belatedly spread to Europe at a point when its popularity was ebbing in America'. This type of architecture was characterised by uniformity; although it was modern in style, its anonymity made it 'acceptable to the cautious taste' of corporation directors and property developers.

J Jacobus *Twentieth century architecture: the middle years 1940-65* (Thames & Hudson, 1966).

166 'GOOD DESIGN': In the years since 1945 well-intentioned designers, and officials attached to institutions such as the *Design Council* in London and the Museum of Modern Art in New York, have espoused the cause of modern design in articles, lectures, exhibitions, and also by means of design awards and seals of approval given to selected products. Its advocates described modern design in terms of its 'honesty', 'integrity', 'truth to materials', by adjectives such as 'decent', 'modest', 'wholesome', and thus good modern design came to be regarded as good in a moral as well as an aesthetic sense. In the beginning the adjective was a compliment, but consumer goods, manufactured for a mass public, have to appeal to the average man; this fact, coupled with the selection of approved products by committee, resulted in a middle-brow aesthetic. Good Design became a cliché and the term acquired its disparaging inverted commas, or was called 'Easy Art'; it became boring and dowdy—as Christopher Cornford puts it 'like cold rice pud: plain, nutritious, high-minded and off-white'—especially when contrasted with the *Post-Modern Design* of Carnaby Street, *Pop Art,* customising, and the zest of the *Supersensualists.* Some writers have noted a cult of the ugly, of *Kitsch,* and call it 'anti-design'.

L B Archer 'What is Good Design?' (I) *Design* (137) May 1960 28-33.

L B Archer 'What is Good Design?' (II) *Design* (140) August 1960 26-31.

C Cornford 'Cold rice pudding and revisionism' *Design* (231) March 1968 46-48.

F MacCarthy *All things bright and beautiful* . . . (Allen & Unwin, 1972) 178-179, 214-215.

167 **GRASS ROOTS ART:** Work by untrained artists; an alternative term for 'primitive', 'folk', or 'naïve' art, coined by G N Blasdel.

G N Blasdel 'The Grass Roots artist' *Art in America* 56(5) September/October 1968 24-41.

168 **GROUP FORM:** An architectural term devised by the Japanese architect Fumihiko Maki to refer to the sum of relationships between a number of buildings. In other words, the form of individual buildings is subordinated to the form of the group as a whole.

F Maki 'The theory of group form' *Japan architect* February 1970 39-42.

169 **GROUP ONE FOUR:** A London based group of painters and sculptors formed in 1964 by Brian Yale and Mauro Kunst while they were teaching at Hornsey College of Art. The group has two other members: John Berry and Ron Grayson. Its name derives from the flat where discussions were held. Group One Four has produced *Multiples,* in an attempt to combine art and industrial techniques, and has promoted itself by means of business methods; that is, it has issued its own publicity material and designed a packaged exhibition of work for international circulation.

4*

E Rowan ' Group One Four ' *Studio international* 178(917) December 1969 228-229.

E Wolfram ' Group One Four ' *Art & artists* 3(2) May 1968 50-53.

170 **GROUP ZERO** (or Group O, often referred to simply as ' Zero '): An influential German group formed in Düsseldorf in 1957 by Otto Piene and Heinz Mack; a third member, Gunther Uecker, joined in 1960. The word ' zero ' does not equal ' nothing ', but a ' zone of silence for a new beginning '; it derives from the countdown sequence of a rocket take-off. The German artists were strongly influenced by the work of the *Nouvelle Tendance,* especially artists like Yves Klein, Jean Tinguely and Lucio Fontana, and reacted against the prevailing fashion for *Tachisme.* They developed a form of *Kinetic Art* exploiting light and motion, which attempted to re-establish a harmonious relationship with the forces of nature. The group disbanded in 1966.

See also Düsseldorf School, Light Art.

C Barrett ' Group Zero ' *Art & artists* 1(9) December 1966 54-57.

J A Thwaites ' The story of Zero ' *Studio international* 170(867) July 1965 2-9.

171 **GROUPE DE RECHERCHE D'ART VISUAL** (GRAV) was founded in Paris in 1960 to encourage research into light, illusion, movement and perception. Its chief members were Yvarel, François Morellet, and Julio le Parc. GRAV was largely inspired by the work and theories of Victor Vasarely; it was also closely associated with the Gallery ' Denise René '. Its members were opposed to *L'Art Informel,* they replaced spontaneity with pseudo-scientific research techniques and substituted group activity and anonymous works for individual creation. In addition they sought to involve the spectator by participatory activities, and to reach a mass market by the production of *Multiples.* Essentially they were dedicated to the abolition of the art object, and sought an art that would blend with the environment to end the division between art and life. Much of their work seems to fall into the category of *Kinetic Art.* GRAV became defunct in 1969 because its members, having developed their ideas in different directions, could no longer agree on a common policy.

See also Participatory Art.

C Barrett 'Mystification and the Groupe de Recherche' *Studio international* 172(880) August 1966 93-95.

172 GROUPE INTERNATIONAL D'ARCHITECTURE PROSPECTIVE (GIAP):

A group that has met since 1965 under the leadership of Michel Ragon to discuss visionary and futuristic concepts of architecture.

M Ragon 'Le Groupe International d'Architecture Prospective' *Cimaise* (79) January/March 1967 42-51.

173 GUERRILLA ART ACTION: A New York art

and politics group (or concept—anyone may use its name and ideas); members include Jean Toche and Jon Hendricks. They criticise current art on the grounds that it is merely a commodity of the capitalist society, and that museums and artists in their present roles are adjuncts to fascism. In order to challenge this state of affairs, the group performs *Actions* in public places, hoping to provoke a reaction from the authorities. One such Action, called 'Blood Bath', was performed at the Museum of Modern Art, New York in 1969.

See also Art Workers Coalition, Cultural Art.

G Battcock, 'Guerrilla Art Action' *Art & artists* 6(11) February 1972 22-25.

174 GUTAI GROUP: An organisation of Japanese artists

devoted to the cause of experimental art, which was founded in Osaka in 1954. The word 'gutai' approximates to the German 'gestalt'. The original members of the group were young artists influenced by the master Jiro Yoshihara. The Gutai Group are particularly noted in the West for their theatre art, or public spectacles, which pre-dated the *Happenings* of New York. In 1957 contacts were established between the Gutai Group and *L'Art Informel* of Europe via Michel Tapié who visited Japan in that year.

M Cohen 'Japan's Gutai Group' *Art in America* 56(6) November/December 1968 86-89.

A Kaprow *Assemblage, Environments, Happenings* (NY, Abrams, 1965).

J Langster 'Gutai: an on the spot report' *Art international* 9(3) April 1965 18-24.

J Love 'The group in contemporary Japanese art: Gutai and Jiro Yoshihara' *Art international* 16(6-7) Summer 1972 123-127, 143.

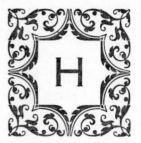

175 **HABITAT:** A vogue word among architects and designers in the 1950's and 1960's. According to the dictionary, 'habitat' refers to the natural environment or locality in which plants and animals develop, hence a place of abode. For human beings 'habitat' generally means an artificial environment designed by architects, such as Le Corbusier's 'Unite d'Habitation', Marseilles 1945-1952, a village in one vertical structure. The ninth assembly of the 'Congrès Internationaux d'Architecture Moderne' (CIAM) held in Aix en Provence in 1954 made Habitat its theme.

In 1967, for the Expo at Montreal, the Israel architect Moshte Safte built a cliff-like structure using mass production methods to create modular housing units which were then stacked in a variety of ways. The structure, called 'Habitat', accommodated a large population in a limited space without restricting human needs for privacy and comfort.

Terence Conran, an English designer trained at the 'Central School of Arts and Crafts' opened a shop in London in 1964, named 'Habitat', in order to sell tastefully designed household goods to 'switched-on people'.

176 **THE HAIRY WHO:** A group of Chicago painters formed in 1966; members include Gladys Nilsson, James Nutt, Suellen Rocca, and Karl Wirsum; they specialise in gruesome images inspired in many cases by comics, their work has been described as 'rotgut Dada' and 'a pictorial counterpart of *Funk Art*'.

F Schulze 'Art news in Chicago' *Art news* 70(7) November 1971 45-55.

F Schulze 'Chicago' *Art international* 11(5) May 20 1967 42-44.

177 **HAPPENINGS** (also called Action Theatre, Event Art, Painters' Theatre, Total Art or Total Theatre, Theatre of Mixed Means): The name 'Happenings' derives from

Allan Kaprow's earliest public work, 'Eighteen Happenings in six parts', which was performed in New York in 1959.

Happenings integrate several media (hence the description 'Mixed Means' and 'Total Art'); they are a cross between an art exhibition and a theatrical performance developed by painters and sculptors, and consequently they emphasise visual, tactile, and olfactory responses, rather than literary or verbal experience. Generally they avoid such features of traditional theatre as plot, character, actors, and repetition of performance, but they do make use of scripts, themes, and rehearsals, (they are not merely improvised events). Happenings are not fixed in time (their duration tends to be uncertain), or venue (they can be performed in galleries, private houses, back yards or in the country-side). Great stress is laid on materials, and participants are often made to look like objects, performances usually result in a great deal of mess and destruction, and impermanence is an essential part of the aesthetic of Happenings. Audiences at these events have to be prepared to endure physical discomfort and possible abuse.

Happenings lack rational plots or storylines; their structures are compartmentalised like a collage, or *Assemblage,* a dreamlike conjunction of situations and events. Precedents for the phenomena of Happenings can be found in the Dada 'Cabaret Voltaire' and the unlikely juxtapositions typical of Surrealism. Also it is possible to trace a line of development from the Cubist Collage via *Junk Sculpture/ Assemblage—Tableau—Environmental Art* to Happenings, but this explanation is probably too pat. Perhaps more important was the influence of the idea of the artist's creative performance before the canvas to be found in *Action Painting,* and also the influence of John Cage; several artists later associated with Happenings attended his courses at ' Black Mountain College ' in the early 1950's.

The major centre for Happenings was New York, and artists working there during the 1960's included Allan Kaprow, Jim Dine, Red Grooms, Claes Oldenburg, George Segal, Robert Whitman, Al Hansen and George Brecht; but similar events have taken place in Japan (see Gutai Group) and in cities throughout Europe (see Fluxus, Direct Art, Presentological Society, Décollage, Actions).

Happenings & Fluxus (Cologne, Kölnischer Kunstverein, 1970).

A Kaprow *Assemblage, Environments and Happenings* (NY, Abrams, 1965).

M Kirby *Happenings: an illustrated anthology* (NY, Dutton, 1966).
R Kostelanetz *The theatre of mixed means* (Pitman, 1970).

C Tisdall 'Life copying art (Happenings)' *The guardian* June 2 1972 p 8.

178 HARD-EDGE PAINTING: This expression, first used by the Californian critic Jules Langster in 1959, describes an aspect of American abstract painting produced by a number of artists reacting against the brushy, gestural quality associated with *Abstract Expressionism*. According to Lawrence Alloway, a critic who has extended the Hard-Edge concept, this type of painting treats the whole picture surface as one unit: forms extend across the canvas from edge to edge, and therefore Hard-Edge Painting has no 'figures on a field' or other depth effects. Paint is applied evenly to produce an immaculate finish, colours are restricted to two or three saturated hues and delineations between areas of colour are abrupt (hence Hard-Edge); often this creates optical shimmer. (If by 'Hard-Edge' we mean merely a technique of painting with sharp edges of colour rather than blurred edges—some writers use the term in this sense—then it is also applicable to many of the paintings of *Pop Art*). The main practitioners of the style are Ellsworth Kelly, Alexander Liberman, Al Held and Jack Youngerman; their precursors were Joseph Albers, Ad Reinhardt and Barnett Newman (see Colour-Field Painting). At first sight, Hard-Edge Painting appears to continue the linear *Geometric Abstraction* of artists like Malevich or Mondrian, but in fact it developed out of the American painting that immediately preceded it rather than the European tradition. Many painters and sculptors outside the United States have been influenced by Hard-Edge, or have arrived at a comparable style, especially in England (see Situation). See also Non-Relational Painting.

L Alloway 'On the edge' *Architectural design* 30(4) April 1960 164-165.

J Coplans 'John McLaughlin, Hard-Edge and American painting' *Artforum* 2(7) January 1964 28-31.

179 HAUS-RUCKER-CO. (House-mover company): An experimental Austrian architectural design group formed in 1967 by two architects, Laurids Ortner, Zamp (Gunter Kelp), and Klaus Pinter, a painter/designer; they are also assisted by a staff of five with other skills. Haus-Rucker-Co is located in an old house in Vienna; there the group create *Participatory Art* works ' to be lived in, worn, played with, and jumped on '. The group has performed *Actions* and presented exhibitions in cities throughout Germany and also in New York. Their particular specialities are plastics—they are sometimes referred to as the ' plastics people '—pneumatic structures, air mattresses and life support systems.

' Conceptual architecture ' *Design quarterly* (78/79) 1970 29-33.

' Haus-Rucker-Co-Live ! ' *Craft horizons* 30(4) August 1970 30-33.

180 HERMETICISM: A term used by Werner Haftmann to describe a variety of post-war European painting exemplified by the work of artists such as Jacques Villon, Jean Bazaine, Alfred Manessier, Ernst W Nay, Theodor Werner, Fritz Winter, and Guiseppe Santomaso. The word ' hermetic ' derives from alchemy and means ' airtight ', ' closed in ', ' absolutely sealed ', and many critics use it in this sense to describe self-contained, self-referring styles of painting. However Haftmann's term refers to painting that appears abstract, but which is pregnant with representational content. He distinguishes two kinds of such painting: (1) Representational Hermeticism, in which artists work towards abstraction from a motif, and (2) Abstract Hermeticism, in which artists work from formal problems and discover as they proceed representational references. See also Homeless representation, Intrasubjectives.

W Haftmann *Painting in the twentieth century* vol 1 (Lund Humphries, 1960).

181 HISTORICISM: Nikolaus Pevsner uses this word to describe a post-modern, anti-rational tendency in twentieth century architecture and design which relies on historical precedents as a source of inspiration. In Pevsner's view Historicism marks an unfortunate retreat to those nineteenth century values that the *Modern Movement* architects sought to replace. As examples of recent stylistic revivals Pevsner lists Neo-Accommodating, *Neo-Liberty,* Neo-German Expressionism, Neo-Perret, Neo-De Stijl, Neo-Art Nouveau and Neo-School of Amsterdam.

P Collins ' Historicism ' *Architectural review* 127(762) August 1960 101-103.

N Pevsner ' The return of Historicism ' *Studies in art architecture and design vol 2: Victorian and after* (Thames & Hudson, 1968) 242-259.

182 HOLOGRAPHS: Three-dimensional images can be reconstructed by passing a beam of laser light through a hologram wave interference photograph. The British artist Margaret Benyon has made use of this technical achievement to produce what are called ' Holographs ' or ' Stereo-Paintings '.

Holography is also claimed to be a new tool of value to architectural designers. See also Laser Art, Imaginary Architecture.

J Benthall ' Laser holography and interference patterning '—chapter in—*Science and technology in art today* (Thames & Hudson, 1972) 85-98.

D Dickson 'Art: holographs by Margaret Benyon ' *New scientist* May 20 1971 p 480.

L Fader & C Leonard ' Holography: a design process aid ' *Progressive architecture* 52(6) June 1971 92-94.

H Wilhelmsson ' Holography: a new scientific technique of possible use to artists ' *Leonardo* 1(2) April 1969 161-169.

183 HOME ART: Ritual objects produced by the British artist Terry Setch ' for the solace and comfort of the home maker '. His work is based in art clichés and *Kitsch* motifs to be found in the decoration of the average British home.

T Hudson ' Terry Setch . . .' *Studio international* 176(904) October 1968 p 163.

184 HOMELESS REPRESENTATION: A trend in American and European painting of the 1950's identified by Clement Greenberg: painterlessness which tends towards abstraction but which continues to suggest representation. An example would be Willem De Kooning's series of ' Women ' paintings executed between 1952 and 1955. Subsequently this approach to painting became a mannerism adopted by artists outside the Abstract Expressionist style.

See also Bay Area Figuration, Hermeticism.

185 L'HOMME TÉMOIN: A group of young French painters, including Bernard Buffet and Paul Rebeyrolle, exhibiting in Paris in 1949, whose work was described as a kind of ' pictorial existentialism bearing witness to the emptiness and desolation of the world '.

186 HOUSE STYLE (also called Group Identity, Company Handwriting): A design trend that emerged in the 1950's. Alec Davis defines a House Style as ' a visual character—in all means whereby an organisation comes into contact with people—which is recognisable as belonging to that organisation '. Designers are usually specially commissioned by large industrial concerns and public enterprises to impose a common design style on items such as publications, advertising, signs, letter headings, packaging, symbols, exhibition stands, name plates, labels, overalls or uniforms, and colour schemes. In the United States, House Style is usually referred to as ' Corporate Design '.

A Davis ' House Style: a special issue ' *Design* (95) November 1956.

187 HYBRID ENTERPRISES: A market research approach to art initiated by two English artists, Peter Phillips and Gerald Laing, while resident in New York in 1964/65. They compiled kits of materials—colour samples, optical patterns, choice of forms, statistical sheets—and issued them to a number of critics, dealers, and collectors. When the data was returned it was processed by computer and art objects constructed in accordance with the specifications provided. The objects that resulted were three dimensional but unlike traditional sculpture, for they were made of glamorous materials such as perspex and aluminium.

See also Custom Painting.

M Amaya *Pop as art: a survey of the New Super Realism* (Studio Vista, 1965) 129-130.

' Hybrid Consumer Research Project ' *ICA bulletin* (151) October 1965 17-18.

188 HYPER-REALISM: An international trend in art on display at the seventh Paris Biennale in 1971. A form of extreme realism often combined with alterations of scale: wall-size photographs transferred to canvas, the image of a crumpled bed on canvas which itself is crumpled; paintings of corners of rooms sited to create trompe l'oeil effects; life-size three dimensional figures. Many European writers use the term ' Hyper-Realism ' as an equivalent of the American *Photo-Realism*.

U Kultermann & P Faveton ' La révolte des realistes ' *Connaissance des arts* (244) June 1972 118-123.

189 ICOGRADA: Acronym for 'International Council of Graphic Design Associations', a body founded in 1963.

190 ICSID: Initials of the 'International Council of Societies of Industrial Design', a body founded in 1957.

191 IMAGINARY ARCHITECTURE (also called invisible Architecture, Nowhere Architecture): A proposal by Friedrich St Florian of the 'Rhode Island School of Design' for an architecture of synthetic space, as an alternative to permanent buildings, to be activated only for specific purposes. Such architecture would consist of space-defining conceptual structures (he quotes the world airway network and stacking zones above airports as examples of imaginary structures which retain the conventional engineering parameters of height, width, and depth, but which exist physically only when used by aircraft, and then only as readings on instruments). Florian has also suggested 'simulated architecture', to consist of holographic images of monuments projected into the sky by laser beams. A demonstration of his ideas was held at the Moderna Musset, Stockholm in 1969. See also Aerial Architecture, Conceptual Architecture.

'Imaginary Architecture' *Domus* (491) October 1970 48-54.

192 INDEPENDENT GROUP (IG): An informal ideas group composed of members of the *Institute of Contemporary Arts*, London, who met intermittently between the years 1952 and 1954. Participants included Lawrence Alloway, Reyner Banham, Magda and Frank Cordell, Theo Crosby, Toni Del Renzio,

Richard Hamilton, Nigel Henderson, John McHale, Eduardo Paolozzi, Colin St John Wilson, Alison and Peter Smithson and William Turnbull. Thus the IG represented a wide cross section of the visual arts: architecture, painting, sculpture, photography, and art criticism. Its purpose was to examine the implications of science, technology, the mass media, and popular culture for art at mid-century. Topics discussed included the machine aesthetic, *Action Painting*, popular music, car styling, consumer goods, fashion and communication theory. American mass circulation magazines, advertising, cinema, and science fiction periodicals provided much source material. The term *Pop Art* was used, but in the beginning it referred to popular, mass culture arts rather than fine art exploiting popular culture for imagery and technique.

The IG mounted two exhibitions to make their ideas public, ' Parallel of Life and Art ' held at the ICA in 1953, and *This is Tomorrow* held at the Whitechapel Gallery in 1956.

F Whitford ' Paolozzi and the Independent Group '—essay in—*Eduardo Paolozzi*: catalogue (Tate Gallery, 1971) 44-48.

193 **INDETERMINATE ARCHITECTURE:** A new approach to architectural design propounded by the English architect John Weeks in the early 1960's. His buildings—in particular the Northwick Park Hospital of 1961—were designed to provide ' inbuilt potential for growth and change which is matched to the growth and change in the organisation which the buildings house '; therefore their form is ' indeterminate ' from the outset. The notion of ' indeterminacy ' derives, ultimately, from the uncertainty principle of physics formulated by W Heisenberg in 1927.

Weeks' idea for a completely flexible architecture has been developed further by the *Archigram* group.

See also Random Art, Endless Architecture.

J Weeks ' Indeterminate Architecture ' *Transactions of the Bartlett Society* 2 1963-1964 85-106.

194 **INFORMATION:** Title of a major exhibition held at the Museum of Modern Art, New York in 1970. The show presented an international report on the activities of younger artists working mainly in the area of *Conceptual Art*. The choice of the word 'Information' as a title probably reflected the interest artists have shown in the mathematical theory of communication known as 'information theory', and also the increasing use of documentation as a means of presenting art works.

G Battcock 'Informative exhibition at the Museum of Modern Art' *Arts magazine* 44(8) Summer 1970 24-27.

K L McShine—editor—*Information* (NY, MOMA, 1970).

195 INSTALLATION: A word frequently used in art magazines, especially American ones, in captions to photographs of galleries showing the layout and disposition of artworks in exhibitions. Its use reflects the dependence of much recent art, especially *Minimal Art,* on particular gallery spaces or settings. An installation show is normally a once-only affair and close-up photographs of single works would not reveal their crucial relationship to the environment. The word also has industrial or mechanical associations appropriate to Minimal sculptures, which are often fabricated in factories according to specifications supplied by the artist.

196 THE INSTITUTE FOR RESEARCH IN ART AND TECHNOLOGY LTD (IRAT): An administrative organisation working on behalf of various autonomous groups that from time to time make up the institute. IRAT was founded in 1968 and was first located at the New Arts Lab, London. Later it moved to an old dairy in Kentish Town, London. The institute provides studio space for individual artists, and assists groups concerned with alternative theatre, alternative television, film and photography co-operatives, printing, electronics, computers, plastics, children's workshops; it also co-operates with related groups such as *Project 84, Continuum,* and *Space Provision for Artists (Cultural and Educational).* The television department of IRAT has published a report on the influence of video in community development. Trustees of IRAT include the writer J G Ballard, Reyner Banham and Joe Tilson; its secretary-general is Michael Julian.

See also Technological Art, Arts Lab.

197 THE INSTITUTE OF CONTEMPORARY ARTS, LONDON (ICA): The ICA was founded in 1947 by Herbert Read and Roland Penrose to encourage new developments in the arts. Its programmes include art exhibitions, films, concerts, poetry readings, lectures, and discussions. Many leading British artists have been members of the ICA and have formed fruitful associations under its auspices (see Independent Group). Currently, the ICA is suffering a financial crisis and some uncertainty concerning the role it should play in the artistic life of London.

S Braden ' Malaise in the Mall ' *The guardian* June 23 1972, p 10.

198 INTER-ACTION: A community arts association, established in 1968, located in houses due for redevelopment in Kentish Town, London. Inter-Action has forty associates and is led by an ex-Rhodes scholar, Ed Berman. Its aim is to involve ordinary people in local affairs, to give them a sense of belonging to a community and of living in a particular neighbourhood. Their methods of achieving this aim include game techniques, *Street Art*, or Street Theatre, a Fun Art Bus, ' technological folk art ' forms such as Media Vans, Video, photography, and films. The intention is to communicate positive social messages via entertainments and spectacles; primarily these forms are directed at children and adolescents in the hope that through them adults will become involved.

A plan exists for a more permanent structure to house Inter-Action, to be designed by Cedric Price.

See also Action Space, Actions.

' Invisible London ' *Time out* (116) May 5 to 11 1972.

199 INTER-MEDIA, MIXED-MEDIA, MULTI-MEDIA: Three expressions which art critics use more or less synonymously, they all reflect a trend towards an integration of the traditional forms of art—painting, sculpture, poetry, music, dance, theatre, etc—a trend characteristic of much art activity since 1945.

' Mixed-Media ' is probably the broadest term of the three because it refers to fairly conventional art works composed of different materials —oil paint, fabric, sand, metal and wood collaged together—and also to performances combining say, dance, film, light and sound. The latter phenomena are also called ' Multi-Media ', meaning many media used simultaneously.

Dick Higgins, a member of *Fluxus,* has popularised the term ' Inter-Media ', which he defines as ' media between media '. Higgins is proprietor of ' Something Else Press ', a publishing concern which promotes all forms of Inter-Media art. It is claimed that there has been an 'Inter-Media revolution', whose prophet was John Cage; parallels have also been drawn with the development of interdisciplinary sciences such as Cybernetics.

Inter-Media appears to have become formalised into an art form in its own right, if the number of groups devoted to it are any guide: in 1965 Otto Beckmann founded a group in Vienna called 'Art Intermedia'; in 1968 Joe Kyle founded a group in Vancouver called 'Intermedia'; the American artists' collective known as USCO has recently formed a group called 'the Intermedia Systems Corporation'.

Many writers regard the Inter, Mixed, Multi-Media trend as indicating the ultimate disintegration of the traditional art forms, and they talk constantly about the 'death of painting'; but, as Susan Sontag points out, while there are artists who break down distinctions between genres, there are always other artists and critics, equally radical, who differentiate ever more precisely between genres, and who strive to isolate the essential characteristics of each art form (see, for example, Modernist Painting).

See also Assemblage Art, Happenings, Environmental Art, Combine Painting.

L Warshaw 'Intermedia workshop' *Arts in society* 6 (3) Fall/Winter 1969 448-451.

G Youngblood *Expanded cinema* (NY, Dutton, 1971) 345-398.

200 INTERVENTIONS: A trend in art on view at the seventh Paris Biennale in 1971. Random, ritualistic acts were performed, extraordinary sights and sounds were presented to the public during the course of the exhibition by groups such as the 'Paradiso' from Amsterdam. One critic compared these artists to itinerant medieval troubadours, because they travel from museum to museum in order to give their performances.

201 INTRASUBJECTIVES: Title of an exhibition of paintings by American artists held in New York in 1949, including work by Willem De Kooning, Hans Hofmann, Arshile Gorky, Mark Tobey and others. The show was organised by Harold Rosenberg and Samuel Kootz in an attempt to delineate a cohesive movement. The name 'Intrasubjectives' derives from an essay by

Jose Ortega y Gasset and refers to a method of arriving at abstraction via subjective experience rather than by an objective study of the external world. The label did not catch on, but later the majority of these artists were subsumed under the name *Abstract Expressionism*. See also Hermeticism.

The Intrasubjectives: catalogue (NY, Kootz Gallery, 1949).

202 **INVISIBLE CITY:** The networks and structures of urban life—transportation and communication services, cultural and social networks—and its resources of people, places and processes, as opposed to the physical elements—buildings, roads —usually thought of as the city. The Invisible City was the theme of the 1972 'International Design Conference' held at Aspen, USA.

'Invisible London' *Time out* (116) May 5-11 1972.

203 **INVISIBLE PAINTING:** A description applied to paintings by three American artists—Ad Reinhardt, Paul Brach and Ludwig Sander—that have colour or tonal values so closely attuned that they exist on the threshold of human perception. At first glance Invisible Paintings appear to the viewer to be uniform in tone, but if time is allowed for the eye to accommodate to the subtle differences, then the image contained in the painting, usually a cross form, becomes visible. Reproductions of such painting in art books are virtually worthless, they give no indication of their merit. It is part of the programme of these artists that they oppose the easy assimilation of art via illustrations in art books and magazines.

204 **ITALIAN CRAZE** (or Expresso Style): In Britain during the years 1953 to 1960 a mania developed for Italian design—Olivetti typewriters, Espresso coffee-making machines, Piaggio 'Vespa' scooters, Gio Ponti furniture, Nebiolo typefaces, Italian clothes and Italian films—especially among young, newly affluent, teenagers. In 1956 Cecil Gee introduced Italian male fashions into England: narrow trousers, winkle-picker shoes, short 'bumfreezer' jackets with narrow lapels, and striped shirts.

Italian products continue to excite interest. One writer claims that there is a 'design explosion' in Italy called the 'poltrona (armchair) boom '. Leading Italian designers include Gio Ponti, Ettore Sottsass, Joe Colombo, Bruno Munari, Gae Aulenti and Achille Castiglioni. They are particularly admired for the high quality and elegance of their architecture, interior design, furniture, and ceramics, all of which are regularly featured in ' Domus ' magazine.

See also the Supersensualists.

M Laski ' Espresso ' and S Gardiner ' Coffee bars ' *Architectural review* 118 (705) September 1955 165-173.

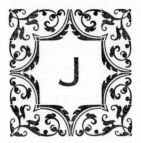

205 **LA JEUNE PEINTURE:** A group of young artists based in Paris, formed in 1965, who use their art as a means of political protest. A work which received a great deal of publicity concerned Marcel Duchamp, an artist La Jeune Peinture regard as the epitome of art for art's sake, and consisted of the 'murder' of Duchamp. The group has also protested about American involvement in the Vietnam war, and about the repressive role of culture in France—in 1968 the painters of the group worked as members of the *Atelier Populaire*. The best known artists of La Jeune Peinture are Gillies Allaud, Eduardo Arroyo, Antonio Recalcati and Bernard Rancillac.

M Gibson '"La Jeune Peinture"—protest and politics' *Art in America* 58(6) November/December 1970 142-145.

206 **JUDD'S DICTUM:** A remark by the American sculptor and writer Don Judd in answer to the perennial question 'but is it art?' to the effect that 'if someone calls it art, it's art' (to which one is tempted to reply 'if someone else says it is not art, it's not art'). Judd's Dictum has been discussed at length in the literature of *Conceptual Art*.

P Pilkington & D Rushton 'Don Judd's dictum and its emptiness' *Analytical art* (1) July 1971 2-6.

207 **JUNK CULTURE:** Lawrence Alloway coined this term in the 1950's to describe art that rescues the waste products of city life, art that incorporates objects that accumulate in drawers, cupboards, and attics, discarded but still retaining the history of their human use.

See also Junk Sculpture, Assemblage, Le Nouveau Realisme.

L Alloway 'Junk culture' *Architectural design* 31(3) March 1961 122-123.

208 JUNK SCULPTURE: A form of *Assemblage Art* popular in Europe and the United States during the 1950's. Metal objects, automobile parts and other debris taken from refuse dumps were used as a basis for sculpture by artists such as John Chamberlain, César, Richard Stankiewicz, Eduardo Paolozzi and Lee Bontecou. Some artists presented objects as found, others transformed their discoveries, usually by welding metal parts together to form abstract scupltures. The method of collaging junk together can be seen as reaction against the carving and modelling traditions of sculpture. It derives primarily from the work of Kurt Schwitters, the first great exponent of the artistic exploitation of street debris.

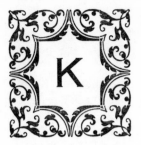

209 **KINETIC ARCHITECTURE:** In their book published in 1971 William Zuk and R H Clark argue that the static, fixed forms of traditional architecture are unable to respond to the pressures exerted on them by a society in a state of flux, and therefore they make a plea for a new type of architecture, called 'Kinetic', which would be dynamic, adaptable, and responsive to the changing demands of its users. The broad category of Kinetic Architecture includes a number of other concepts: 'Reversible Architecture', 'Incremental Architecture', 'Deformable Architecture', 'Disposable Architecture' and *Mobile Architecture*. Zuk and Clark quote examples of the work of R Buckminster Fuller, Pier Luigi Nervi, the *Metabolists*, *Archigram* and others, to show that forms of Kinetic Architecture already exist.

See also Additive Architecture, Indeterminate Architecture, Plug-In Architecture.

W Zuk & R H Clark *Kinetic Architecture* (NY, Van Nostrand Reinhold, 1971).

210 **KINETIC ART** (also called the Movement Movement): The word 'kinetic' derives from the Greek for 'moving'. In the nineteenth century it was applied to movement phenomena in physics and chemistry; in the twentieth century it was used sporadically in the context of plastic arts, but Kinetic Art as a distinct movement did not emerge until the 1950's. Kinetic Art has been described as four-dimensional because it adds the dimension of time to sculpture. According to Frank Popper, various kinds of movement can be identified (a) actual movement—mobiles, moving lights, machines, (b) virtual movement—a response within the spectator's eye to static visual stimuli, (c) movement of the spectator in front of the art work or manipulations of parts of the art work by a spectator (see Option Art). Kinetic Art can be seen as a logical extension of the virtual movement characteristic of *Op Art* paintings, and the two movements are often discussed together.

Kinetic Art requires technical proficiency, and therefore Kinetic artists seek a union of art and technology. They have a natural tendency to form groups and claim to pursue ' visual research ' rather than art activities (see for example Groupe de Recherche d'Art Visuel, Group Zero, Nouvelle Tendances). Unfortunately, merely to ape the teamwork and techniques of science does not by itself produce comparable results. Many kinetic artists seem to believe that static art is inherently inferior to art that moves, while critics who believe the opposite refer to Kinetic Art disparagingly as ' turntable art '. Kinetic Art is an international movement, but is especially favoured in Europe and South America, and the major artists associated with it are Yaacov Agam, Nicolas Schöffer, Jean Tinquely, Victor Vasarely, Yvaral, Raphael J Soto, Frank Malina and Pol Bury.

See also Electronic Art.

M Compton *Optical and Kinetic Art* (Tate Gallery, 1967).

G Kepes—editor—*The nature and art of motion* (Studio Vista, 1965).

F Popper *Origins and development of Kinetic Art* (Studio Vista, 1968).

211 **KITCHEN SINK SCHOOL:** A label applied by David Sylvester to the realist paintings of John Bratby, Derrick Greaves, Jack Smith and Edward Middleditch—four English artists, ex-students of the ' Royal College of Art '—exhibiting at the ' Beaux Arts Gallery ', London in the middle 1950's. These painters specialised in depicting domestic squalor; their work resembled, to some extent, Social Realist art, but they disavowed any political intentions. Their banal subject matter—tables loaded with food and cereal packets—anticipated the content of *Pop Art*, but their vision and manner of painting were fundamentally academic. Edward Lucie Smith described Kitchen Sink as ' an eccentric detour ' in the history of British painting; he also included under this heading two followers of David Bomberg (see Bomberg School): Frank Auerbach and Leon Kossoff.

The Kitchen Sink trend was not restricted to painting; it was also manifested in the films of the period and in plays by John Osborne and Harold Pinter; in fact they were all part of a general movement in English culture, inward-looking, self-critical, with a refreshing honesty and directness, but unfortunately shortlived.

'The Beaux Arts Gallery and some young British artists' *The studio* 154(775) October 1957 110-113.

212 **KITSCH:** Most writers on Kitsch state that the word derives from the German 'Verkitschen'—to make cheap. Hence Kitsch is artistic rubbish, or 'low art' that apes the effects of past fine art styles, and in the process cheapens them. However, Gilbert Highet has suggested that the word may derive from the Russian 'Keetcheetsya' meaning to be haughty and puffed up. Harold Rosenberg describes Kitsch as the daily art of our time—all those cheap, sentimental, cute artifacts found everywhere in Western industrialised societies—an art form that follows established rules when the genuine modern artist puts into question all rules in art. Clement Greenberg remarks that if the avant garde represents the forefront of art, Kitsch represents the rearguard, or, as another writer expresses it, Kitsch is the mirror image of formalism.

Kitsch is a form of art pollution, or pseudo-art, created for mass consumption. It is a commodity among commodities, and its audience and effects are utterly predictable; it is one-dimensional and therefore unable to provide an authentic aesthetic experience. Since the vast majority of the populations of Western societies are now 'middle-class', Kitsch is an expression of their taste in striving to possess the opulence previously enjoyed only by the aristocracies. Examples of Kitsch include cheap replicas of famous artworks, factory-produced paintings sold in Woolworths, most 'art' sold in 'art' shops, the enormous output of products associated with the gadget, gift, souvenir, and tourist industries, as exemplified by the garden gnome and Disneyland. Kitsch manifests itself in every media—films, advertising, interior decoration, music, fiction, etc. Most critics regard Kitsch as an inevitable consequence of the industrial revolution—a mass produced art catering for millions who wish to embellish their environment, but who are philistine in their tastes because they lack formal education and have lost contact with traditional folk culture. Abraham Moles, who has undertaken the most complete analysis to date of the phenomenon of Kitsch, claims that it satisfies the bourgeois values of security, self-esteem, ownership, geniality, and the need for daily rituals.

Mass taste is manipulated above all by advertising, and the latter is frequently geared to the exploitation of sex, hence the expression 'Porno Kitsch' coined by Gillo Dorfles. Most critics discuss Kitsch in a tone of moral disapproval—Kitsch has been called the cultural revenge of the lower classes—but it does have its appreciators; for example, *Camp* taste delights in outrageously bad art. Many artists and designers are also attracted to Kitsch as a contrast to the over-refined quality of much fine art—Yves Klein expressed his intention to produce art in bad taste, Claes Oldenburg has made use of Kitsch decoration in his environmental sculptures, and the Italian design groups *Archizoom* and *Superstudio* exploit similar sources. The American architect Morris Lapidus builds highly successful Kitsch hotels, the decoration of which bastardises many styles; they provide, according to one critic, a ' medium for visceral and tactile fulfilment, the pornography of comfort '.

K Allsop ' Of gnomes and plaques and plastic thatch and fairy lights and things ' *Nova* September 1970 54-57.

G Dorfles—editor—*Kitsch: an anthology of bad taste* (Studio Vista, 1969).

G Highet *Talents and geniuses* (OUP, 1954).

A Moles *Le Kitsch: l'art du bonheur* (Paris, Mame, 1971).

B N Schwartz 'Art confrontation: the sacred against the profane ' *Arts in society* 9(1) Spring/Summer 1972 149-158.

J Sharpe ' It's new, it's different, it's been here all the time ' *Ark* (41) 1967 24-27.

J Sternberg *Les chefs d'oeuvre du Kitsch* (Paris, Editions Planète, 1971).

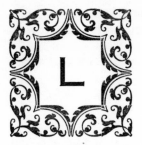

L

213 **LANDSCAPE SCULPTURE:** A new type of sculpture identified by the magazine 'Landscape architecture' in 1971, and defined as 'designed landscape forms which embody more than one sculptural medium beyond earth itself; an organic system of materials used to express a unified aesthetic concept, and responsive to conditions set by its physical environment'.

See also Earth Art, SITE.

'Landscape sculpture' *Landscape architecture* 61(4) July 1971 special issue.

214 **LASER ART** (laser = acronym for 'light amplification by stimulated emission of radiation'): According to Dr Leon Goldman, lasers—devices for producing coherent, high intensity beams of radiation, or light—provide artists and craftsmen with a new tool for use in the fields of design, etching and sculpture. Lasers have already been used to carve jade and plastic and a helium/neon laser has been used, in association with optical and acoustic systems, to produce a form of *Kinetic Art*. Laser holography enables three-dimensional sculpture to be presented when the original is unavailable.

Light beams of various colours, produced by lasers, have been employed to create examples of *Environmental Art*. For example, Rockne Krebs, in collaboration with the American industrial company, 'Hewlett-Packard Inc', made a 'Laser Environment' as part of the 'Art and Technology' programme organised by the 'Los Angeles County Museum of Modern Art'; the artwork was displayed at the 1970 Expo in Japan. A similar work, entitled 'Laser Beam Environment', was created by Keji Vsami in 1969.

See also Holographs, Imaginary Architecture, Technological Art.

L Goldman 'Lasers—a coherent approach to art' *New scientist* January 21 1971 146-148.

L Goldman 'Progress of Laser Art in lapidary work' *Lapidary journal* 25(2) May 1971 328-329.

215 LETTRISM:

An international avant garde movement, based in Paris, established in 1950 by Isidore Isou (a Roumanian writer who came to France in 1945) and Maurice Le Maitre. Lettrists publicise their ideas with 'aggressive megalomania'; they believe that the word in poetry has been exhausted and concentrate instead on the letter. Similarly they believe that figuration and abstraction in painting and sculpture are dead ends, and as an alternative they propose a new formal structure based on the letter or sign. In fact Lettrism 'claims to be able to revolutionise every aesthetic discipline of its time', including, besides those already mentioned, the novel, the theatre, the cinema, architecture, and even politics!

The term 'Lettrism' is also employed by art critics in a wider sense; that is, to describe the introduction of words, letters, signs and pictographic symbols into paintings by artists such as Jasper Johns, On Arakawa, Robert Watts and Robert Indiana.

See also Concrete Poetry.

N & E Calas 'Lettrism'—chapter in—*Icons and images of the sixties* (NY, Dutton, 1971) 131-148.

C Cutler 'Paris: the Lettrist movement' *Art in America* 58(1) January-February 1970 116-119.

I Isou 'The creations of Lettrism' *Times literary supplement* (3,262) September 1964 796-797.

216 LIGHT ART

(also called Lumia or Luminism): Willoughby Sharp believes that Light Art—the literal use of light in art—is the only totally new art form of our time. The term itself is a broad concept encompassing such diverse phenomena as colour organs, fireworks, projected light, and sculpture made of neon tubes. Light Art is usually treated as a sub-division of *Kinetic Art*, but some writers claim it is such a large movement that it deserves a separate status. A more pertinent reason for such a separation is the fact that not all artists who use light are concerned with movement or a changing display of lights in time; for example, Dan Flavin's austere neon sculpture relates to *Minimal Art*, and Chryssa's neon tube lettering relates to *Pop Art*, not to *Kinetic Art*.

Among the best known Kinetic artists who have exploited light in the years since 1945 are Lucio Fontana, Nicholas Schoffer, Julio Le Parc, Bruno Munari, Frank Malina, and those artists associated with the German *Group Zero*, and the French *Groupe de Recherche d'Art Visuel*.

See also Electrographic Architecture.

F Popper ' Light and movement '—chapter in—*Origins and development of Kinetic Art* (Studio Vista, 1968) 156-189.

W Sharp ' Luminism and Kineticism '—essay in—*Minimal Art: a critical anthology* edited by G Battcock (Studio Vista, 1969) 317-358.

A T Spear ' Sculptured light ' *Art international* 11(10) Christmas 1967 29-49.

217 LIVING ART: In its straightforward sense this expression means the art of now, art by living artists; hence it has been chosen as a title by periodicals dealing with contemporary art—for example, ' Living art ' published by the *Institute of Contemporary Arts*, London during the early 1960's, and the French journal, ' L'art vivant ' currently being issued.

More profoundly, the expression refers to an attempt to transcend the division (that Robert Rauschenberg believes exists) between art and life, by substituting ' the real for the aesthetic object ' (see, for example, Actions, Actualism, Direct Art, Living Sculpture). In effect, Living Art seeks the end of art. However, as Ad Reinhardt noted, ' art is always dead, and a " living art " is a deception '. Herbert Marcuse agrees that the notion is absurd, because art ' must retain, no matter how " minimally ", the Form of Art as different from non art, and it is the Art Form itself which frustrates the intention to reduce or even annul this difference . . . Art cannot become reality, cannot realise itself without cancelling itself as Art in *all* its forms . . .'

H Marcuse 'Art as a form of reality '—essay in—*On the future of art* edited by E Fry (NY, Viking Press, 1970) 123-134.

A Reinhardt—quoted in—*Conceptual art* by U Meyer (NY, Dutton, 1972) p 167.

218 LIVING SCULPTURE: An example of the persistent tendency in the art of recent years for the artist to abandon the production of physical objects and to present himself, or a tableau vivant, as the artwork. In 1961, for example, the Italian artist Piero Manzoni signed nude models and also declared his friends to be works of art. In 1962, during the *Fluxus*-inspired 'Festival of Misfits' held in London, the French artist Ben Vautrier exhibited himself in the window of 'Gallery One' for fifteen days and nights as an example of 'Living Sculpture'. In Stockholm in 1969, Pi Lind provided a number of pedestals in a gallery so that real people could sit motionless pretending they were statues. The Greek artist Jannis Kounelli, who works in Rome, has introduced parrots and cacti into artworks; in 1969 he exhibited a number of horses in an art gallery. The English artist Stuart Brisley has in recent years presented himself in various gallery settings described as 'life situations'.

In London in 1972 Ann James mounted an exhibition called 'Sculpture in Reverse' based on the idea that visitors to the show themselves constituted the exhibition; Ann James provided a setting of cobwebs. In exhibitions of extremely realistic sculpture it has become a cliché to include a motionless live human in order to induce uncertainty in the spectator about what is, and what is not, real.

See also Gilbert & George, Performance Art.

219 LOS ANGELES FINE ARTS SQUAD: A group of four painters—Victor Henderson, Terry Schoonhover, Jim Frazin, and Leonard Korin—who live and work in Venice, Los Angeles. The squad was founded in 1969 and specialises in the creation of large-scale murals on the blank walls of buildings. One of their paintings may take as long as a year to complete; scenes depicted include views of local streets rendered in a trompe l'oeil, signpainter's style, but while they are life-scale and realistic, they usually contain incongruous additions; for example, a street scene may be given a layer of snow (which has never fallen in Venice, California).

See also Street Art.

T H Garver 'Venice in the snow . . .' *Artforum* 9(7) March 1971 91-92.

G Glueck 'Art notes: the art squad strikes again' *The New York times* July 9 1972 p 16.

220 LOS ANGELES PROVOS (or LA Provos):
A group of Los Angeles artists active in 1966 who were
inspired by the ideas of Allan Kaprow and the example of the Dutch
Provos. The group, led by Michael Agnello, performed anarchistic and
provocative acts, such as taking from the poor to give to the rich,
planting marijuana joints in public library books, and so on.

K Von Meier 'Los Angeles: the failure and future of art' *Art
international* 11(5) May 20 1967 54-57.

221 LOST SCULPTURES (or Invisible Sculptures):
'Lost' is used as the opposite of 'found' in 'found
objects'. A term applied by Max Kozloff and others to the *Minimal
Art* of Don Judd, Carl Andre, and Robert Morris, whose sculptures
are so sparse in their visual appeal that they may easily be read
as real, nondescript objects of the everyday world. A work by Carl
Andre exhibited at the Sonsbeek tri-annual at Arnhem in 1971 was
mistaken for rubbish by a park attendant and cleared away. Claes
Oldenberg created an Invisible Sculpture called 'Placid City monument' for the 'Sculpture in Environment' exhibition held in New
York in 1967. It consisted of a trench 6' × 6' × 3' excavated by two
gravediggers and then filled in again. A similar project for a buried
cube has been put forward by Carl Andre. Spectators would have to
take the existence of such works on trust.

222 LYRICAL ABSTRACTION: A phrase suggested by the French painter Georges Mathieu as a
title for a exhibition held in Paris in 1947 (the show was in fact called
'The Imaginary') of work by Wols, Hans Hartung, Jean-Paul
Riopelle, Camile Bryen, Jean Atlan and others. Pierre Rastany and
other critics employed it to refer to the more decorative, non-violent,
poetical painters of *L'Art Informel* and of *Abstract Expressionism*—
Sam Francis, Philip Guston and James Brooks (Lyrical Abstraction in
America has been called an emasculinated version of *Abstract Expressionism*).

See also The New Informalists.

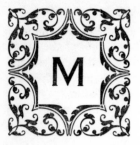

M

223 **THE MADI MOVEMENT:** A South American *Kinetic Art* movement founded in Buenos Aires in 1946 by Gyula Kosice and others. The word ' madi ' is a contraction of the cry ' Madrid!'. Kosice and his colleagues attempted to create a totality of the arts based on the common denominator-movement. Their ideas were expressed in manifestos and in a magazine called ' International Madi Art ', eight numbers of which appeared between 1947 and 1954.

M Ragon ' Kosice the poorly known precursor and the Madi Movement ' *Cimaise* (95/96) January/April 1970 30-45.

224 **MAGICAL ARCHITECTURE:** A proposal put forward by Frederick Kiesler for a unity of painting, sculpture and architecture to be achieved by collective artistic effort. Kiesler is an architect of Austrian origin who has been closely associated with French Surrealism, especially the design of Surrealist exhibitions. It is therefore not surprising to find that he is opposed to functional architecture, which he dismisses as ' the mysticism of hygiene '.

V Conrads—editor—*Programmes and manifestoes on 20th century architecture* (Lund Humphries, 1970) 150-151.

225 **MASS ART:** Harold Rosenberg used this expression to describe popular art consumed by a mass audience: Hollywood movies, pulp fiction, television shows . . . (see also Kitsch). More recently, Jasia Reichardt has applied it to psychedelic posters, or non-utilitarian objects, produced for a mass market but not necessarily created by professional artists.

226 **MATTER ART:** An aspect of *L'Art Informel.* During the 1950's European painters such as Jean Dubuffet, Jean Fautrier, Antonio Tàpies, Enrico Donati and Alberto Burri made use of ' unworthy materials (*ie* non-fine art) such as cinders, sand, old sacking, charred wood, etc, in place of, or in addition to, oil paints. The surface of their paintings resembled a hardened crust, a rind. Matter artists wanted to incorporate 'reality' in a non-illusionistic way, thus matter was not only the medium but also the subject. A similar attitude is evident in the work of those artists belonging to the *Art Povera, Earth Art* and *Anti-Form* movements. Recent paintings (1971) by Larry Poons suggest a revival of interest in Matter Art among younger artists.

227 **MEC ART** (or Peinture Mécanique) is short for ' Mechanical Art '. It is a term used by the French painter Alain Jacquet and the Italian artist Mimmo Rotella to describe ' paintings ' produced entirely by the creative manipulation of photo-mechanical reproduction processes. Such works are issued in editions of 200 or more. Mec Art reflects the influence of techniques pioneered by the American painters Robert Rauschenberg and Andy Warhol.

See also Multiples, Silk Screen Printing.

P Restany 'Alain Jacquet: the big game of reality and of fiction ' *Domus* (510) May 1972 51-55.

228 **MEDIA ART** (or Media Inversion): A form of art practised by an avant garde group based in Berkley, California called ' Sam's Cafe '. The group consists of three artists, Marc and Terri Keyso and David Shine. Sam's Cafe makes use of existing structures or institutions such as the postal system, the Press and television in order to reach a huge, non-art audience. For example, in 1971 the group pretended to be a debt collection agency and distributed 20,000 mythical bills giving the address of the local television station as the centre for all enquiries. Naturally enough within a short time the Press, television, radio and police were embroiled in the art work, creating a great deal of documentation. Media Inversion—the feeding of alien elements into sophisticated communications systems in order to turn the network against themselves—was a political idea fashionable in the 1960's.

See also Correspondence Art.

T Albright ' Visuals ' *Rolling stone* (85) June 24 1971 36-37.

229 MEGASTRUCTURES: A variety of *Utopian Architecture*. During the 1960's a number of architects, in response to the daunting urban problems of the twentieth century, proposed vast new structures (mega=great) to replace existing cities, on the grounds that large problems require large technological solutions. In the design of Megastructures individual buildings become merely components or lose their separate identity altogether; these designs also attempt to allow for the demand for universal mobility and for rapid change, their overall purpose being to provide a total environment for work and leisure. The best known architects associated with the Megastructure concept are Kenzo Tange (Tokyo Bay Project), Leonardo Ricci, Paolo Soleri (see Arcology), Yona Friedmann and *Archigram*. The American architect Robert Venturi has dismissed Megastructures as designs for ' fashionable hill towns with technological trappings '. The origin of the word ' Megastructure ' is uncertain. The earliest mention of it that I can trace is in a letter by Don Kingman published in ' Progressive architecture ' in June 1967.

230 METABOLIST GROUP: A Japanese experimental architectural group formed under the direction of Kenzo Tange in 1960. Members include Norboru Kawazoe, Noriaki Kurokawa, Kiyonori Kikutake, Fumihiku Maki and Masato Otaka. The Metabolists envisage an architecture whose principles are analogous to those of biology. They are concerned with the design of urban systems, services and connections between buildings rather than with individual buildings themselves. Kukokawa has designed a plant type community with living space above ground and production facilities below ground level. In a project for the development of the Tokyo Bay area the Metabolists planned a linear, open system capable of responding to different rates of change.

G Nitschke ' The Metabolists of Japan ' *Architectural design* 34(10) October 1964 509-524.

231 METAMATICS: Jean Tinquely constructed between 1955 and 1959 a number of humorous *Kinetic Art* works which were both sculptures and painting machines. Coin operated Metamatics which were displayed at the 1959 Paris Biennale scribbled in coloured inks on sheets or rolls of paper; stylistically the results resembled the abstractions of *L'Art Informel* and *Tachisme*.

J Reichardt 'Art at large: The painting machines' *New scientist* 53 (786) March 9 1972 p 563.

232 MINIMAL ART (also called ABC Art, Anti-Illusionism, Bare Bones Art, *Cool Art*, Literalist Art, Know Nothing Nihilism, Idiot Art, *Object Art*, Reductive Art, Rejective Art, Primary Structures): The term ' Minimal Art ' is thought to have been used first by Richard Wollheim in 1965, though some writers ascribe it to Barbara Rose. It describes a major art movement of the 1960's, primarily American—its supporters claimed that it was the first American movement to owe nothing to Europe—though British artists, such as Anthony Caro, were sometimes included in discussion. The chief exponents of Minimal Art were Robert Morris, Don Judd, Sol Le Witt, Robert Smithson, Ronald Bladen, Walter De Maria, Tony Smith, Dan Flavin, Larry Bell and John McCracken. A major exhibition of Minimal Art called ' Primary Structures ' was held at the Jewish Museum, New York in 1966.

Minimal Art was essentially sculptural, despite the inclusion of painters such as Kenneth Noland and Frank Stella by some critics, because the literal, physical space occupied by sculpture was regarded as intrinsically more powerful in the perception of art works than the illusionary space of painting. The most outstanding feature of Minimal Sculpture was its clarity and simplicity, characteristics which reflected the influence of older artists such as Barnett Newman, Ad Reinhardt and David Smith; it also marked a reaction against the emotional self-expression of *Abstract Expressionism* and *Assemblage Art*. Minimal artists, by their cooler, blander approach, hoped to create works which would be more resistant to assimilation and so avoid the rapid obsolescence of modes such as *Op Art* and *Pop Art*.

Art critics have disagreed as to whether the adjective ' minimal ' applies to the finished sculpture—Wollheim's view and also Clement Greenberg's who says that Minimal Art aspires to the condition of non-art (*cf* Lost Sculptures)—or whether it refers to the means by which the sculpture is produced, the opinion held by John Perrault.

Yvonne Rainer has conveniently listed those sculptural qualities which Minimal artists reject or minimise—left hand column—and those they substitute or emphasise—right hand column:

figurative references	non-referential forms
illusionism	literalness
hierarchical relationship of parts	unitary forms or modules
complexity, detail	simplicity
monumentality	human scale
hand craftsmanship	factory fabrication
texture	uninterrupted surfaces

The purpose of such criteria was to establish the autonomous nature of sculpture, to isolate those qualities of scale, shape, proportion and mass considered specific to it and to avoid those qualities appropriate to architecture, monuments and ornaments. Sculpture that was dependent on internal part to part relationships—the Cubist aesthetic—was eschewed on the grounds that it was fundamentally anthropomorphic. In its place the Minimal artist presented unitary, gestalt like forms—for example a cube—which could be perceived at once. In such works aesthetic interest shifts from internal to external relationships, for example to the relationship between the mental concept ' cube ' and the varying perceptual shapes of the object as one moves around it, or that between the sculpture and the negative space of its architectural setting: sculpture as place. Many Minimal sculptures were produced for particular gallery or exhibition spaces and were not transferable, thus making *Installation* a crucial factor.

Often Minimal artists submitted plans or instructions to industrial firms for their pieces to be fabricated. The skilled handwork traditionally associated with sculpture was totally superseded by the process of making aesthetic decisions. This method of working influenced the development of *Conceptual Art*.

Minimal Art has been strongly attacked for, it is claimed, lacking genuine surprise, for being merely *Good Design* reflecting the influence of *Basic Design* courses in art colleges. It has also been criticised on political grounds for being an art form entirely appropriate to big business and right wing attitudes.

See also Art Povera, Earth Art.

'Aspects of Art called " Minimal " ' *Studio international* 177 (910) April 1969 165-189.

G Battcock—editor—*Minimal Art: a critical anthology* (Studio Vista, 1968).

233 **MOBILE ARCHITECTURE:** A new type of architecture proposed by a number of young architects from France, Holland, Poland and Israel who met in Paris in 1957 and formed an organisation called ' Groupe d'Études d'Architecture Mobile ' (GEAM). In a manifesto published in 1960 GEAM suggested the reform of property and land rights to make possible constructions that would be variable and interchangeable, buildings with moveable floors and ceilings, buildings on rafts, etc. The demand for such extreme flexibility was made in response to the overwhleming problems of modern town planning. Mobile Architecture would not be expected to be constantly on the move, only to be capable of being moved if required.

M Ragon 'Architecture Mobile ' *Cimaise* (64) March/June 1963 106-115.

234 **MODERN ART:** A complex notion scrupulously ignored by most art dictionaries. In a broad sense it is a chronological concept describing all the painting and sculpture of present and recent times; more narrowly it is an ideological concept referring to that art of our era which self consciously rejects past modes and aggressively asserts its claim to be the only art truly reflecting our age. No two critics or historians agree exactly on a date for the birth of Modern Art but it is generally located in the middle, or second half, of the nineteenth century because the revolutionary changes in science, in industry, and in society during that period profoundly influenced the arts and resulted in the formulation of new aesthetic theories, in the development of new techniques and materials, and in changes in the social status of the artist.

Modern architecture and design are also considered to have originated in the nineteenth century but not to have become a fully fledged movement until the twentieth century (see The Modern Movement).

The intensive use of any adjective in relation to the art of a particular historical period inevitably links the word with that period; hence ' modern ' is most closely associated with European art movements appearing between 1910 and 1938. Consequently there is a constant search for a term to replace ' modern '. ' Contemporary ' was tried but critics claimed it was suggestive of only one generation of artists and therefore too limited in scope. In Britain during the late 1940's and early 1950's ' contemporary ' was overworked and became indelibly

5*

associated with the art and design of that period (see Contemporary Style). The feeble expression ' new art ' is generally employed when critics and exhibition organisers are at a total loss for a name; it has been popular at least since the 1890's (Art Nouveau), was used to greet the arrival of *Minimal Art* during the 1960's, and in 1972 it was used as the title of a major exhibition of the latest trends in British art held at the Hayward Gallery, London.

' Modernism '—entry in—*Encyclopedia of World Art* Vol 10 (NY, McGraw Hill, 1965) 201-209 columns.

235 THE MODERN MOVEMENT: A phrase popularised by Nikolaus Pevsner's book ' Pioneers of the Modern Movement ', published in 1936. (The 1960 revised edition is entitled ' Pioneers of Modern Design '.) Like *Modern Art*, modern architecture and design are believed to have originated in the nineteenth century but they did not become a fully fledged movement until after the first world war. Some authorities regard Art Nouveau as the first modern style because it avoided the eclecticism of Victorian design; others equate ' modern ' solely with the clear rational designs associated with the Bauhaus and regard 1936 as the height of the modern period. Hence ' The Modern Movement ' refers primarily to architecture and design produced in the 1920's and 1930's according to the prevailing functionalist aesthetic, which was thought by its adherents to yield forms without style, forms that would be permanently valid (see ' Good Design '). Modern architecture is also credited with an ' heroic period ', according to Alison and Peter Smithson dating precisely from 1915 to 1929.

Since 1945 it has become clear that the pre-war notions of functionalism were naïve. The masters of modern architecture have continued to produce elegant buildings but it is now seen that their work constituted a style like any other. By 1960 Modern design had become an established tradition against which a younger generation of architects and designers have reacted vehemently.

See Post-Modern Design.

N Pevsner *Pioneers of Modern Design from William Morris to Walter Gropius* (Penguin, 1960).

A and P Smithson ' The heroic period of Modern Architecture ' *Architectural design* 35 (12) December 1965 590-639.

236 **MODERNISM:** The ideological theory of *Modern Art*, architecture and design, a theory which rejects past styles and claims it is the only true reflection of our age. The term 'modernistic' is often used disparagingly to refer to the style called *Art Deco* which combined elements of modern design with past motifs for decorative purposes, or used functional ideas for their visual appeal, for example streamlining static objects; hence the expression 'bogus modernism'.

'Modernism'—entry in—*Encyclopedia of World Art* Vol 10 (NY, McGraw Hill, 1965) columns 201-209.

237 **MODERNIST PAINTING:** The influential American art critic Clement Greenberg, leader of the school of *Formalist Criticism,* has developed an aesthetic of painting based on the ideological concept of *Modernism*. Greenberg defines the essence of modernism in painting as 'the use of the characteristic methods of a discipline to criticise the discipline itself . . . to entrench it more firmly in its area of competence'. He regards Modernist Painting as the mainstream of painting since Manet, painting which openly acknowledges as virtues its physical constraints: flat surface, properties of pigments, shape of support. Movements in painting outside this narrow category Greenberg tends to dismiss as *Novelty Art*.

C Greenberg 'Modernist Painting' *Art and literature* (4) Spring 1965 143-201.

238 **MODULAR ART:** Paintings and sculpture based on a module, that is a unit of size or measurement that is repeated throughout the art work. Architects have used the modular concept for centuries, especially since the development of standardised building components. In recent years furniture designers have also produced many ranges of modular or unit furniture.

The explicit use of modules in the fine arts only developed during the 1960's. The term 'modular' has been applied by critics to sculpture by Carl Andre, Tony Smith and Sol Le Witt, and to paintings by Robert Mangold and Brice Marden. In 1970 an exhibition entitled 'Modular Painting' was held at the Albright Knox Gallery, Buffalo, New York. Its curator, Robert M Murdock, described the modular approach as ' the use of structural elements; a technique in which physically separate modules are constructed as opposed to those represented on a surface '.

See also Serial Art.

G Kepes—editor—*Module, symmetry, proportion* (Studio Vista, 1966).

239 **MOMA:** Initials standing for ' Museum of Modern Art ' (New York), an influential institution noted for its exhibitions and publications. In 1971 the American artist Les Levine parodied MOMA by creating the ' Museum of Mott Art Inc ', located at 181 Mott Street, New York.

240 **MONOCHROMATIC AND MONOTONAL PAINTING:** Since 1945 many painters have followed Kasimir Malevich and Alexander Rodchenko's example and produced a series of paintings in a single colour or a single tone. Among these artists are Piero Manzoni, Lucio Fontana, Yves Klein, Frank Stella, Robert Rauschenberg, Robert Mangold, Philip Guston, Robert Ryman and Ad Reinhardt. Monochromatic paintings can be regarded as extreme instances of the reductivist aesthetic. Perhaps the most famous series of monochromatic canvases were those produced by Yves Klein in the 1950's, for which he created and patented, special colours: International Klein Gold, International Klein Rose, and International Klein Blue. Udo Kultermann organised an exhibition of monochromatic paintings in 1960; it was held at the Schloss Morsbroich, Leverkusen, Germany.

See also Colour-Field Painting, All-Over Painting.

241 **MULTIPLES:** In the past etchings, lithographs, bronzes and china ornaments have been produced in edition form. They provided—and still provide—collectors with signed artworks cheaper than unique originals. Such editions were strictly limited in order to preserve reproduction quality but there have been signed editions of graphics up to 5,000. Multiples, an extension of the edition concept, are works created by artists that can be repeated—multiplied—in production, theoretically without limit; they are manufactured from a design or matrix.

The idea of Multiples was first suggested by Agam and Jean Tinguely. They put their idea to the Parisian gallery dealer Denise René in 1955 but none were produced until 1962. René tried, unsuccessfully, to patent the word 'multiple' for the exclusive use of her stable of artists; René's multiples are always issued in strictly limited editions.

During the 1960's many artists produced Multiples: Claes Oldenberg, Daniel Spoerri, Julio Le Parc, Joe Tilson and others. Usually Multiples are a minor stylistic version of an artist's painting or sculpture.

New materials, such as plastics, and new industrial techniques, such as vacuum forming, make possible the mass production of artworks. This, together with the possible utilization of non-art outlets like supermarkets, have caused some critics to view Multiples as a means of democratising art. However, the idea is shallow for, as Jasia Reichardt points out, Multiples are not cheap enough to appeal to a mass market and are still sold through the established gallery system. They are in fact merely another élite category of decorative objects. Other writers have pinpointed the basic problem: Multiples occupy a no man's land between unique artworks and ordinary shop commodities; objects of such uncertain identity are unlikely to sell to a mass market.

See also Cultural Art.

'Multiples Supplement' *Art & artists* 4(3) June 1969 27-65.

New Multiple Art (Whitechapel Gallery, 1970).

J Reichardt 'Multiples' *Architectural design* 41 (2) February 1971 p 71.

242 **MUSEUM WITHOUT WALLS:** The French writer André Malraux has examined the way museums condition our experience of art—we see works divorced from their original context and thus become aware of style above all the other qualities—and believes that reproductions of works of art on cards, in books and periodicals constitute a 'musée imaginaire', an imaginary museum. The Museum Without Walls extends the process set in motion by the physical museum, making available to the private individual the art of all times and of all peoples, though at the cost of providing substitutes for the originals.

See also Slide Culture.

A Malraux *The voices of silence* (Secker & Warburg, 1954).

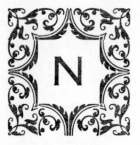

243 **N. E. THING COMPANY** (NETCO): An avant
garde Canadian group established in Vancouver in
1966. 'Anything' is structured like a business company with a 'president'—Iain Baxter—and a number of departments—Research,
Things, Accounts, ACT (Aesthetically Claimed Thing), ART (Aesthetically Rejected Thing), Photography, Films, Projects, Consultations and
COP. The last department is concerned with 'Cop Art', that is, the
use, exploitation or annexation of other artists' work, for example, a
chevron by Kenneth Noland was extended by fifteen feet, a carrying
case was designed for one of Andy Warhol's pillows. NE Thing is not
interested in the production of art objects, it regards itself as an
alternative device for exploiting cultural knowledge. Information on
Baxter's recent activities can be found in Lucy R Lippard's essay 'Art
within the Arctic Circle '—in—*Changing: essays in art criticism* (NY,
Dutton, 1970) 277-291.

'N E Thing Co Ltd '—in—*Information* (catalogue) (NY, MOMA,
1970) 88-91.

244 **NARRATIVE FIGURATION:** Narration in art
has been out of favour since its ' misuse ' by Victorian
genre and history painters, but from 1963 onwards a number of
painters, mostly based in Europe, developed a new form of Narrative
art. The French critic Gerald Gassiot-Talabot organised an exhibition
at the Galerie Europe, Paris in 1965 to define the new tendency.
Modern narrative art represents events in time—with or without a
storyline—on a single canvas. Frequently its imagery is distorted and
its subject content fragmented: several sequences may be compressed
into one painting. Jasia Reichardt, an English critic who has employed
the comparable term ' Narrative Art ', claims that it can also include

abstract paintings that deal with successive transformations of an image (see Systemic Painting). Narrative Figuration blends aspects of *Pop Art* with illustration; it has been influenced by the Cinema and comic strip cartoons. The major artists associated with it are Oyvind Fahlstrom, Gianfranco Baruchello, David Powell, Dado, Hervé Télémaque and Bernard Rancillac.

P Couperie and others *Bande dessinee et figuration narrative* (Paris, Musée des Arts Decoratifs, 1967) 233-253.

G Gassiot-Talabot 'Everyday mythologies . . .'—essay in—J P Hodin and others *Figurative art since 1945* (Thames & Hudson, 1971) 272-302.

245 NART: Mario Amaya's alternative description for *Cool Art* and *Minimal Art*. His neologism is a combination of ' Nothing ' and 'Art ' and means less equals more. Nart is characterised by impersonality and boredom of repetition; its objects have no development or climax, it is unphotogenic and mechanical. Amaya includes in his category a number of works in different media: 'Dance', a construction by Robert Morris, visual poems by Dieter Rot, musical compositions by La Monte Young, Andy Warhol's eight hour films ' Sleep ' and ' Empire ', Carl Andre's *Clastic Art* sculptures, and paintings by Mark Lancaster. According to Amaya, Nart reflects the influence of Ad Reinhardt, Frank Stella and Zen philosophy.

M Amaya ' Views/Reviews : Mario Amaya on Nart ' *Vogue* (British) 123(11) September 1966 18-20.

246 NATURAL SCULPTURE: A concept postulated by four British artists—Terry Atkinson, David Bainbridge, Michael Baldwin and Harold Hurrell—a sculptural 'object' to consist of electromagnetic lines of force invisible to the human senses except by readings on instruments. According to the artists such an ' object ' would possess ' sculptural morphology '.

See also Conceptual Art, Lost Sculptures.

247 NEO-DADA: A label applied in the late 1950's to the work of two American painters—Jasper Johns and Robert Rauschenberg—by unsympathetic critics. Johns painted banal images—flags, targets, numbers and maps—filling the whole surface of the canvas. These pictures create a degree of uncertainty in the spectator's mind about the identity of the object he confronts. Rauschenberg incorporated industrial refuse into his *Combine Paintings* in a manner that reminded critics of Kurt Schwitters' collages. These works were thought to be *Anti-Art* like Dada, hence the label 'Neo-Dada'. However, the comparison was superficial since the American artists had little in common with the pre-war European movement. Their work, in fact, marked a reaction to *Abstract Expressionism* (though Rauschenberg retained its splashy brushwork) and heralded the arrival of *Pop Art,* hence its other label 'Proto-Pop'.

248 NEO-LIBERTY: During the 1950's there occurred a revival of interest in the Art Nouveau style, especially in Italy. Architects such as Vittorio Gregotti, M D Bardeschi, Raffaello Lelli, and Leonardo Savioli came under its influence; also the furniture designer Gae Aulenti. Their work was described as ' sensuous, decorative, with flowing lines and flower like profiling'. Reyner Banham attacked it as a retreat from the ideals of the *Modern Movement* and dismissed it as ' an infantile regression '.

The expression ' Neo-Liberty ' was first used by Paolo Portoghesi in 1958 and was derived from ' Stile Liberty ', the Italian name for Art Nouveau (after the British firm of ' Liberty's ' which had supplied Art Nouveau style goods to Italy).

R Banham ' Neo-Liberty: the Italian retreat from Modern Architecture ' *Architectural review* 125(747) April 1959 231-235.

T Del Renzio ' Neo-Liberty ' *Architectural design* 30(9) September 1960 375-376.

' Neo-Liberty: the debate ' *Architectural review* 126(754) December 1959 341-344.

249 NEO-PICTURESQUE: In Britain in the middle 1940's a revival of interest in the picturesque developed among architects and writers associated with the journal 'Architectural review'. As a result of the wartime bombing, Britain's towns had many ruins and in accordance with the picturesque taste for crumbling remains architects were encouraged to retain them.

For example, Basil Spence in his plan for the new Coventry Cathedral incorporated the shell of the old building into his design instead of demolishing it.

250 NEO-ROMANTIC PAINTING: An aspect of British art that developed during the 1930's and continued in the immediate post-war period. A number of painters—John Piper, Edward Burra, Paul Nash and Graham Sutherland—and the sculptor Henry Moore created works, usually in watercolour, depicting landscapes in a highly theatrical and emotional manner influenced by the romantic tradition of English art.

Probably this tradition was revaluated during the 1930's as a result of the impact of Surrealism on English artists. In the 1940's younger painters such as John Minton, Robert MacBryde and Robert Colquhuon worked in the same Neo-Romantic vein.

R Ironside ' Painting since 1939 '—essay in—*Since 1939* (Phoenix House, 1948) 147-181.

251 NEW AMERICAN PAINTING: The title of an influential exhibition of American painting that toured Europe in 1959. The expression is synonymous with *Abstract Expressionism.*

252 THE NEW BRUTALISM: A movement in British architecture primarily associated with Alison and Peter Smithson—especially their work during the years 1953 to 1955—and the critical writings of Reyner Banham. The New Brutalism was not so much a style as ' a programme or an attitude to architecture '; as the Smithsons put it, ' an ethic, not an aesthetic '. Above all, the New Brutalists waged a moral crusade against the diluted versions of modern architecture produced in England in the immediate post-war period, and against the compromises they felt even the masters of the *Modern Movement* were making; the Smithsons set out to re-establish the original integrity and strength of modern architecture. They tried, in buildings like the Hunstanton secondary school, to express structure and services honestly, to use materials truthfully in the tradition of Le Corbusier and Mies van der Rohe. They also admired the sensuous use of materials in Japanese architecture and were conscious of certain classical canons of proportion.

The phrase ' The New Brutalism ' emerged in the early 1950's and was used by young architects who had adapted it from the term ' Neo-Brutalists ' coined by the Swedish architect Hans Asplund. The phrase has other shades of meaning besides the one given above: it is used in a superficial sense to refer to an international architectural style, popular in the late 1950's, concerned with a Corbusier like treatment of building surfaces (the word 'Brutalism' has been associated with Le Corbusier's béton brut—rough honest brickwork, exposed concrete imprinted with the grain of wooden shuttering—an approach to building design reflecting his intention 'to construct moving relationships out of brute materials'); on other occasions the phrase was linked with *L'Art Brut* of Jean Dubuffet, the paintings of Magda Cordell, and the sculpture of Eduardo Paolozzi.

R Banham 'Brutalism'—essay in—*Encyclopedia of Modern architecture* (Thames and Hudson, 1963) 61-64.

R Banham *The New Brutalism: ethic or aesthetic?* (Architectural Press, 1966).

R Boyd 'The sad end of New Brutalism' *Architectural review* 142(845) July 1967 9-11.

253 THE NEW EMPIRICISM: A term applied by British writers to Scandinavian architecture produced during the immediate post-war period. Also described as 'gentle and self effacing' and 'Welfare State Architecture '.

E De Maré and others 'The New Empiricism' *Architectural review* 103(613) January 1948 8-22.

'The New Empiricism: Sweden's latest style' *Architectural review* 101(606) June 1947 199-204.

254 NEW FIGURATION: In the early 1960's, after a decade of abstraction, art critics noted a resurgence of figurative painting in Paris, London and New York. In 1961 the French critic Michael Ragon called this tendency 'Nouvelle Figuration'. A wide spectrum of artists fall into this category, most of them of little merit, the exception being Francis Bacon.

It is claimed that the artists associated with New Figuration continue the 'figural experiments' of Jean Dubuffet, the *Cobra* painters, and Willem De Kooning. Some writers include the whole *Pop Art* movement under the heading of New Figuration.

A Pellegrini *New tendencies in art* (NY, Crown, 1966) 197-210.

M Ragon *Vingt cinq ans d'art vivant* ... (Paris, Casterman, 1969).

255 **THE NEW FORMALISM:** In the late 1950's several critics noted a new classicising trend in American architecture, manifested in buildings by Mies van der Rohe, Philip Johnson, Paul Rudolph and Minoru Yamasaki. This tendency was labelled ' The New Formalism '.

W H Jordy ' The formal image USA ' *Architectural review* 127(757) March 1960 157-165.

256 **THE NEW INFORMALISTS** (or New Colourists, Lyrical Colourism, Beautiful Painting): In the last few years a wave of American painters—David Diao, Robert Duran, Alan Shields, Ken Showell, James Sullivan, David Cummings, Donald Lewallen and others—have challenged the view that painting is dead by producing large scale pictures using acrylic pigments sprayed or stained onto the canvas. These works are abstract and extremely decorative. The New Colourists apply paint in multiple layers, a method which ' imitates a natural way of forming matter '. Their emphasis on work procedures reflects the influence of the *Process Art* aesthetic.

Critics have compared these new works to the painting styles of the 1950's—*Action Painting, L'Art Informel, Lyrical Abstraction,* Painterly Abstraction—especially the more decorative aspects of these modes. In 1970 Carter Ratcliff called these painters ' The New Informalists ' because their work sidestepped the ' formalist ' concerns of American painting of the previous decade. He also noted a connection between their use of colour and texture and certain mannerisms associated with youth cult light shows, drug sensibility and tie dye fabrics. Another critic dismissed the new paintings as ' a wave of viual muzak '; nevertheless the influence of this American style has already been registered in work done by fine art students in British colleges of art.

L Aldrich ' Young lyrical painters ' *Art in America* 57(6) November/ December 1969 104-113.

D Ashton ' Young Abstract painters: right on ' *Arts magazine* 44(4) February 1970 31-35.

R Channin ' New directions in painterly abstraction ' *Art international* 14(7) September 20 1970 62-65.

C Ratcliff ' The New Informalists ' *Art news* 68(10) February 1970 46-50.

257 **THE NEW MATERIALISM:** An extremely broad label devised by William Feaver to describe art that is part painting, part sculpture and part stage prop, made of unworthy materials such as dirt, refuse, slag and perishables. His category includes work by artists such as Keith Milow, Stephen Buckley, David Medella, Jeff Nuttall and Kenneth Price. Further details on the kind of art Feaver is referring to can be found under the headings Art Povera, Food Art, Funk Art.

W Feaver ' The New Materialism ' *London magazine* 10(8) November 1970 77-85.

258 **NEW REALISM:** In spite of the dominance of abstraction in twentieth century art many painters and sculptors continue to work in representational or figurative modes. Periodically groups of such artists are ' discovered ' by art critics and hailed as embodiments of the New Realism or the *New Figuration*. For example, since about 1970 a number of American painters (discussed in this glossary under the heading Photo-Realism) have been labelled New Realists.

Critics also claim, from time to time, that a variety of abstract art reveals a new insight into reality, and consequently the words ' real ' and ' realism ' are in constant use.

See also Le Nouveau Réalisme and under Realism in the Index.

259 **THE NEW SENSUALISM:** A broad movement in modern architecture identified by ' Progressive architecture ' magazine in 1959, and essentially the post-war work of the architects Le Corbusier, Paul Rudolph, Eero Saarinen, Minoru Yamasaki, Felix Candela, Pier Luigi Nervi, Jorn Utzon and others. The buildings are sculptural in design and possess a sensuous plasticity of form in contrast to the rectilinear, modular, or flat-surfaced style usually considered typical of modern architecture.

T H Creighton ' The New Sensualism I ' *Progressive architecture* 40(9) September 1959 141-147.

T H Creighton ' The New Sensualism II ' *Progressive architecture* 40(10) October 1959 180-187.

260 THE NEW YORK SCHOOL: A phrase that dates from the 1940's. The growth of the New York School of painting and sculpture since the end of the second world war has largely been responsible for the American domination in art, paralleling the United States' political, economic and military leadership of the West. The New York School usurped the position previously held by the School of Paris.

According to Harold Rosenberg the term is a neutral geographical description referring to a cluster of styles—but primarily *Abstract Expressionism*—that developed in New York or were given a special inflection there. It is difficult to identify the characteristics of New York painting but Rosenberg suggests a largeness of scale, a direct or crude method of execution, a hardness of light.

H Geldzahler *New York painting and sculpture 1940-1970* (Pall-Mall, 1969).

H Rosenberg 'École de New York'—chapter in—*The de-definition of art: Action art to Pop to Earthworks* (Secker and Warburg, 1972) 188-200.

M Tuchman *The New York School: Abstract Expressionism in the 40's and 50's* (Thames and Hudson, 1970).

261 NO ART (also called Shit Art, Doom Art): Paintings, sculpture, collages and *Assemblage Art* by a group of American artists—Boris Lurie, Stanley Fisher, Sam Goodman, Michelle Fisher—exhibiting in New York between 1959 and 1964. Their exhibitions, at the March Gallery and at the Gallery Gertrude Stein, were given provocative titles—'The Doom Show', 'The No Show', 'The Vulgar Show', 'The Involvement Show'—and consisted of chaotic assemblages of rubbish, bloody dismembered toys and sexual fetishes designed to shock the viewer. No Art occurred during the McCarthy era in American politics; essentially it was a form of social protest. No artists disliked uncommitted art, especially *Pop Art*. They said 'No' to exploitation and pollution of all kinds: advertising, armaments, hunger, poverty, pornography, religion . . . Their preoccupation with feces—a work by Lurie consisted of mounds of excrement—has prompted the usual psychoanalytical explanation 'anal fixation'.

G Glueck 'The Non Gallery of No Art' *The New York times* Section 2 January 24 1971.

149

L R Lippard and others *Pop Art* (Thames and Hudson, 1966) 102-103.

B Lurie ' No Art ' (statements)—in—W Vostell *Aktionen: Happenings und Demonstrationen seit 1965* (Hamburg, Rowohlt, 1970).

E K and R S Schwartz ' No Art: an American psycho-social phenomenon ' *Leonardo* 4(3) Summer 1971 245-254.

262 NON-RELATIONAL ART: According to Lawrence Alloway, relational paintings, for example Cubist paintings or Hans Hofmann's colourful abstractions, contain a hierarchy of forms—large, medium, small—related one to another. Such paintings exploit the depth effects of ' figures on a field '. In contrast, Non-Relational paintings, for example Frank Stella's canvases of the 1960's, have a single uniform space and avoid depth effects by means of forms which stretch across the picture from edge to edge. Other painters avoid depth by means of an even distribution of accents —see All Over Painting—or by means of single colours—see Monochromatic and Monotonal Painting.

Because there is a dearth of internal relationships in Non-Relational Painting more importance comes to be attached to the external shape of the support and the rectangle, or *Shaped Canvas,* which itself becomes a ' figure ' against the ' field ' of the wall on which it is hung. The lack of depth in Non-Relational painting tends to emphasise the lateral reading of pictures, that is left to right or right to left across the surface of the canvas.

To the layman it may seem perverse that painters deny those qualities of pictorial illusion inherent in the act of making marks on canvas, but there is no intellectual challenge in repeating past achievements, and for this reason the modern painter is compelled to address himself to different pictorial problems.

The term ' Non-relational ' has also been applied to *Minimal Art* because Minimal sculptors claim that their work is non-figurative, non-symbolic, non-illusionistic, and does not *relate* to anything outside of itself.

See also Push and Pull, Colour-Field Painting, Hard-Edge Painting.

263 LE NOUVEAU RÉALISME: A movement in European art, centred on Paris and active during the period 1960 to 1963, sponsored by the French critic Pierre Restany. The expression 'New Realism' was first used by Restany in a manifesto

published in April 1960 in anticipation of an exhibition taking place in Milan the following month. In October of the same year at the home of Yves Klein in Paris, Restany formally constituted the New Realist group in the presence of Arman, François Dufrêne, Raymond Hains, Klein, Martial Raysse, Daniel Spoerri and Jean Tinquely; several other artists—J M De La Villeglé, César, Mimmo Rotella, Niki de Saint-Phalle, Gérard Deschamps and Christo—participated in later manifestations of the group.

Many diverse personalities are included in this list. They worked in a variety of different modes (see for example Destructive Art, Metamatics, Monochromatic Painting, Performance Art, Packaging, Snare Pictures, Affiche Lacérees) and despite Restany's rhetoric it is difficult to see what they had in common. A number of these artists were practitioners of *Assemblage Art* and were called ' Realists ' because they appropriated material from the urban environment and incorporated it, unadulterated, into their art works. New Realism has been described as ' art de constant ', an art of factual affirmation, an art of precise testimony.

Other activities of the group included a number of spectacles, *Actions* or *Happenings*. The title of an exhibition—' Forty degrees above Dada '—held in Paris in 1961 indicated the major source of the New Realist aesthetic. Restany's group were contemporaneous with the American *Neo-Dada* artists and joint shows were organised in Paris and New York in 1962; thus one finds the terms ' Neo-Dada ' and ' New Realism ' used interchangeably by some critics. Both movements are seen as presaging the development of *Pop Art*.

P Restany *Les Nouveaux Réalistes* (Paris, Editions Planète, 1968).

P Restany ' The New Realism '—essay in—J P Hodin and others *Figurative Art since 1945* (Thames and Hudson, 1971) 242-271.

264 NOUVELLE TENDANCE: An international *Kinetic Art* movement formed in Europe in the early 1960's. The name derives from the title of an exhibition organised by Matko Mestrovic in Zagreb in 1961. Artists from France, Spain, Holland, Yugoslavia, Switzerland, Germany and South America banded together into groups to produce collective or anonymous work, to exploit new materials and techniques, to explore the use of movement, light and spectator participation in art.

The loose association of these groups and their shared attitudes formed the Nouvelle Tendance.

F Popper *Origins and development of Kinetic Art* (Studio Vista, 1968) p 102.

265 **NOVELTY ART:** Clement Greenberg's derogatory term for those art movements of the 1950's and 1960's—*Kinetic Art, Pop Art, Op Art, Funk Art*—which, in his opinion, avoid the essential problems of *Modernist Painting*. He claims that they are self consciously innovatory, and that they are only capable of offering a one-time aesthetic surprise.

266 **NUAGISTES:** A minor group of French gestural painters formed by Julien Alvardin in the early 1950's. Members of the group included Frédérick Benrath, Jean Messagier and René Duvillier. Their work employed cursive lines and circular rhythms reminiscent of cloudscales; 'nuage' is the French word for cloud.

267 **NUCLEAR ART:** A short lived movement associated primarily with the Italian artists Enrico Baj (whom Italian critics claim is the father of *Pop Art*) and Dangelo. Their first manifesto was issued in 1952. A further statement dated 1957 declared its opposition to all forms of geometric abstract art and indeed to any fixed style of art; it proposed instead experimentation with tachist, calligraphic and automatic techniques. The language employed by the Nuclearists refers to 'atomised situations', 'states of matter' and '"heavy water" colours', but exactly what connection was intended with nuclear physics is not clear.

The British abstract relief artist, Mary Martin has also employed the term 'nuclear' to describe her method of working, that is building up part by part around a central core or theme.

'The end of style' *Leonardo* 3(4) October 1970 465-466.

T Sauvage *Art Nucléaire* (Paris, Editions Vilo, 1962).

268 **NUL GROEP:** A Dutch group established in 1962 by Henk Peeters and Armando. 'Nul' is the Dutch equivalent of 'zero' and the group was directly inspired by the work of the German *Group Zero*.

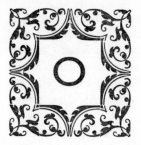

269 **OBJECT ART** (or Object Sculpture): This term was used before 1945 to describe paintings or constructions by Futurists, Dadaists and Surrealists incorporating real, non-art objects. It has been employed occasionally in this sense since the war and is essentially an alternative to *Assemblage Art*. In 1965 the French critic Alain Jouffrey labelled a group of artists, incorporating objects into their work or taking moulds of objects, ' Objecteurs '; the artists concerned were Antonio Recalcati, Jean Pierre Raynaud, Tetsumi Kudo and Paul Van Hoeydonck.

In the late 1960's in the United States, ' Object Art ' was employed as an alternative for *Minimal Art;* this usage derives from the expression ' specific objects ' coined by Donald Judd.

270 **OBJECTHOOD:** A word that frequently occurs in *Formalist Criticism*, especially in the writings of Michael Fried. It is Fried's contention that there is a conflict between our readings of physical works of art as art, and as objects; he claims that when we view a painting as an object we are regarding it as a non-art entity. He believes that *Modernist Painting*, to be valid, must find means to defeat or suspend its own objecthood but without resorting to illusionistic pictorial devices of the past.

The problem is complicated by the fact that the whole trend of art since Gauguin has been to stress the literal, object qualities of painting.

During the 1960's Frank Stella emphasised the box-like quality of the picture support by the use of very thick stretchers. Minimal sculptors banish illusion from their work and stress its Objecthood. They are accused by Clement Greenberg of cultivating a non-art look.

M Fried 'Art and objecthood '—essay in—*Minimal Art: a critical anthology* edited by G Battcock (Studio Vista, 1968) 116-147.

271 **OP ART** (also called Perceptual Abstraction): The term 'Op Art'—short for Optical Art—was first used by 'Time' Magazine in 1964 and popularised by James Canaday, art news editor of the 'New York times'. It describes an international movement in painting that emerged during the 1960's and specialised in the production of violent optical effects within the visual system of the viewer.

Op paintings are abstract. They make use of parallel lines or patterns of squares or circles, all painted with sharp precision, and employ strong colour contrasts, or black and white contrasts, to produce optical shimmer. Illusions, after-images, moiré patterns, periodic structures, ambiguous figures are all illustrated in the text books on the psychology of perception and all feature in Op Art. *Kinetic Art* and Op Art are closely related and are often discussed together; Op Art provides many examples of virtual movement and its effects are accentuated by the movement of the spectator in front of the canvas.

A large scale exhibition of Op Art called 'The Responsive Eye' was held at the Museum of Modern Art, New York in 1965. The best known practitioners of Op painting are Victor Vasarely, Bridget Riley, Richard Anuszkiewisz, Larry Poons, Reginald Neal and Jesus Raphael Soto.

Some critics regard Joseph Albers as a precursor of Op Art, but he objects strongly to the term, claiming that all pictorial art is 'optical' and that it would be just as nonsensical to speak of 'acoustic music' or 'tactile sculpture'. As an alternative he proposes 'perceptual painting', but this does not seem to be an improvement since all painting is, presumably, perceived.

For a short period of time Op Art was extremely fashionable; to the distress of some of the painters, their designs were adopted by the textile and clothing industries and eye dazzling patterns appeared everywhere. However, the movement lacked staying power, according to Lucy Lippard because of its 'essential dullness, predictability and spurious contemporaneity'.

See also Retinal Art.

C Barrett *An introduction to Optical Art* (Studio Vista, 1971).

C Barrett *Op Art* (Studio Vista, 1970).

R G Carraher and J B Thurston *Optical illusions and the visual arts* (Studio Vista, 1966).

M Compton *Optical and Kinetic Art* (Tate Gallery, 1967).

L Lippard ' Perverse perspectives '—essay in—*Changing: essays in art criticism* (NY, Dutton, 1971) 167-183.

R Parola *Optical art: theory and practice* (NY, Van Nostrand Reinhold, 1969).

W C Seitz *The responsive eye* (NY, Museum of Modern Art, 1965).

272 **OPTION ART:** A name devised by Lawrence Alloway to describe a form of *Participatory Art* which allows the artist and the spectator a number of options in the arrangement of the elements that make up the work. His term is applicable to ' Variable Paintinges ' by the Swedish artist, Oyvind Fahlstrom. These paintings are composed of detachable figures and images, hinges and magnets permitting of endless permutation; characters can even be dressed and undressed. The term is also applicable to ' Change Paintings by the English artist, Roy Ascott; to ' Transformables ' by the Israeli artist, Agam; and to the contour shapes that Timothy Drever, an English sculptor, spreads out on floors or lawns for spectators to rearrange.

An exhibition of such work, called ' Options ', was held at the ' Museum of Contemporary Art ', Chicago in 1968.

L Alloway ' Options ' *Art and artists* 4(7) October 1969 16-21.

L Alloway ' Interfaces and options: participatory art in Milwaukee and Chicago ' *Arts magazine* 43(1) September/October 1968 25-29.

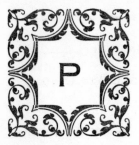

P

273 PACKAGING (or Wrapping, Bagging): The Surrealist Man Ray invented this technique with his mysteriously wrapped object called 'The enigma of Isidore Ducasse'. At least one post-war artist—Christo—has devoted his whole œuvre to this idea; he has wrapped chairs, nude girls, whole buildings and even stretches of coastline. The significance of this technique may be indicated by market research studies which reveal that the packaging of a product is almost as important as the product itself to a potential customer. The Canadian artist, Iain Baxter also wraps or 'bags' whole rooms and all their contents using transparent polythene; the result is called a 'bagged place'.

274 PAINTERS ELEVEN: A Canadian group founded in Montreal in 1953. Jack Bush and Harold Town are two internationally recognised painters who were members of this group.

275 PARTICIPATORY ART: All art works require the involvement of a spectator before they are complete —a point emphasised by Marcel Duchamp at a discussion session on the creative act held at Houston, Texas in 1957—and to this extent all art is participatory. However, the traditional artist did not make spectator participation his prime aim. In contrast, since 1945 many avant garde artists have created objects, or structured situations, explicitly to encourage adult play, to invite spectators to join in games and in physical activities.

The participation tendency can be detected in *Op Art* (which involves vision more actively than traditional oil painting); in some forms of *Kinetic Art* (those which make use of spectator movement);

in *Cybernetic Art* sculptures (those which respond to sounds made by spectators); in *Environmental Art* (inflatables which require athletic ability to be appreciated); in *Happenings* and *Street Art* (where the audience is often an integral part of the art work.)

From this general tendency has emerged the concept of 'Part Art'. An exhibition called 'Pioneers of Part Art'—featuring the artists John Dugger, David Medella, Lygia Clark, Helio Oiticica and Li Yuan Chia —was held at the 'Museum of Modern Art', Oxford in 1971. Medella uses the word 'art' as in 'articulation', not as in 'art object'. The American sculptor Robert Morris designed a series of objects— described by one critic as an assault course—for his show at the 'Tate Gallery', London in 1971 to be physically used instead of contemplated. In this instance the works were too successful: the audience participated over vigorously and to prevent further destruction and injury this section of the exhibition was closed.

In the United States Part Art is called 'Fun Art'. According to Thomas Meehan it is a new art form that has excited large crowds of visitors to American galleries and museums in 1970. Fun Art is often expensive because of its technical complications—it may employ plastics, currents of air, strobe lights, electronic devices, feed back systems—hence it tends to be created by artists versed in engineering skills. Mostly these artists are young and unknown, but three— Howard Jones, Stanley Landsman and Jean Tinguely—are established names. Clearly the name 'Fun Art' stresses spectator enjoyment. However, the pleasure provided by this type of art does not seem to be primarily aesthetic.

Experimental groups such as the *Haus-Rucker-Company*, the *Situationists*, the Event Structure Research Group and *Groupe de Recherche d'Art Visuel* are also dedicated to the idea of spectator participation, as are community art associations such as *Action Space* and *Inter-Action*. In 1972 *Inter-Action* transformed a London Transport double decked bus into a mobile theatre, equipped it with video, and called it the 'Fun Art Bus'.

The concept of participation in art has aroused much adverse criticism, for example, Michael Billington claims that 'the notion of physical participation' is 'one of the great myths of contemporary art' and is not to be 'equated with spiritual involvement' because 'more often than not ... it's a substitute for it'.

See also Option Art, Technological Art.

L Alloway ' Interfaces and Options: participatory art in Milwaukee and Chicago ' *Arts magazine* 43(1) September/October 1968 25-29.

M Billington ' Life Copying Art ' *The guardian* June 2 1972 p 8.

M Duchamp ' The Creative Act '—essay in—*Marcel Duchamp* by Robert Lebel (Paris, Trianon Press 1959) 77-78.

A Forest ' Popa at Moma ' *Art & artists* June 1971 46-47.

E Lucie-Smith 'Art and playpower: a new philistinism ' *Encounter* (8) August 1971 58-60.

T Meehan ' Fun Art ' *Daily telegraph magazine* (276) January 30 1970 18-23 + cover.

276 PAVILIONS IN THE PARKS (PIP): In 1968 six British artists founded an organisation called ' The Pavilions in the Parks Advisory Service ' to make painting, sculpture, films, poetry, music and mixed-media events available to the general public in informal settings such as parks. Lightweight, demountable structures are used to display art works and to house events. The pavilions move from site to site during the summer but remain in one place for up to three months. This scheme enables local artists —selected by a random method—to show their work to local communities and provides an alternative to the commercial gallery system.

Finance is provided by local authorities and arts associations. Not everyone is impressed by the PIP project; one writer dismissed it as ' random art for a random audience '.

S Braden ' Pavilions in the Parks ' *Studio international* 178(914) September 1969 p 94.

' Pavilion Design Competition ' *Architectural design* 41(3) March 1971 183-184.

' Pavilions in the Parks ' *Catalyst* January 1971 p 39.

' Pavilions in the Parks Project ' *Leonardo* 2(2) April 1969 209-210.

S W Taylor ' Pavilions in the Parks ' *Art & artists* 3(5) August 1968 58-59.

277 PENTAGRAM (A star shape with five points): The name of Britain's largest design group, formed in London in 1972 by five mature designers—Theo Crosby, Colin Forbes, Alan Fletcher, Mervyn Kurlansky and Kenneth Grange—each of whom have international reputations in their own special fields.

Pentagram blends graphic, product and architectural design skills in order to provide a comprehensive service for large companies.

R Carr ' Main Line Merger ' *The guardian* June 16 1972 p 12.

Pentagram Design Partnership—editors—*Pentagram : the work of five designers* (Lund Humphries, 1972).

278 PEOPLE'S DETAILING: According to Charles Jencks People's Detailing was a style of house building popular in Britain during the 1950's characterised by ' pitched roofs, bricky materials, ticky-tacky, cute lattice work, little nooks and crannies, picturesque profiles all snuggled within a cardboard-like rectitude '.

C Jencks ' Pop-non Pop ' (1) *AAQ* 1(1) Winter 1968/1969 48-64.

279 PERFORMANCE ART may be generally defined as the execution of a prescribed course of action before a live audience. Apart from isolated examples in Japanese art— the painting of huge scrolls in the presence of the Emperor and his court—traditional painting and sculpture had nothing in common with the performing arts, but in the years since 1945 the situation has altered drastically. An element of performance has appeared in much recent art, especially since so much stress was placed on the artist's creative act in *Action Painting*. In 1956, for example, the French painter, George Mathieu created a large work entitled ' Homage to Louis XIV ' before a theatre audience. The painting was executed on the anniversary of a battle and the time spent on the canvas equalled the time taken by the conflict.

A popular art film made in 1953 showed Pablo Picasso displaying his graphic skill by drawing in paint on glass, and in darkness with a light source. In 1960 Yves Klein directed the production of a series of paintings called 'Anthropometrics '. They were made by three naked models rubbing their paint covered bodies against canvas; these activities were accompanied by music and performed before an invited audience. Other artists whose work includes a strong element of performance are discussed under the headings Actions, Auto-Destructive Art, Body Art, Gilbert and George, Process Art, Street Art; a total merger of the plastic and performing arts is attempted in *Happenings*.

According to Lucy R Lippard, the performing arts have become a neutral territory in which visual artists with different styles can meet and agree. In New York three American artists—John Perreault, Marjorie Strider, and Scott Burton—have formed the 'Association for Performances' to promote, present and preserve new forms of artists' theatre.

See also Living Sculpture.

V Acconci ' Some notes on activity and perfomance ' *Interfunktionen* (5) November 1970 138-142.

L R Lippard ' The dematerialisation of Art '—essay in—*Changing: essays in art criticism* (NY, Dutton, 1971) p 256.

' Performance at the limits of performance ' *The drama review* 16(1) March 1972 70-86.

280 THE PERIPATETIC ARTISTS GUILD

(PAG): A New York organisation advertising its services in art magazines like ' Studio international ' in the 1970's. Artists such as Robert Morris and R Craig Kauffman declare that they are available for commissions anywhere in the world. They list projects in which they are qualified to engage and request hourly wages plus expenses from patrons willing to sponsor their art projects.

281 THE PHASES MOVEMENT: Since 1952 the

French poet, Eduouard Jaguer has presided over an international movement centred on Paris devoted to the art of the imaginary, that is, continuing the principles of Surrealism. It is known as ' the Phases Movement ' after a review published in 1954 called ' Phases '. Jaguer has organised a number of exhibitions which included artists as various as Enrico Baj, Pierre Aelchinsky, Antonio Tàpies, and Oyvind Fahlstrom.

G Ollinger-Zinque ' Phases '—paragraph in—' The Belgian contribution to Surrealism ' *Studio international* 183(937) October 1971 p 155.

A Pelligrini *New tendencies in Art* (NY, Crown, 1966) 283-292.

282 PHENOMENAL ART: A term used by the

American sculptor James Seawright to describe those of his works that undergo changes with the passage of time, for example changes of illumination, spatial relationships or sound production. He specifically disclaims any connection with the philosophical notion of phenomenology discussed in the following entry.

J Seawright 'Phenomenal Art: form, idea and technique'—essay
in—*On the future of art* edited by E Fry (NY, Viking Press, 1970)
77-93.

283 PHENOMENOLOGICAL ART: The French philosopher Maurice Merleau-Ponty is noted for his

writings on phenomenology, a theory concerned with the primacy of
perception. In the middle 1960's the work of American sculptors,
notably Robert Morris and Donald Judd (associated at that time with
the *Minimal Art* movement), was interpreted by critics such as Rosalind
Krauss and Marcellin Pleynet in terms of Merleau-Ponty's theory.
These artists were not interested in the internal formal relationships
of sculpture but rather with drawing the attention of the spectator
to certain perceptual experiences of form.

Another American artist, Bruce Nauman, has been described as a
'phenomenologist'—hence Marcia Tucker's pun 'PhenNaumanology'
—because he isolates sensory phenomena—sound, light or colour—
for our contemplation. (Artists who work with natural phenomena are
discussed under the heading Ecological Art.)

J Burnham *Beyond Modern Sculpture* . . . (Allen Lane, The Penguin
Press, 1968) 172-174.

N Calas 'The phenomenological approach'—chapter in—*Icons and
images of the sixties* by N & E Calas (NY, Dutton, 1971) 249-257.

P Smith 'Phenomenology as a hermeneutic of art' *Analytical Art* (1)
July 1971 50-56.

284 PHOTO-REALISM (also called Artificial Realism, New Realism, New New York Naturalism, Radical Real-

ism, New Academicians, Post-Pop Realism, Super-Realism, Sharp-
Focus Realism): In recent years group shows of American figurative
painters and sculptors have given rise to a rash of new labels usually
incorporating the word 'realism'. Their work has been qualified by
adjectives such as 'super', 'radical' and 'hyper' because of its extreme
verisimilitude and thoroughness of technique. Some critics regard
Photo-Realism as a continuation of the pre-war tradition of American
realist art, while others see it as an extension of the heightened realism
of some *Pop Art* painting. Paradoxically it probably owes more to
abstract art than to preceding naturalism.

Most of the painters called Photo-Realists use photographs as a source of imagery, commonly of banal subjects like the urban landscape, the human face and animals. Malcolm Morley also employs coloured reproductions of old master paintings. These images are rendered meticulously in acrylic paints, and the results closely resemble trompe l'oeil painting. Their cold, mechanical finishes result in strangely arresting and surreal effects.

The subject matter of the photographs does not seem to be crucial. Photo-Realists are interested in the formal problems of rendering the changing tones across a surface, of capturing reflections and highlights. The photograph is primarily a flat image for use on a flat surface. All parts of the image are treated in an abstract fashion—Morley turns his photographs sideways to negate subject matter or cuts them into small squares for transposing to canvas.

The major Photo-Realist painters are Ralph Goings, Paul Sarkisian, Don Eddy, Lowell Nesbitt, Richard McClean, John Salt, John Clem Clarke, Richard Estes, Chuck Close, Philip Pearlstein, Robert Bechtle and Robert Cottingham.

Realist sculptors such as John De Andrea and Duane Hanson create life size replicas of the human figure in glass fibre and polyester resin; their works have the same disconcerting illusionism as waxworks. Some other artists linked with the American movement are Jann Haworth, Marilyn Levine and Roland Delcol.

See also Hyper-Realism.

D Ashton 'New York commentary: realism again?' *Studio international* 183(942) March 1972 126-127.

N & E Calas 'Artificial Realism '—in—*Icons and images of the sixties* (NY, Dutton 1971) 149-162.

G Henry 'The *Real* thing' *Art international* 16(6-7) Summer 1972 86-91 and 144.

U Kultermann *New Realism* (Mathers Miller Dunbar, 1972).

J P Marandel 'The deductive image: notes on some figurative painters' *Art international* 15(7) September 20 1971 58-61.

C Ratcliff 'New York Letter' *Art international* 16(3) March 20 1971 28-29.

285 PLACE: An early form of *Environmental Art* shown at the *Institute of Contemporary Arts,* London in 1959. Spacial divisions were created by the use of large scale abstract paintings by Robyn Denny, Ralph Rumney and Richard Smith.

R Coleman 'The content of environment' *Architectural design* 29(12) December 1959 517-518.

286 LES PLASTICIENS: A movement in Canadian painting established in Montreal in 1954 by the painter/critic Rodolphe de Repentigny. Les Plasticiens reacted against gestural painting and produced a style of *Geometric Abstraction* continuing the tradition of Mondrian and Malevich. The best known artist of the movement was Guido Molinari.

287 PLUG-IN ARCHITECTURE: A design for a new type of architecture evolved by Peter Cook of the *Archigram* group. Plug-in architecture consists of a basic structure—to contain transportation and communication services—and a series of separate units—domestic environments, shops, leisure centres—that can be plugged into it. These plug-in units can be added to or replaced as required. The design claims to take account of the need for expansion and also the fact that various systems are semi-autonomous and change at different rates.

288 POLIT ART: Paintings that make political comment on such subjects as pollution, racialism, gay liberation . . . a term devised by the English community artist Mick Shrapnell in 1972.

See also Prop Art, Activist Art.

289 THE POMPADOUR STYLE: A description applied by Brian O'Doherty to the environment of Miami Beach—the design of hotels, night clubs, shop products—and to the life style of its inhabitants, especially their clothes. The Pompadour Style is, he claims, a woman's style based on excessive decoration and opulence exploiting glitter and transparent materials. It is vernacular style that originated in the 1930's and reached a peak in the 1960's.

B O'Docherty 'Miami and the iconography of the Pompadour Style' *Art international* 13(7) September 1969 23-25.

290 POP ARCHITECTURE: This expression is used by architectural writers to refer to at least four distinct types of architecture:

(1) Buildings that are popular with large sections of the general public and/or property developers and spec builders, for example SPAN Housing; Centre Point office block, London; Coventry Cathedral . . . this type of architecture has also been called ' commercialised modern '.

(2) Buildings or structures that are symbolically styled, for example a hamburger stall in the shape of a hamburger; the Brown Derby restaurant, Los Angeles; Granada and Odeon cinemas; large scale illuminated signs (see Electrographic Architecture); advertising hoardings . . . according to Reyner Banham this type of architecture is a branch of commerce packaging ' imagery of dreams that money can buy '. Robert Venturi, discussing Las Vegas, describes it as ' autoscape architecture ' and claims it is based on communication, not form.

(3) Buildings by professional architects who have been influenced by the example of the Pop Architecture of commerce described in (2) above; examples include the ' House of the Future ' project designed by Alison and Peter Smithson in 1956, which incorporated ideas of styling, expendability and annual model changes; the Windsock Schooner Inn, Dunstable; and certain projects by Robert Venturi and by Charles Moore.

(4) Fantastic designs and projects by artists (mainly Pop artists such as Claes Oldenburg) for vast sculptures on an architectural scale, or images of destructive transformations of existing architecture and landscapes.

Architectural theorists, like fine artists, have been interested in popular culture as a source of ideas since the 1950's. Many architects reacted against the purist tradition of modern architecture and envied the vitality of Las Vegas; its chaos and vulgarity appealed particularly to Robert Venturi, who made a plea for greater complexity and contradiction in architectural design. In the view of architectural theorists, associative and symbolically styled architecture meets genuine psychological needs and they believe modern functionalist theory needs to be revised in the light of this.

R Banham ' On trial 5: the spec builders, towards a pop architecture ' *Architectural review* 132(785) July 1962 43-46.

G Broadbent ' Towards a Pop Architecture ' *RIBA journal* 72(3) March 1965 142-143.

C Jencks ' Pop-non Pop (1) ' *AAQ* 1(1) Winter 1968/1969 48-64.

C Jencks ' Pop-non Pop (2) ' *AAQ* 1(2) April 1969 56-74.

G M Lehmann ' Pop Architecture ' *Architecture Canada* 45(6) issue No 513, June 1968 69-71.

' Pop Architecture ' *Architecture Canada* 45(10) issue No 517, October 1968 (Special issue) 35-56.

P Reilley ' The challenge of Pop ' *Architectural review* 142(848) October 1967 255-259.

F Schulze ' Chaos in architecture ' *Art in America* 58(4) July/August 1970 88-96.

R Venturi *Complexity and contradiction in architecture* (NY, MOMA, 1966).

F Vostell & D Higgins *Fantastic Architecture* (NY, Something Else Press, 1969) German edition published as ' Pop Architektur '.

291 POP ART

(also called Commonism, O K Art, Industrial Art, Consumer Style, Factualist Art, New Super Realism, New Sign Painting, Commodity Art, Gag Art): The term ' Pop Art ' is credited to the English critic Lawrence Alloway. It was first used during meetings of the *Independent Group* in the middle 1950's, in the beginning to refer to the popular arts of mass culture and later to a fine art movement drawing inspiration from mass culture sources.

Pop Art celebrated the affluent consumer society, its stars and its culture heroes. Motifs were derived from commercial photography, advertising, packaging, supermarkets, comic strips, films, automobile styling . . . but as several critics have pointed out, such subject matter is not particularly new in painting. What was distinctive about the Pop Art of the late 1950's and early 1960's was that its techniques and visual vocabulary were also derived from the same sources. Fine artists are professionally interested in the ways reality can be coded for representational purposes and were impressed by the highly sophisticated and abbreviated codes used by commercial artists (Warhol and Rosenquist were commercial artists before they became fine artists). Pop artists treated their subject matter in an impersonal way, avoiding moral judgements, and frequently echoed the mass production techniques used in industry to manufacture consumer goods (see Silkscreen Printing).

Variations of Pop Art occurred in most Western capitalist societies but the major centres were Great Britain and the United States. American Pop Art developed out of *Neo-Dada* and was usually stronger and more direct than the English variety, which tended to be over complicated, whimsical and nostalgic. The major artists of Pop Art: Roy Lichtenstein, Andy Warhol, Claes Oldenburg, Robert Indiana, Jim Dine, James Rosenquist, Tom Wesselmann, Richard Hamilton, David Hockney, Eduardo Paolozzi, R B Kitaj, Derek Boshier, Allen Jones, Patrick Caulfield, Peter Blake and Peter Phillips.

Initial reaction to Pop Art was unfavourable but it rapidly gained wide public acceptance. Its popular success was probably due to the appeal of its subject matter, although few of its appreciators recognise the extent to which Pop artists transform or manipulate their subject content, despite the fact it is on these formal achievements that their reputation as artists must stand.

See also Capitalist Realism.

M Amaya *Pop as art: a survey of the new super realism* (Studio Vista, 1965).

M Compton *Pop Art* (Hamlyn, 1970).

C Finch *Pop Art: object and image* (Studio Vista, 1968).

C Finch *Image as language: aspects of British art 1950-1968* (Harmondsworth, Penguin, 1969).

L R Lippard & others *Pop Art* (Thames & Hudson, 1966).

G Melly *Revolt into style: the pop arts in Britain* (Allen Lane, The Penguin Press, 1970).

J Rublowsky *Pop Art: images of the American dream* (NY, Nelson, 1965).

J Russell & others *Pop Art redefined* (Thames & Hudson, 1969).

292 POST-ART ARTIST: A highly critical phrase used by Harold Rosenberg in 1971; it refers to ' " the artist " in a pure state, without the benefit of art. Having put aside the art of the past to the point of putting aside art itself, he has passed beyond art to its essence . . . this Post-Art Artist has no need of art since, by definition, he is a man of genius, sensitive, open to experience, a communicator and a perceiver of social realities.'

H Rosenberg ' The artist as perceiver of social realities: the Post-Art Artist ' *Arts in society* 8(2) Summer/Fall 1971 501-507.

293 POST-MINIMALISM AND ANTI-MINIMALISM: The first of these two expressions refers to art forms appearing after *Minimal Art,* namely

Process Art, Conceptual Art, Body Art, trends which began to make their mark in the literature on art from approximately 1969 onwards. Anti-Minimalism refers to modes of art that appeared at the same time as Minimal Art but which opposed its aesthetic, for example *Eccentric Abstraction* and *Funk Art.*

294 POST-MODERN DESIGN (or Pop Design):

Since 1945 many young architects and designers have reacted against the values established by the masters of *The Modern Movement.* Modern architecture and design is seen by them to constitute a tradition. They believe that the functional theories of modern design —fitness for purpose, truth to materials, functional efficiency—have proved inadequate because they fail to allow for the emotional, psychological and irrational needs of human beings, needs that are clearly revealed by the existence of popular culture, by the continued appeal of *Kitsch,* and by the demand for consumer products.

In recent years the history of the development of modern architecture has been rewritten to correct an imbalance; too much weight had been given to rational forms of architecture at the expense of expressionistic and fantastic traditions.

During the 1960's the emergence of Pop Art and ' Pop Design '— exemplified by Carnaby Street, London—indicated the extent of the reaction to the modern tradition and initiated the Post-Modern Design era.

K & K Baynes ' Behind the scene ' *Design* (212) August 1966 18-29.

C Cornford ' Cold rice pudding and revisionism ' *Design* (231) March 1968 46-48.

C Hughes Stanton ' What comes after Carnaby Street?' *Design* (230) February 1968 42-43.

P Reilly ' The challenge of Pop ' *Architectural review* 142(848) October 1967 255-257.

295 POST-PAINTERLY ABSTRACTION (or

The New Abstraction): The title of a major exhibition of American painting, organised by Clement Greenberg, held at the County Museum of Art, Los Angeles in 1964. Greenberg's phrase ' painterly abstraction ' was an alternative to *Abstract Expressionism* (he derived ' painterly ' from Heinrich Wolfflin's ' malerische ', a word

Wolfflin had used about Baroque art to distinguish it from preceding linear and geometric styles). Therefore 'Post-Painterly Abstraction' refers to work produced after *Abstract Expressionism,* namely paintings by a younger generation of artists: Paul Feeley, Frank Stella, Ellsworth Kelly, Al Held, Alexander Liberman, Sam Francis, Helen Frankenthaler and others.

Most of these younger painters rejected the brushy, gestural qualities of the Abstract Expressionists and sought a greater clarity and openness of design. Greenberg's category is a broad one and includes several trends more pedantically described as *Hard-Edge Painting, Systemic Painting* and *Stain Painting.*

G Greenberg *Post-Painterly Abstraction* (Los Angeles, County Museum of Art, 1964).

296 PRESENCE: According to American critics, Presence is an attribute of *Minimal Art* sculpture. William S Rubin defines it as 'the ability of a configuration to command its own space'; Michael Fried believes it is basically theatrical: a stage presence; Clement Greenberg, the first writer to analyse Presence, claims that it is not an artistic quality, and that the Presence of Minimal sculpture is a result of its size and non-art look.

M Fried 'Art and Objecthood'—essay in—*Minimal art: a critical anthology* edited by G Battcock (Studio Vista, 1969) p 127.

W S Rubin *Frank Stella* (NY, MOMA, 1970) p 37.

297 PRESENTOLOGICAL SOCIETY: An avant garde group concerned with *Happenings* and *Street Art* formed in Prague in 1968 by Rudolf Nemec and Eugen Brikcius.

298 PROCESS ART (or Procedural Art): Recently an English art critic noted that the word 'process' had topped the art terminology charts. However, the notion it refers to dates back to 1950 and the emphasis placed on the artist's creative behaviour in *Action Painting.* As Robert Motherwell said at the time —during a discussion on the question of when a painting could be regarded as finished—'We are involved in "process" and what is a "finished" object is not so certain'. In other words, to Action painters the final object was primarily a record of their creative performance and they thought of the painting as ' unfinished ' because their performance could be continued, or repeated, on other occasions. Furthermore, as in the *Drip Painting* of Jackson Pollock and the later *Stain Painting* of Morris Louis, the end results were predicated by the nature of the materials and procedures used to create the work. Robert Morris has emphasised the fact that many American artists have, in order to make art, adopted systematic methods of behaving as an alternative to the tasteful arrangement of forms (though taste remains in the choice of materials and procedures). The essence of Process Art is that the process of making the work becomes the subject of the work; fairly simple techniques are employed so that the viewer can mentally reconstruct, from the final object, the procedure by which it was made.

Several critics maintain that Process Art tends towards the production of series, hence *Systemic Painting* has been included in this category. Two English painters whose works have been interpreted as an enquiry into the process of painting are Bernard Cohen and Mark Lancaster. However, the process aesthetic is not restricted to the realm of painting. During the 1960's it was adopted by a number of sculptors—Richard Serra, Keith Sonnier, Robert Morris—and in the 1970's by artists working in several international modes.

A number of exhibitions held in 1969 marked the ascendency of Process Art: the *Anti-Form* show; the travelling exhibition ' When attitudes become form '; the 'Anti-Illusion: procedures/materials ' show held at the Whitney Museum, New York; the ' Place & Process ' exhibition held at the Edmonton Art Gallery. A typical example of a Process piece, by Robert Morris, consisted of firing a shotgun at a wall, photographing the result, then firing a shotgun at the enlarged photograph, photographing the result, etc.

Morris believes that once an artist has adopted systematic procedures, including some that rely on the element of chance, he has, to a certain extent, automated art making; this he regards as an advantage because it provides ' coherence '. The Process artist has a special regard for materials and the natural laws that affect them. Rafael Ferrer has created works with blocks of ice which, over a period of time, alter their shape and finally disappear; Carl Andre welcomes the fact that his open air pieces are in a constant state of change, for example steel units that rust; thus the ' work becomes a record of everything that happened to it '.

According to Thomas Albright, Process Art is 'the act of change, the process of creation itself'. He distinguishes two kinds—*Performance Art,* which he regards as an extension of theatre, and 'Force Art', which makes use of natural forces or elements (see Ecological Art).

The popularity of the Process concept in recent art is based on the fact that it allows the visual artist to deal with time and also to de-materialise the now despised art object. The artist himself, as the embodiment of the creative process, becomes the art work, as in *Body Art.* He ceases to manufacture commodities for a consumer society, simulating instead the ecological processes of nature.

T Albright ' Visuals' *Rolling stone* (85) June 14 1971 36-37.

J Burnham *The structure of art* (NY, George Braziller, 1971).

R Motherwell—remarks in—*The New York School: Abstract Expressionism in the 40's and 50's* edited by M Tuchmann (Thames & Hudson, 1970) p 26.

W Sharp ' Place and Process ' *Artforum* 8(3) November 1969 46-49.

Tate Gallery *Robert Morris* (catalogue) (Tate Gallery, 1971).

299 PROGRAM PARTNERSHIP: An English group of artists—John Bowstead, Gary Crossley, Roger Jeffs, Tony Rickaby and Ron Sutherland—continuing the customising ideas of *Fine Artz.*

' Softy softly ' *Ark* (44) Summer 1969 28-31.

300 PROGRAMMED ART: A description applied by the Italian artist/designer Bruno Munari to certain of his own works produced since 1945. His art objects generally take the form of small viewing screens displaying changing combinations of colour and shape. These transformations are produced by electric motors turning moveable parts. Programming, a word derived from computer terminology, consists in deciding operating speeds and the length of time required to complete a cycle of transformations. According to the artist, Programmed Art ' aims to show forms in the process of becoming '; it seems to be a variety of *Kinetic Art* but Munari denies this hypothesis.

Art critics have also described certain recent art—*Op Art, Systemic Painting, Serial Art*—as ' programmed ', meaning that their forms and relationships are often pre-determined by the use of mathematical series.

The term 'Programmed Art' refers most aptly to *Computer Art* since this form of art is literally programmed.

B Munari *Design as art* (Penguin, 1971) p 174.

B Munari 'Programmed art' *Times literary supplement* (3262) September 3 1964 p 793.

301 **PROJECT 84:** A centre established in London in 1971 to promote co-operation and understanding between artists and scientists. The centre organises discussions, lectures and working groups; in the future it hopes to set up a reference library and workshop facilities. Project 84 is co-ordinated by the mathematics graduate and science journalist David Dickson; its organising committee includes Conrad Atkinson, Guy Brett, Peter Byrne and Alan Campbell.

D Dickson 'Project 84' *Studio international* 181(931) March 1971 90-91.

'Exhibitions: Project 84' *Time out* (115) April 28-May 4 1972 p 61.

302 **PROP ART:** Short for 'Propaganda Art', the kind exemplified by political posters.

See also Polit-Art, Activist Art.

G Yanker: *Prop Art: international political posters* (Studio Vista, 1972).

303 **PSYCHEDELIC ART:** A trend in the painting and *Light Art* of the late 1960's coincident with the Hippy and Flower Children drug culture, international in scope but primarily an American West Coast phenomenon. Drugs such as LSD and techniques of sensory deprivation produce states of consciousness very different from normal waking experience. Drugs, it is claimed, enhance perception, increase aesthetic sensitivity, improve creativity, unlock the subconscious mind. The Psychedelic artist is one whose works are influenced by his altered consciousness. Often he attempts to communicate, via a visual analogue, the drug experience itself. Admirers of this kind of art postulate a psychedelic sensibility to account for stylistic precedents in the work of Hieronymus Bosch and

171

William Blake, and in Art Nouveau and Surrealism. Drug influenced art was not exclusive to the 1960's: the Decadent and Symbolist painters of the late nineteenth century sought inspiration from similar substances.

Characteristics of modern Psychedelic Art—and all over decorative patterning, a melange of abstract and figurative motifs, snaky, dissolving forms, ambiguous spacial effects, irredescent or acid colours. Timothy Leary summarised their impact as 'retinal orgasm'. Other writers found the style 'tedious', its forms 'niggling' and its colours 'emetic'. The Psychedelic style was quickly assimilated by advertising, the cinema, by clothing and textile manufacturers. No major artist emerged from the movement, perhaps the best known is Isaac Abrams.

The kaleidoscope effects sought by Psychedelic painters were more successfully reproduced by light shows; these are now obligatory at any Pop music concert or dance. Multi-media performances attempt to induce synaethesia, making use of sound, coloured smoke and strobe lights to assault several senses at once. The extreme loudness of the music and the intensity and frequency of the light oscillations are designed to produce sensory overload, a disorientation of normal consciousness—in fact, a synthetic trip.

'Are we suffering from psychedelic fatigue?' *Design* (229) January 1968 p 21.

N Gosling 'Snakes in the grass' *Art & artists* 4(9) December 1969 26-31.

R E L Masters & others *Psychedelic Art* (Weidenfeld & Nicolson, 1968).

304 PULSA: An American art, research, and technology group formed in 1967 by ten artists but now (1970) consisting of seven: Michael Cain, Patrick Clancy, William Crosby, William Duesing, Peter Kindlmann, David Rumsey and Paul Fuge. Pulsa makes use of electronic technology to produce sensory phenomena in programmed environments. For example, in a sculpture court at the 'Spaces' Exhibition, Museum of Modern Art, New York, in the winter of 1969-1970, they created an environment of computer linked light, sound and heat systems responsive to spectator behaviour and to the noise of the urban setting.

See also Technological Art, Environmental Art.

J Burns *Arthropods: new design futures* (NY, Praeger, 1972) 138-142.

305 PUSH AND PULL: A dynamic theory of pictorial tensions devised by Hans Hofmann, a German/American painter who has been called 'the dean of *Abstract Expressionism*'. 'Push and Pull' refers to those 'in and out' forces that occur in abstract paintings composed of many patches of colour. This kind of pictorial depth is achieved not by means of perspective or tonal gradation, but by the control of colour relationships. The forces of Push and Pull operating three dimensionally must also be balanced against other forces functioning across the canvas in the two dimensional plane.

H Hofmann *Hans Hofmann* (NY, Abrams, 1964).

306 PUSH PIN STUDIO: An influential American graphic design organisation of twenty artists founded in 1964 by Milton Glaser and Seymour Chwast. Admirers of the Push Pin style claim that it combines wit, superb draughtsmanship and diverse imagery.

A Ferebee & M Genehell 'Revivalism revisited' *Design* (242) February 1969 32-37.

The Push Pin style (Palo Alto, California, Communication Arts Magazine, 1970).

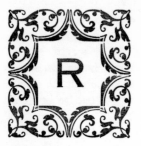

307 RADICAL ART:

The adjective 'radical' is becoming increasingly popular in art criticism. It has two connotations: (1) art that is extreme or advanced in its aesthetic or technique, (2) art that reflects extreme political attitudes; often the word is used in both senses simultaneously. To quote examples of its popular use, the extreme form of American realist painting of recent years (see Photo-Realism) has been labelled 'Radical Realism'; in 1969 Ursula Meyer described the latest trends in American sculpture as 'Radical Abstraction' because it was 'art without form, or aesthetics without art'; Germano Celant has used the term 'Radical Architecture' in reference to the work of Italian architectural and design groups who take ideas to extreme conclusions in order to challenge the established notions of architecture.

A Mendini 'Radical design' *Casabella* (367) July 1972 p 5.

U Meyer 'De-objectification of the object' *Arts magazine* 43(8) Summer 1969 20-22.

308 RANDOM ART:

A concept announced by the Dutch artist Hans Koetsier in 1969, referring to art based on the laws of probability or chance. Artists have always been willing to take advantage of happy accidents or to incorporate random elements into their creative procedures, for example Marcel Duchamp's 'Standard Stoppages', Hans Arp's collages (created by dropping scraps of paper on to a paper ground), or the technique called *Drip Painting*, but in recent years chance procedures have become much more formalised. Science orientated artists have employed statistical techniques derived from probability theory and information theory, giving rise to expressions such as 'Aleatory Art' or 'Stochastic Painting'.

See also Computer Art, Indeterminate Architecture.

A M Bork 'Randomness and the twentieth century' *ICA bulletin* (175) November/December 1967 7-16.

M Challinor 'Change, chance and structure: randomness and formalism in art' *Leonardo* 4(1) Winter 1971 1-11.

F L Whipple 'Stochastic painting' *Leonardo* 1(1) January 1968 81-83.

309 **RETINAL ART:** Paintings that appeal primarily to the eye and emphasise sensuous painterliness. Marcel Duchamp, an artist who tried consistently to reintroduce intellectual content into art, used the word 'retinal' disparagingly. He believed that Impressionist painting—indeed all painting since Courbet, apart from Surrealist—was retinal. As *Op Art* is the retinal style par excellence, Retina Art is sometimes used as an alternative description of it.

P Cabanne *Dialogues with Marcel Duchamp* (Thames & Hudson, 1971) p 43.

310 **ROBOT ART:** A form of *Kinetic Art* developed by the Israeli artist P K Hoenich which makes use of the forces of the sun, the wind and the movement of the earth to activate mobiles and to structure light and shadow. The operating period for such works can be as long as six months.

The American artist and art historian Jack Burnham, in his book on the impact of science and technology on modern sculpture, uses the expression 'Robot Art' to describe sculpture produced by artists such as Eduardo Paolozzi and Ernest Trova which combine robotic and human forms. Burnham discusses mock-robin sculpture as a preliminary to a full examination of working robots operating according to Cybernetic principles (see Cybernetic Art).

J Burnham *Beyond modern sculpture* . . . (Allen Lane, The Penguin Press, 1968).

P K Hoenich 'Kinetic Art with sunlight . . .' *Leonardo* 1(2) April 1968 113-120.

P K Hoenich ' "Robot Art ": using the rays of the sun' *Studio international* 175(901) June 1968 306-309.

M Myers and P K Hoenich 'Robot Art' *Ark* (35) Spring 1964 30-33.

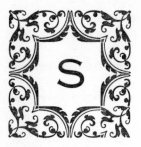

311 **ST IVES SCHOOL** (or Cornish School, or West Country School: St Ives is a fishing village situated in a part of England noted for the quality of its light. In the twentieth century it has been the only significant visual art centre in Britain outside of London. During the pre-war years a mixture of abstract and naïve art prevailed: artists who lived there included Ben Nicolson, Barbara Hepworth, Naum Gabo, Alfred Wallis, and the potter Bernard Leach. During the late 1940's and early 1950's a number of younger artists, working in a wide variety of styles, took up permanent residence in St Ives or visited the village for the summer months: John Wells, Peter Lanyon, Bryan Wynter, Terry Frost, Victor Pasmore, William Scott, Roger Hilton, Patrick Heron, Robert Adams and Merylyn Evans.

D V Baker *Britain's art colony by the sea* (George Rowland, 1959).

312 **SAINT MARTIN'S SCHOOL OF ART: SCULPTORS:** This description refers to a number of talented British sculptors—David Annersley, Michael Bolus, Philip King, Tim Scott, William Tucker and Isaac Witkin—all of whom, except Tucker, studied under Anthony Caro in the late 1950's and early 1960's at St Martin's School of Art, London. Like Caro, they rejected the modelling and carving traditions of sculpture represented in England by Henry Moore. They rejected also the *Geometry of Fear* style, submitting instead to the influence of American artists such as the sculptor David Smith and the abstract painter Kenneth Noland.

The British sculptors first attracted public attention at the 'New Generation' exhibition held at the Whitechapel Art Gallery, London in 1965. Their work is generally open in format and stands directly on the floor rather than on plinths (see Floor Art). It is made up of basic elements in the Constructivist tradition but also stresses physical qualities such as colour, surface texture, volume and topology. Most of the sculpture is abstract but a vein of Surrealist imagery is discernable in some works. Industrial materials such as sheet steel, metal pipes or netting, fibre glass and acrylic plastic are employed in preference to marble or wood. The sculpture is brightly coloured with commercial gloss paints (it has been called 'Colour Sculpture') and presents a cheerful appearance (it has also been called 'Fun Sculpture').

The New British Sculpture in some respects resembles American *Minimal Art* but generally it avoids the extreme severity of Minimal Sculpture. Anthony Caro is highly regarded by many American critics but the St Martin's School as a whole has been dismissed by them as 'British lightweights'.

D Dickson 'Art: the Alistair McAlpine gift' *New scientist* July 22 1971 p 221.

'Some aspects of contemporary British sculpture' *Studio international* 177(907) January 1969 10-37.

Whitechapel Gallery *The New Generation* (catalogue) (Whitechapel Gallery, 1965).

313 SCANDINAVIAN STYLEOR DESIGN:

During the 1950's a vogue for Swedish, Finnish, Danish and Norwegian products—glassware, silverware, textiles, jewellery, enamels, and furniture—swept Britain; their style was quickly copied by the Arts and Crafts Movement and also pioneering new research internationally famous include Alvar Aalto, Tapio Wirkkala, Bruno Mathsson, Arne Jacobson, Eward Hald and Hans J Wegner.

Scandinavian Design had been developing on the lines laid down by the Arts and Crafts Movement and also pioneering new research techniques, such as anthropometrics, throughout the inter-war years; 'Swedish Modern' had achieved international recognition in the 1930's. Unlike their British counterparts, Scandinavian artist/designers were highly regarded by employers and the general public; their higher professional status permitted greater artistic freedom. The relatively small scale of Scandinavian industries made it possible for designers to be closely involved with the production processes. As a result of these factors, Scandinavia achieved a union of mass production and handicraft traditions.

The design products of Scandinavia were attractive in appearance and functional. Furniture designers made sensitive use of natural woods and woven fabrics. Generally designers sought purity and simplicity of form. Italy is currently the source of the best design in Europe (see Italian Craze and the Supersensualists) and Scandinavian products nowadays tend to be dismissed as dull and unexciting.

314 SCIART: A blend of 'Science' and 'Art' proposed by the American physicist, poet, and art gallery dealer Bern Porter. In a manifesto appended to his book 'I've left' (NY, Something Else Press, 1971), Porter lists a series of scientific discoveries —such as polarised light and nuclear particle beams—which he believes should be exploited by artists.

J Reichardt 'Art at large: the union of science and art' *New scientist* January 6 1972 p 46.

315 SEE-THROUGH FURNITURE: Transparent furniture dates back to the 1920's when objects such as pianos were constructed of glass (with a steel framework) although at that time such items were curiosities.

Since 1945 the development of new clear materials has made transparent furniture commonplace. Inflatable or Blow-up chairs have been made in clear PVC, rigid chairs have been constructed out of perspex sheets and tables made of glass. A designer particularly noted for his See-Through Furniture is Quasar Khanh, a Vietnamese working in Paris.

316 SEMIOLOGICAL SCHOOL (or Semiotic School): The English architectural writer Charles Jencks and others believe that the urban environment can be regarded as a 'communicating system, a tissue of signs and symbols'. Therefore they maintain that semiology—the science of signs—is of fundamental importance to modern architecture. Jencks predicts the development of a Semiological School of architecture which will attempt to 'make a complex environment significant' and analyses the work of Robert Venturi and José Luis Sert in terms of this theory.

A number of essays on the application of semiology to the theory of architecture are collected in the anthology 'Meaning in architecture'.

C Jencks *Architecture 2000: predictions and methods* (Studio Vista, 1971).

C Jencks & G Baird—editors—*Meaning in architecture* (Barrie & Rockliff, 1969).

317 SERIAL ART: A term associated with two important exhibitions held in the United States: 'Art in Series', Finch College Museum, 1967 and ' Serial Imagery ', Pasadena Art Museum, 1968. The dictionary defines a series as ' a number of things, events, etc ranged or occurring in spatial or temporal, or other succession '. The traditional notion of art was to perfect a single unique work—what John Coplans calls ' the masterpiece concept '—but since the 1880's, when Claude Monet painted the ' Haystack ' series and Eadweard Muybridge published his series of photographs depicting animal and human locomotion, many modernist artists have worked in series. Generally these artists have no stylistic or other qualities in common apart from their use of the series procedure. However, it was an idiom especially favoured in the 1960's by certain artists associated with the *Minimal Art* movement: Mel Bochner, Sol Le Witt, Don Judd, Carl Andre.

The main intention of artists employing serial imagery is to play variations on a theme; this can be achieved in a number of ways. Andy Warhol has created many works in which an image is repeated again and again within the confines of one canvas. The images are applied mechanically by the *Silk Screen Printing* process and individual variations (equivalent to the ' handwriting ' of traditional art) are provided by the ' errors ' of the printing, and also in some cases by the addition of colour by brush. Josef Albers is famous for a series of paintings called ' Homage to the Square ', in which one variable of painting (image) is held constant while another (colour) is manipulated. Jasper Johns' 'American Flag ' series is another example of the Albers approach: the flag image remains constant while Johns varies colour, brushwork and placement of image.

In order to appreciate art in which an idea is exhausted through a series of paintings, it is necessary to see the complete set so that they can be read in sequence. Individual elements of the set are relatively unimportant compared with their relation to the whole concept (the latter is generally called the system (see Systemic Painting). Consequently the work of many modern painters appears shallow when judged from single examples in mixed exhibitions but gains in stature in the context of one man shows.

Gerald Gooch, a San Francisco artist, has parodied serial imagery in a work consisting of twenty panels showing a professor of aesthetics getting on and off a bicycle!

No element of levity is found in discussions of *Minimal Art* sculpture. Mel Bochner characterizes Serial Art as 'highly abstract', an 'ordered manipulation of thought . . . self contained and non-referential . . . Serialism is premised on the idea that the succession terms (divisions) within a single work are based on a numerical or otherwise predetermined derivation (progression, permutation, rotation, reversal) from one or more of the preceding terms in that piece. Furthermore the idea is carried out to its logical conclusion, which, without adjustments based on taste or chance, is the work . . . The only artistic parallel to this procedure would be in music . . .' Bochner cites Sol Le Witt's 'Series A' 1967 sculpture as a prime example of these ideas. Clearly Minimal artists adopt a much more rigorous approach than those painters interested in serial imagery.

Some examples of Minimal sculpture consist of a series of identical units (*cf* Clastic Art) spaced at regular intervals, like the teeth of a comb. Such a series is a segment of the infinite, a continuum with no particular beginning or end; variety is provided not by the artist but by the interaction of the work and its environment, and by the spectator's perceptual experience of the work as he moves about the gallery. A good example is Don Judd's wall piece 'Untitled' 1965.

M Bochner 'Serial art, systems, solipsism'—essay in—*Minimal Art: a critical anthology* edited by G Battcock (Studio Vista, 1969) 92-102.

M Bochner 'The serial attitude' *Artforum* 6 (4) December 1967 28-33.

N Calas 'Art and strategy'—essay in—*Icons and images of the sixties* by N and E Calas (NY, Dutton, 1971) 218-221.

J Coplans *Serial imagery* (NY, Graphic Society, 1968).

L March 'Serial Art' *Architectural design* 36 (2) February 1966 62-63 and cover design.

318 SHAPED CANVAS (also called Topological or Sculptural canvas): The traditional shape of portable oil paintings has generally been rectangular in order to match the walls from which they derive and upon which they are displayed. Nevertheless other shapes, such as diamond, cross and tondo, have been employed by painters from time to time. In the twentieth century, Georgio de Chirico used triangular and trapezoid shapes, Jackson Pollock worked on exceptionally long horizontal rectangles and Barnett Newman produced very narrow, vertical paintings, but despite these examples there was little experimentation with shape of support before the 1960's.

Various artists are given credit for the 'invention' of the modern shaped canvas; H H Arnason cites Lucio Fontana, William S Rubin cites Barnett Newman. Painters as different as Richard Smith, Bernard Cousinier, Anthony Green, Derek Boshier, Joe Tilson, Trevor Bell, Neil Williams, Harvey Quaytman, Charles Hinman, David Hockney and James Rosenquist have created shaped canvases, but the chief practitioner is Frank Stella.

In non-relational painting the 'figure on the field' effect is banished from the interior of the picture. This tends to emphasise the external shape of the canvas, which itself becomes a figure against the background wall, and the environmental setting of the work consequently assumes greater importance. (Patrick Heron criticises Shaped Canvases on the grounds that the artist's control does not generally extend to the settings in which his works are displayed.)

In 1960 Frank Stella began his famous series of notched canvases, the shapes of which were determined solely by the pattern of stripes of colour crossing the picture surface. Since then he has methodically explored the reciprocal relationship between internal pattern and external profile. Lawrence Alloway points out that Shaped Canvases stress the object quality of art and that despite their environmental space Stella's works have great internal solidity, emphasised by the use of thick stretchers. Alloway maintains that the contoured edges are ambiguous, keeping in suspense the balance between interior and external space. He also claims that Shaped Canvases are a mixture of painting, sculpture and craft. Despite the critical attention paid to this development, many art commentators remain unimpressed by the Shaped Canvas, regarding it as the terminal agonies of an exhausted art form.

See also Deductive Structure, Dimensional Painting, Objecthood.

319 SILK SCREEN PRINTING: A technique used in the textile and graphic arts, expropriated by a number of easel painters in recent years, notably Robert Rauschenberg, Andy Warhol and Richard Hamilton.

Photographic images transposed on to canvas by means of the silk screen process eliminate the necessity of drawing as a preliminary to painting. In many instances painting becomes a form of tinting. The silk screen technique multiplies the image-making capacity of the artist: the same image can be repeated many times within one work or over a series of works. Such possibilities have been exploited to the full by Andy Warhol.

See also Mec Art.

320 SITE: Acronym for ' Sculpture In The Environment ', a New York organisation established in 1969 consisting of five sculptors—Dana Draper, James Wines, Cynthia Eardley, Nancy Goldring and Marc Mannheimer—who operate like an architectural team, working collectively and individually on different projects. SITE artists have no pre-conceived aesthetic or style, and produce sculpture best suited to the characteristics of each individual site, hence the name of the group.

' People ' *Landscape architecture* 61 (4) July 1971 282-283.

J Wines ' The case for site orientated art ' *Landscape architecture* 61 (4) July 1971 317-319.

321 SITUATION: The title of two important exhibitions of painting held in London in 1960 and 1961 representing the British version of *Post-Painterly Abstraction*. The work was large in scale, abstract and made use of flat fields of colour (though some paintings were still gestural). It reflected the influence of Barnett Newman and American *Hard-Edge Painting*. Situation, a loose association of twenty artists, included Gillian Ayres, Bernard and Harold Cohen, Robyn Denny, John Hoyland, Henry Mundy, Richard Smith, Anthony Caro and Peter Stroud. The exclusion of those British painters associated with the *St Ives School* indicated the emergence of a new generation of artists.

A new London gallery, or bureau, called ' Situation ' was established in 1971 by Robert Self and Anthony de Kerdrel to encourage ' openness, new directions '; it acts as an outlet for films, *Video Art* and *Performance Art*.

L Alloway ' Situation in retrospect ' *Architectural design* 31 (2) February 1961 82-83.

' Exhibitions: Situation ' *Time out* (103) February 4-10 1972 p 36.

322 SITUATIONISTS: An alliance of European avant garde artists, architects and poets called the 'Internationale Situationiste' (IS) was formed at a conference in Italy in 1957 by amalgamating two existing organisations: 'Lettriste Internationale' (see Lettrism) and the 'International Union for a Pictorial Bauhaus'. Members of IS included the architects Debord and Constant and the ex-*Cobra* painter Asger Jorn. The aim of IS was to cut across existing political and nationalistic divisions. They refused to proclaim any sort of doctrine (which makes them rather hard to define) but they did believe in a totality of the arts, an art of interaction, of participation, a spatial art or 'Unitary town planning' which would take account of the needs of different localities and specific situations. The ideal Situationist was envisioned as an amateur expert, an anti-specialist. The volatile Situationists soon split into competing groups however. One such breakaway faction, called the 'Bauhaus Situationiste Drakabygzet', was established in Sweden in 1961, and based itself on Soren Kierkegaard's philosophy of situations.

M Bernstein 'The Situationist International' *Times literary supplement* (3, 262) September 3 1964 p 781.

U Conrads (ed) *Programmes and manifestoes on 20th century architecture* (Lund Humphries, 1970) p 161 and p 172.

J Nash 'Who are the Situationists?' *Times literary supplement* (3,262) September 3 1964 782-783.

323 SLIDE CULTURE: This term reflects the influence of colour photography on contemporary taste, particularly the use of colour slides in art and design education. Disturbing events, such as nuclear explosions and unsightly environments, become tolerable, even ravishing, as coloured images. Similarly, slides glamourise art works and many viewers express disappointment when they see the originals.

See also Museum without Walls.

324 SLURB: A word combining 'slum' and 'suburb', coined in California during the 1960's. It describes 'urban slums being created by the sprawl of new housing in America'.

See also Subtopia.

'Public opinion versus " Slurb "' *Design* (232) April 1968 p 24.

325 SNARE PICTURES (or Trap Pictures): A name given by the Italian artist Daniel Spoerri to his own work. Accumulations of objects, such as those remaining on a table at the end of a meal, are 'snared' by Spoerri, that is affixed to boards, hung vertically from walls and presented as art objects.

326 SOFT ARCHITECTURE: A proposal by the studio of Arata Isozaki, a Japanese architect, for a living space with as few fixed elements and permanent divisions as possible, to be achieved by inflated domes, light and sound machines and plug-in units.

327 SOFT ART OR SOFT SCULPTURE: In the past, finished works of sculpture have generally been made of hard materials—wood, marble, bronze . . .—to ensure permanence. However, modern artists are not so concerned with perpetuity (see Expendable Art) and during the 1960's an increasing number of them have explored the possibilities of soft materials such as vinyl, rubber, fibre glass, latex, feathers, felt, plastic, hair, string and sand.

This departure was triggered by Claes Oldenburg's 'Soft typewriter' of 1963; since that date he has created many works in vinyl, canvas and kapok held together by sewing or lacing. His fellow American sculptor John Chamberlain works with plastic foams such as polyurethane. Oldenburg's innovation was prefigured by the soft objects depicted in Surrealist paintings by Salvador Dali. However, Oldenburg claims that his objects were primarily a new way of pushing space around.

The limpness and pliability of Soft Sculpture are analogous to human flesh and organs: several critics have suggested it has visceral connotations.

The Pop artist Jann Haworth makes life-size human figures out of different pieces of fabric sewn and filled out with stuffing. The British sculptor Barry Flanagan has employed felt, rope and sand in his works, materials which accept the force of gravity as a determinant of form. Recent developments in *Anti-Form, Matter Art* and *Art Povera* share the same interest in softness and the action of natural forces.

An exhibition of Soft Art was held at New Jersey State Museum, Trenton in 1969. Critics have seen the emergence of Soft Art as a mocking attack on the pretentions to permanence of orthodox sculpture, and on the sleek monumentality and durability of consumer goods.

M Kozloff ' The poetics of softness '—essay in—*Renderings: critical essays on a century of modern art* (Studio Vista, 1970) 223-235.

R Pomeroy 'New York: Soft Art' *Art & artists* 4(1) April 1969 26-27.

R Pomeroy ' Soft objects at the New Jersey State Museum ' *Arts magazine* 43 (5) March 1969 46-48.

328 **SOFTWARE:** Title of a major exhibition held at the Jewish Museum, New York in 1970. The exhibition was organised by Jack Burnham and the title suggested to him by Les Levine. Software featured artists concerned with ' machine aided communication or documentation '.

The word ' software ' derives from computer nomenclature, where it generally refers to programmes and artificial languages used to operate hardware, that is, the physical equipment. However, Burnham appears to have used it in a broader sense. In his essay ' Real Time systems ', for example, he claims that ' the entire art information processing cycle, the art books, catalogues, interviews, reviews, advertisements of art and contracts are all software extensions of art '. The meaning of software and the appropriateness of its application to art was disputed by Robert Mallary, and the matter was debated by Burnham and Mallary at some length in the columns of ' Leonardo ' magazine in 1970.

See also Systems Art, Conceptual Art.

J Burnham 'Real time systems ' *Artforum* 8 (1) September 1969 49-55.

329 **SOUND ARCHITECTURE:** The use of moving sound as a means of defining architectural space. A concept developed by Bernhard Leitner in 1971.

B Leitner ' Sound Architecture ' *Artforum* 9 (7) March 1971 44-49.

330 **SOUND SCULPTURE:** In recent years a number of artists have become aware of the fact that sound can—as in the cinema and theatre—add an extra dimension to visual art forms (for example in 1959 Robert Rauschenberg introduced radios into his *Combine Painting* 'Broadcast'). The role of sound is especially important in time based art such as *Kinetic Art* and *Performance Art*.

Kinetic art works usually produce some noise, whether planned or not. The phrase 'Audio-Kinetic Sculpture' has been coined to describe those works in which sound and movement are deliberately linked. Some artists, especially in North America, have presented sound as a primary sculptural experience: for the 'Magic Theatre' exhibition held at the Nelson Art Gallery, Kansas City in 1968 Howard Jones devised a 'Sonic games chamber' in which alterations of sound patterns were caused by spectator movement; in 1969 Dennis Oppenheim produced a 'sculpture' consisting of a tape recording of the sound of his footsteps as he traversed a specific area of a city; at the Museum of Conceptual Art, San Francisco in 1970 a show entitled 'Sound Sculpture As' featured the sounds of guns being fired, telephones ringing, and an artist urinating into a bucket. Artists such as Tom Marioni, who combines elements of Performance and *Conceptual Art*, often employ amplifiers to pick up the sound of their actions, and by a process of feedback make the sound persist in the roomspace for as long as there is movement.

In 1970 the Museum of Contemporary Crafts, New York, organised the first major exhibition to focus entirely on sound.

A McMillan 'The listening eye' *Craft horizons* 30 (1) January/February 1970 14-19.

C Oliver 'The drug culture' *The guardian* June 26 1972 p 8.

331 SPACE ART AND SPACE AGE ART: The Dutch artist Paul Van Hoeydonck has been described as the 'Giotto of the age of space exploration' because the subject matter and forms of his paintings and sculpture are inspired by the Russian and American space programs; his work is for this reason called 'Space Art'.

The scientist and Kinetic artist Frank Malina prefers the expression 'Space Age Art' and defines three types: (1) 'art made on Earth with new techniques or materials developed by astronautical technology, incorporating visual experiences provided by space flight and exploration', (2) 'art made on Earth to express either the resulting new psychological experiences or the possible new philosophical experiences of man and of the universe ', (3) ' art made and used on the moon and on other planets '.

J Van Der Marck ' Paul Van Hoeydonck's ten year Space Art program ' *Art international* 14 (2) February 1970 41-43.

F J Malina ' On the visual fine arts in the space age ' *Leonardo* 3 (3) July 1970 323-325.

332 SPACE PROVISION FOR ARTISTS (CULTURAL AND EDUCATION) LTD:

A London organisation founded in 1968 by Bridget Riley, Peter Sedgley, Professor West, Irene Worth, Peter Townsend and Maurice De Sausmaurez. Its purpose is to provide studio space for artists. The organisation developed out of an awareness of two facts: (1) the lack of large working areas for artists, (2) the availability of facilities in disused schools or factory buildings due for demolition. Within a year SPACE managed to accommodate ninety artists in Saint Katherine's Dock, a disused London warehouse; exhibitions of their work have also been mounted. In 1972 the offices of SPACE and its related organisation *Art Information Registry* were re-located in the Royal Academy of Arts, Piccadilly.

S Braden 'A.I.R. R.A. R.I.P.? S.P.A.C.E.D.' *Time out* (84) September 24-30 1971 20-21.

' Notes on SPACE ' *Catalyst* January 1971 p 56.

'A proposal to provide studio workshops for artists ' *Studio international* 177 (908) February 1969 65-67.

333 SPACE STRUCTURE WORKSHOP: A

British group founded in 1968 and operating from London, concerned with events, collaboration with industry, and *Environmental Art;* members include Maurice Agis, Peter Jones and Terry Scales. The workshop organises events in parks and open spaces in order to reach the general public and provides environmental structures that integrate the elements of space, colour and sound. The group's objective is to liberate the senses of the public and present an alternative aesthetic experience that will, by contrast, reveal the deficiencies of the ugly, dehumanised urban environment in which most people live. By these means Space Structure Workshop hopes to stimulate social and political action.

' Spaceplace: selections from the notes of Agis, Jones, Marigold and Pitt ' *Studio international* 183 (940) January 1972 34-37.

334 SPATIAL ABSTRACTION: A term invented by the French abstract painter Auguste Herbin and used by Nicolas and Elena Calas to describe paintings produced in the 1960's by the American artist Leon Polk Smith.

N & E Calas ' Spatial Abstraction '—chapter in—*Icons and images of the sixties* (NY, Dutton, 1971) 163-168.

335 SPATIALISM: A grandiose doctrine developed by Lucio Fontana—an artist born in Argentina who was educated and worked most of his life in Italy—and first expounded in his 'White Manifesto' of 1946. Fontana advocated a radical break with past aesthetic concerns and proposed to end the separate forms of painting and sculpture by synthesising all physical elements—colour, sound, space, motion, and time—into a new kind of art.

Fontana had been trained as a sculptor and wanted to introduce literal space, as opposed to depicted space, into his paintings; this he achieved by means of holes or slits cut in the surface of the canvas. He also added relief elements to create cast shadows. In the 1950's he became interested in *Matter Art* and attached pebbles, glass and other foreign materials to the paint surface. During the same period he evolved a form of *Environmental Art* making use of neon light in black painted rooms.

The Spatialist movement is generally limited to the years 1951 and 1952; other artists who participated were Roberto Crippa, Enrico Donati and Ettore Sottsass.

See also Concrete Poetry.

336 SPATIO DYNAMISM: A form of *Kinetic Art* practised by the Hungarian/School of Paris artist Nicholas Schöffer, whose work continues the space/motion/light tradition established by Laszlo Moholy-Nagy. Schöffer's metal constructions are electronically guided mobiles or robots. Light is reflected from their highly polished surfaces and the spectacle of their movement is accompanied by tape recordings of urban sounds. Like most Kinetic artists, Schöffer believes in the fruitful co-operation of art and science; he frequently uses the vocabulary of science, calling his works by such titles as ' Cybernetic Tower '. He also employs the term ' Luminodynamism ' to signify the union of light and motion. One critic has described his innovations as 'hiding an incongruous poverty of sculptural ideas '.

J Ernest ' Nicolas Schöffer ' *Architectural design* 30 (12) December 1960 517-520.

337 SPONTANEOUS ARCHITECTURE: Buildings, or additions to existing buildings, erected ' spontaneously' by ordinary members of the public without regard to architects or planning regulations.

See also Architecture without Architects.

T Sieverts ' Spontaneous architecture ' *AAQ* 1 (3) July 1969 36-43.

338 STAIN PAINTING: In 1952 the American artist Helen Frankenthaler, inspired by the example of Jackson Pollock's *Drip Painting,* developed a similar method of painting that exploited soft stains or blots of paint on unsized canvas. Two years later Morris Louis visited Frankenthaler's studio and was so impressed that he changed his style and adopted the stain technique. Later the paintings that he, and others such as Kenneth Noland, Jules Olitski and Paul Jenkins, produced during the late 1950's and early 1960's made the stain method world famous.

Stain painters apply very diluted acrylic paints, such as Magna, to unsized, unstretched cotton duck canvas. The liquid paint is poured, spilt or flooded on to the surface (in the case of Louis these facts are deduced from his paintings: he was secretive about his working methods). Olitski also applied paint with a spray gun and rollers. The unstretched canvas is sometimes folded or pleated to create design variations. On completion canvases are stretched, a process which presents the Stain painter with the problem of placement, that is, the relating of the image to the shape of support. Diluted paint soaks into cloth and therefore stain paintings resemble dyed fabric more than they do traditional oil paintings. Stained pigment is not a skin on the surface of the canvas; it is part of the object, like the coloured skin of a peach. Thus stain paintings have no sense of paint texture or natural sheen, giving their colour a disembodied look. The absence of surface reflections enables the pictures to be viewed from wide angles of vision. In some of his works Louis applied successive waves of paint to produce translucent veils of colour which achieve a merger of figure and ground: foreground and background no longer exist as separate entities.

To a large extent the stain method is 'automatic' in operation. According to American cities certain advantages follow: (1) since no hand or arm movements are involved the painter is freed from the linear quality of drawing and the whole tradition of painting with a brush; (2) since the stained areas of paint exist as pure colour the problem of tonal modulation is transcended; (3) stain paintings are a record of the process by which they have been made, hence they unite pictorial structure with process of production.

Although stained canvases are extremely seductive to the eye (they have been called 'The New Aestheticism'), not all art critics are entranced by them. Some find their beauty 'cosmetic', and Harold Rosenberg dislikes their soaked-in quality, claiming that it affirms middle class values of tidiness and security.

See also Washington Colour School, Colour-Field Painting, Process Art.

339 STOCKWELL DEPOT SCULPTORS: Roland Brener, David Evison, Roger Fagin, Gerard Hemsworth, Peter Hide, Roelof Louw, Alan Barkley and John Fowler: eight young British sculptors who have worked and exhibited since 1967 in a Victorian industrial building called 'Stockwell Depot' situated in South London. These sculptors are not a group in the sense of sharing a common aesthetic but their work does have two points of similarity: it is generally abstract and it is usually too large in scale to be accommodated in private art galleries.

340 STREET ART: In a facile sense this category includes a whole range of art activities from outdoor sculpture displays, murals by groups such as *City Walls* or the *Los Angeles Fine Art Squad,* to forms of street theatre, *Actions, Happenings,* etc. All these have in common the fact that they are presented in public thoroughfares or in public open spaces.

However, the essential significance of the designation 'Street Art' is political: the street belongs to the people and therefore it can be used by artists as a forum to draw attention to urban problems—drugs, rats, police brutality. A New York artist exploiting these themes is Tosun Bayrak. The concept of Street Art in a political sense can be traced to the propaganda art and mass spectacles of the years following the Russian Revolution, when artists were encouraged by Vladimir Mayakovsky ' to make the streets our brushes, the squares our palette '.

See also Presentological Society, Cultural Art.

Hayward Gallery *Art in revolution: Soviet art and design since 1917* (catalogue) (Arts Council of Great Britain, 1971) p 10.

341 STRUCTURALISM AND ART: Structural anthropology—a discipline derived from structural linguistics—is a method of discovering general principles, order, or structure in human culture by an empirical study of social behaviour, myths, sign systems and art. The doyen of Structuralism is the French writer Claude Levi-Strauss. The American art historian Jack Burnham has recently used Levi-Strauss's methodology to analyse a large number of art works—predominantly modern—in an ambitious attempt to reveal the logical structure common to all examples of successful art. Other writings on Structuralism and art are listed below.

J Burnham *The structure of art* (NY, George Braziller, 1971).

G Dorfles ' Structuralism and Semiology in Architecture '—essay in—*Meaning in architecture* edited by C Jencks and G Baird (Barrie & Rockliff, 1969) 38-49.

A Michelson 'Art and the structuralist perspective '—essay in—*On the future of art* edited by E Fry (NY, Viking Press, 1970) 37-59.

A Moles ' Vasarely and the triumph of Structuralism ' *Form* UK (7) March 1968 24-25.

M Pleynet ' Peinture et " structuralisme " ' *Art international* 12 (9) November 20 1968 29-34.

342 STRUCTURISM: A theory and method of creation developed by the American artist Charles Biederman. He coined the term in 1952 to describe his own work from the late 1930's onwards and in order to distinguish it from his earlier concept *Constructionism*. Biederman produces brightly coloured abstract reliefs which attempt to synthesise qualities of painting, sculpture and architecture. He claims that they are created in accordance with the structural processes of nature.

The pre-war traditions of abstract art are continued by a number of other artists resident in Europe and North America, all of whom are admirers of Biederman. They include the English artist Anthony Hill, who has used the expression 'Structural Art' to describe his own work; the Dutch artist Joost Baljeu, founder of the magazine 'Structure' which began publication in 1958; and the Canadian artist Eli Bornstein, who describes his reliefs as 'structurist' and who is editor of an art annual entitled 'The Structurist', published by the University of Saskatchewan since 1960.

The confusion that can arise in art terminology is illustrated by the fact that American art critics have also employed 'Structural Art' and 'Structuralist Art' to refer to paintings and sculpture more generally known as *Minimal Art*. The word 'structure' derives, in this instance, from 'Primary Structures', the title of a large scale exhibition of Minimal sculpture held in New York in 1966.

E Bornstein 'Structurist art and creative integration' *Art international* 11 (4) April 20 1967 31-36.

A Hill—editor—*Data: directions in art, theory and aesthetics* (Faber, 1968).

G Kepes—editor—*Structure in art and science* (Studio Vista, 1965).

343 STYLING: The notion of style—a distinctive visual mode, an idiom shared by a number of works for a limited period of time—is entrenched in the history of art and design. Different styles can co-exist together at one time but it is inherent in the notion of style that they must change and be replaced by others. A stylist is a designer who seizes upon the fact of historically inevitable stylistic change and exploits it fully by conscious operation; he accelerates or induces changes of style.

The industrial and economic structures of Western capitalist countries require an ever increasing output of manufactured goods. These products could be designed to last for many years, but if they did so this would threaten the ever expanding production economy, and therefore customers are supplied with poor quality goods and encouraged to replace them, even before they wear out. This is achieved by 'psychological obsolescence', a technique pioneered in the women's clothing industry, where new style models make previous products out of date, not in terms of utility but by making them appear unfashionable. As a result, Styling has a bad name; it has been called 'superficial design' and dismissed by Raymond Chandler as 'a commercial swindle intended to produce artificial obsolescence '.

Because they are concerned with fashion, stylists concentrate on the 'look' of products, altering exteriors (a procedure called 'shroud design') according to current mannerisms and clichés. They seek to satisfy psychological and symbolic needs of consumers which they have identified by motivation research studies.

Gifford Jackson has identified five different style changes in American product design since the late 1920's: Stepform, Streamform, Taperform, Sheerform and Sculptureform. A striking example of the absurdity of Styling is the application of aerodynamic streamlining to static products such as ashtrays. Styling affected designers in all fields in America in the 1950's and reached a peak in the annual model changes of automobiles manufactured in the last years of the decade. In Germany the term 'Detroit Machiavellismus' was coined to express distaste for this aspect of American design.

'Car Styling' was one of the topics discussed by the *Independent Group* during the 1950's. One of its members, the English artist Richard Hamilton, has expressed great interest in Styling in his writings and in his paintings, the latter being full of imagery derived from American Styling.

J De Syllas ' Streamform . . .' *AAQ* 1 (2) April 1969 32-41.

G Jackson 'Analysis—design styles and clichés' *Industrial design* 9 (9) September 1962 59-67.

R Hamilton ' Urbane image ' *Living arts* (2) 1963 44-59.

G Muller-Krauspe ' Design Ideologien (2) Styling—das Prinzip der Diskontinuität ' *Form* (47) September 1969 31-35.

V Packard *The waste makers* (Penguin, 1963).

E Schaper 'The concept of style: the sociologist's key to art?' *British journal of aesthetics* 9 (3) July 1969 246-257.

M Schapiro ' Style '—essay in—*Aesthetics today* edited by M Philipson (Cleveland, World Publishing Co, 1961) 81-113.

S Sontag ' On Style '—essay in—*Against interpretation and other essays* (Eyre & Spottiswoode, 1967) 15-36.

344 SUBJECTS OF THE ARTIST: An art school established in 1948 by a number of American painters—Barnett Newman, William Baziotes, David Hare, Robert Motherwell, Mark Rothko and Clyfford Still—at 35 East Eight St, New York. These artists were convinced that the problem of subject matter in painting had reached a crisis point, hence the rather strange name of their group, suggested by Barnett Newman. The school lasted only one year, but most of the artists continued to meet at *The Club*.

345 **SUBTOPIA:** This word is a combination of 'Suburb' and 'Utopia' and means 'making an ideal of suburbia. Visually speaking the universalisation and idealisation of our town fringes. Philosophically, the idealisation of the Little Man who lives there.' It was coined in the middle 1950's by the architectural writer Ian Nairn. He used it to describe the blurring of the separate identities of town and countryside caused by urban sprawl; 'a witless chaos—a dumping down of every kind of man-made object, urban, suburban and subrural with no relationship to each other or to the site', 'a desert of wire, concrete roads, cosy plots and bungalows'. The attack on Subtopia mounted by Nairn and the 'Architectural review' had the character of a moral crusade.

See also Slurb.

I Nairn *Outrage* (Architectural Press, 1955).

I Nairn *Counter attack against Subtopia* (Architectural Press, 1959).

I Nairn *Your England revisited* (Hutchinson, 1964).

346 **SUPERGRAPHICS:** A new form of *Environmental Design*, appearing in Western countries from 1966 onwards. Supergraphics are akin to fine art in that they dispense with the communication of direct information. They operate on a huge scale and make use of vivid, rainbow colours. The walls, ceilings and exteriors of shops, offices, restaurants and homes have been decorated with them; they are a cheap way of jazzing up dull architecture.

T Albright ' Visuals ' *Rolling stone* (93) October 14 1971 39-40.

347 **SUPERMANNERISM:** A trend in American interior design and decoration of the late 1960's identified by ' Progressive architecture' magazine. Supermannerism, or ' Mega-decoration ', opposes tasteful design and is characterised by perverse trickery, both optical and intellectual. It operates on an explosive scale and uses transparent, reflective, synthetic materials. As the term indicates, the resulting style is mannerist; it also reveals *Pop Art* as a major source of inspiration: Superman-nerism.

' Revolution in interior design: the bold new poly expanded mega-decoration ' *Progressive architecture* (10) October 1968 148-208.

348 THE SUPERSENSUALISTS: Architectural and design journalists have described a number of European designers and design groups—Gae Aulenti, Ettore Sottsass, Hans Hollein, *Archizoom, Haus-Rucker-Co, Superstudio*—as Supersensualists because their work since 1960 manifests a common approach to design. According to Charles Jencks, it is a blend of extravagant sensuality, metaphysical angst, beauty, advanced technology, and, piquantly enough, Marxism. Many of these designers create fantasy worlds in which ideas are taken to extreme conclusions. Their actual commissions are usually for furniture, and for the design of boutique, apartment and restaurant interiors for the urban middle class.

The Supersensualist characteristics are specially marked in the case of the Italian designers, who have been dubbed the ' Dolce Vita School ' because their permissive approach to aesthetics and good taste echoes the permissive morality of the characters in Fellini's film.

349 SUPERSTUDIO: An Italian experimental architectural and design group formed in 1966 and based in Florence. Members include Adolfo Natalini, Cristiano Toraldo Di Francia, Piero Frassinelli, Allessando and Roberto Magris. The Superstudio group carry ideas to extreme conclusions; they develop anti-functional, visionary projects such as the ' Continuous Monument ', designed to extend across the world; spaceship cities; continuous production/conveyor belt cities; etc. Members of Superstudio and the similar group *Archizoom* are called *Supersensualists*. Their work is variously described as *Conceptual Architecture,* or ' radical architecture ', and is featured regularly in magazines such as ' Domus ' and 'Architectural design '.

350 SUSPENDED PAINTINGS: Canvases without stretchers hung from walls or ceilings at various points and then draped, pleated or twisted to create sculptural forms. An artist particularly noted for such works is the American Sam Gilliam. His paintings are extremely colourful and decorative because he stains his canvas with acrylic pigments. The notion of suspended painting appears to combine elements of *Anti-Form, Stain Painting* and *Process Art.* Other artists who have produced Suspended Paintings are Robert Ryman, Phillip Lewis, David Stephens and Derek Southall.

J Applegate ' Paris letter ' *Art international* 15(1) January 20 1971 p 33.

351 SYMBIOTIC ART: A new art form, or research discipline, proposed by Jonathan Benthall in 1969, concerned with 'an interaction between the (human) organism and the environment . . . analogous to symbiosis in nature '.

Benthall suggests that research might usefully be undertaken first in the area of human perceptual response to sound and light. Symbiotic Art appears to be closely related to *Cybernetic Art*.

J Benthall 'Technology and art 4; Symbiotic Art' *Studio international* 177(912) June 1969 p 260.

352 SYNERGIC SCULPTURE: A proposal for a new form of *Participatory Art* put forward by J J Jehring, to consist of 'a totally designed environment made up of changing forms, moving lights and sound controlled by group participation' made feasible by Cybernetic feedback systems. The word 'synergy', derived from the behavioural sciences, means an increase in effect achieved as a result of combined or co-ordinated action. In other words, group participation in art will replace individual participation and lead, according to Jehring, to greater benefits. 'Synergy' is also one of R Buckminster Fuller's favourite terms.

J J Jehring 'Synergic Sculpture' *Arts in society* 8(1) Spring/Summer 1971 415-418.

353 SYSTEMIC PAINTING: An aspect of *Post-Painterly Abstraction* defined by Lawrence Alloway in an exhibition entitled 'Systemic Painting' held at the Guggenheim Museum, New York in 1966. On show were paintings by twenty-eight American artists including Kenneth Noland, Ellsworth Kelly, Larry Poons, Al Held, Frank Stella and Paul Feeley.

A number of Systemic painters employ a given pictorial device—chevron, cross, quatrefoil—again and again in a series of canvases (see also Serial Art). Alloway suggests they might be called 'One Image Art'. These images are subject to continuous transformations of colour, or variations of form, and require to be read in time as well as in space; the viewer must seek 'variety within conspicuous unity'. According to Alloway the sequence of any particular image constitutes a system—defined by the dictionary as 'a whole composed of parts in orderly arrangement according to some scheme or plan'—hence the label

' Systemic '. The category is extended beyond one image painting to include works consisting of a single field of colour, or to groups of such works, and also to paintings based on modules.

The repetitive use of imagery is also common in *Pop Art,* for example Andy Warhol's paintings show close affinities with the Systemic concept. Artists who employ systems make a number of aesthetic decisions before commencing to paint, and for this reason Systemic Painting has been accused of impersonality. Alloway insists, however, that choices made before beginning to paint are no less human or artistic than those made in the course of painting.

See also Modular Art.

L Alloway ' Systemic Painting '—essay in—*Minimal art: a critical anthology* edited by G Battcock (Studio Vista, 1969) 37-60.

354 **SYSTEMS ART:** The word ' system(s) ' has, in recent years, become extremely fashionable among artists and art critics. Usually it is employed in the straightforward dictionary sense—' a whole composed of parts in orderly arrangement according to some scheme or plan '—for example see Systemic Painting and Systems Group.

In 1972 William Feaver, in a review of the John Moores exhibition, Liverpool, described ' system ' sarcastically as ' son of process ' and claimed that it served to ' reconcile figurative and abstract of all kinds: method and chance, reason and instinct, invoke " system " and a life study, a painterly grid, a scrubbed colour field, all interrelate like magic. Fix yourself up with a systematic circle of rules and you can huddle inside reciting jargon non stop to keep the spell binding.'

In other instances the word ' system ' has a more complex connotation: one reflecting the influence of Ludwig Von Bertalanffy—the scientist most closely associated with General Systems Theory—and the phenomenal growth of the science of systems analysis in the years since 1945. Scientists define a system generally as an ' on going process ' and specifically as ' a set of objects, or subsystems, together with relationships between them and their attributes. Since no system occurs without an environment, a characterisation on this basis is incomplete without reference to the total system, *ie*, the system plus its environment.' Systems Art in this latter sense has been discussed by Jack Burnham, an acute observer of the influence of science and technology on modern art. He believes that ' we are moving from an art centred upon objects to one based on systems, thus implying that sculptured objects are in eclipse ' and that ' many artists have chosen to work with the real world including the art system, so that a monitored or documented situation becomes their art '.

See also Conceptual Art, Ecological Art, Media Art, Process Art.

J Burnham ' Real time systems ' *Artforum* 8(1) September 1969 49-55.

J Burnham ' Systems and art ' *Art in society* Summer/Fall 1969.

J Burnham ' Systems aesthetics ' *Artforum* 7(1) September 1968 30-35.

W Feaver 'Art: System ' *The listener* 87(2250) May 11 1972 p 633.

S L Optner *Systems analysis for business and industrial problem solving* (Englewood Cliffs, NJ, Prentice Hall, 1965).

355 SYSTEMS GROUP: An informal association of British artists—Richard Allen, John Ernest, Malcolm Hughes, Colin Jones, Michael Kidner, Peter Lowe, James Moyes, David Saunders, Geoffrey Smedley, Jean Spencer, Jeffrey Steele and Gillian Wise Ciobotaru—whose work continues the Constructivist tradition and reflects an interest in Structuralism and Semiology. These artists exhibit together as a group with the intention of making clear to the public their idea of a modern classical art based on ' order with endless variety '. The members of the Systems Group use systematic procedures, often based on mathematics. They believe that this approach to art is equally applicable to different modes of expression such as sculpture, painting, music and film. The resultant visual art works are totally abstract and geometric in appearance. Since this kind of work is concerned with syntax—' orderly or systematic arrangement of parts or elements '—it has also been called ' Syntactic Art '.

M Hughes ' Notes on the context of " Systems " ' *Studio international* 183(944) May 1972 200-203.

Whitechapel Art Gallery *Systems* (catalogue) (Arts Council of Great Britain, 1972).

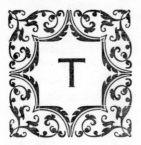

356 TABLEAU: The dictionary defines a Tableau as 'a group of persons and accessories producing a picturesque effect'. The theatrical tradition of 'tableau vivant' dates back to the middle ages.

Representations of such scenes are familiar to us from the displays mounted by shops, museums and waxworks. They usually consist of a shallow stage containing life size figures and real furniture.

In the early 1960's the American sculptor Edward Kienholz began to extend his relief or assemblage constructions from the wall on to the floor. His new works incorporated whole objects, and full size figures. He called them 'tableaux' after the costumed, stop action presentations he had witnessed in rural churches in his youth. Tableau sculpture can be seen as a halfway house between the single, isolated works of tradition and the total enclosures of *Environmental Art*. In general the spectator remains outside a Tableau, preserving the feeling of looking into a picture or through a window into a room. Exceptionally, some of Kienholz's Tableaux are complete rooms that can be entered.

Other sculptors who have made use of the Tableau device: George Segal, Claes Oldenburg, Colin Self, Paul Thek and Duane Hanson.

357 TACHISME: An aspect of *L'Art Informel* that emerged around 1950 and remained fashionable for a decade. Tachist paintings are abstract but non-geometric. Some were produced by throwing or dripping paint on to the canvas (the French noun 'tache' means stain, blot, spot or speckle), others were created by gestural brush strokes. Tachist painters sought fortuitous effects, valuing above all intuition and spontaneity.

The term itself is ascribed by one writer to Pierre Gueguen (1951), while others credit it to Michel Tapié or to Charles Estienne. It was also used about the Nabis painters by Gustave Geffroy in the nineteenth century. Tachisme was the European equivalent of *Action Painting*, but its practitioners were less talented and less adventurous than their American counterparts; consequently Tachist paintings seem too suave and decorative for modern taste. The major artists associated with Tachisme were Pierre Soulages, Wols, Hans Hartung, Jean-Paul Riopelle, George Mathieu, H H Sonderborg, Marcelle Loubchansky and Arnulf Rainer.

See also Drip Painting.

358 **TANTRA ART:** A category of Indian art identified by Ajit Mookerjee, a collecter of Tantra Art and author of two lavish books on the subject. The word ' tantra ' is derived from the Sanskrit ' tan ' (to expand in continuing, unfolding process) and ' tra ' (tool). It refers to a means of extending knowledge. The Tantra religion is a blend of Buddhist, Hindu and Yoga ideas and spans the period fourth century AD to the present day. Therefore, as Robert Fraser points out, Tantra Art provides an insight into an ancient culture whose symbols and myths are alive today. The objects of Tantra Art are various (they include ceremonial vessels, sculptures, icons, paintings, woven fabrics, diagrams, illuminated manuscripts), and have only become known to the general public in the West during the last decade. Philip Rawson stresses, in his introduction to the Hayward Gallery exhibition catalogue, the ecstatic and erotic elements of Tantra Art. As a result of the appeal of these aspects to the drug/Eastern Mysticism/sexual revolution youth cultures of the West, something of a cult has developed. Other groups are attracted by the diagrammatic paintings of Tantra Art, which resemble modern abstract painting.

Arts Council of Great Britain *Tantra* (catalogue) (Hayward Gallery, 1971).

R Fraser ' Tantra revealed ' *Studio international* 182 (939) December 1971 252-253.

O Garrison *Tantra: Yoga of sex* (Academy Editions, 1972).

M Gordon ' Tantra and modern meditative art ' *Art & artists* 3 (10) January 1969 32-34.

A Mookerjee *Tantra Art* (Paris, Ravi Kumar, 1967).

A Mookerjee *Tantra Asana* (Paris, Ravi Kumar, 1971).

P Rawson 'Tantra Art' *Studio international* 176 (906) December 1968 256-259.

F N Souza 'Tantra Art' *Studio international* 172 (884) December 1966 306-311.

V Whiles 'Tantric imagery: affinities with twentieth century abstract art' *Studio international* 181 (931) March 1971 100-107.

359 TEAM 10: An international alliance of young, radical architects who admired each others work and shared certain ideas about the future of architecture. They were called 'Team 10' because they were given the task of preparing a programme for the tenth gathering of the 'Congrès Internationaux d'Architecture Moderne' (CIAM) at Dubrovnik in 1956. During the congress it became evident that a wide divergence of opinion existed between Team 10 and the older founder members of CIAM concerning the purpose of the congress. Team 10 believed the congress had become too large, too diffuse and only produced vague generalisations. The disagreements led to the dissolution of CIAM but the Team 10 continued to meet. The original members of the group were G Candilis, R Gutmann, William G Howell, Alison and Peter Smithson, Aldo Van Eijck and John Voelcker.

R Banham *The New Brutalism: ethic or aesthetic?* (Architectural Press, 1966) 70-72.

A Smithson—editor—'Team Ten Primer 1953-63' *Architectural design* 32 (12) December 1962 559-602.

360 TECHNOLOGICAL ART (also called Tech, or Tek Art, Corporate Art): As most art requires some kind of technology to bring it into being, it could be called 'technological'. But today the word 'technology' signifies a much broader concept than merely the skills of a particular craft: it denotes the techniques, processes and methods of applied science combined with the massive resources of materials, capital and labour deployed by modern industry; 'advanced technology' refers to such fields as lasers, aerospace, plastics, drugs, electronics and computers.

7*

As Jack Burnham describes in his book 'Beyond Modern Sculpture', twentieth century artists have adopted many different attitudes to the growth of technology, ranging from ironic detachment (Marcel Duchamp) to enthusiasm (the Futurists). The Bauhaus encouraged contact with industry so that their designs could be mass produced, but this contact did not extend to fine art. Despite the dependence of *Kinetic Art* on mechanical and electrical engineering, most Kineticists have made only minor use of the huge potential of technology. Only in the middle 1960's was there a significant impetus among artists, especially in the United States, towards collaboration with modern industry; it is the results of such collaboration that are called 'Technological Art'.

The new dialogue between artists and industry was manifested in the development of *Computer Art* and in the founding of a number of new organisations—*Experiments in Art and Technology, Pulsa, Institute for Research in Art and Technology, Artist Placement Group* —dedicated to the task of fostering co-operation between artists and engineers, artists and industrial companies. Fine art magazines also became interested in the topic, for example 'Studio international' began publishing a regular feature on 'Technology and Art' written by Jonathan Benthall. In 1966 Billy Kluver organised in New York a festival of Art and Technology called 'Nine evenings: theatre and engineering'. However, the most elaborate scheme was that organised by Maurice Tuchman, curator of the Los Angeles County Museum. His programme of collaboration between artists and Californian industries was initiated in 1966 and culminated five years later when an exhibition called 'Art and Technology' was held at the L A County Museum in 1971.

Artists such as Claes Oldenburg, Robert Rauschenberg, R B Kitaj, Roy Lichtenstein, Andy Warhol, Tony Smith, Robert Whitman, Newton Harrison and many others selected industrial corporations with whom they worked for periods of many months. The artists did not merely use the facilities of these companies to fabricate preconceived designs, the art works were the result of a genuine participation of both artist and corporation (hence 'Corporate Art') in exploiting the particular technological facilities of the company in question. Tuchman's project was apparently a great success but the exhibition coincided with a change in attitude on the part of artists towards technology, from envy and respect to disillusion and suspicion. Some artists feared that they would become subservient to science and technology as once artists were subservient to the church, while others regarded the industrial modes of production as dehumanised and likely to produce only 'interior design art'. There was also in the 1960's a growing political consciousness among artists. The financial complicity of American industry in the Vietnam war and the pollution of the environment by industry offended their consciences and made the prospects of collaboration with industry, in the near future, unlikely. Many artists, in particular those associated with *Conceptual Art,* are convinced that art essentially does not require elaborate technology in order to yield viable aesthetic results.

J Benthall *Science and technology in art today* (Thames & Hudson 1972).

J Burnham *Beyond Modern Sculpture* . . . (Allen Lane, The Penguin Press, 1968).

N Calas ' Recent developments in Tek Art '—chapter in—*Icons and images of the sixties* by N & E Calas (NY, Dutton 1971) 308-315.

D M Davis 'Art & Technology—the new combine' *Art in America* 56 (1) January/February 1968 28-47.

E Lucie-Smith & others 'Artists in steel towers' *Studio international* 177 (910) April 1969 158-161.

J Livingston ' Some thoughts on "Art and Technology" ' *Studio international* 181(934) June 1971 258-263.

M Tuchman 'An introduction to "Art and Technology" ' *Studio international* 181 (932) April 1971 173-180.

G Youngblood *Expanded Cinema* (NY, Dutton, 1970).

361 **TENSILE ARCHITECTURE:** Structures held rigid by cables or rods under tension. Examples of tensile structures have been known for centuries but only during the 1950's have architects begun to exploit them on a large scale. The chief exponent of Tensile Architecture is the German Frei Otto. He has created vast tents composed of steel netting held under tension, which Peter Cook calls 'membranes' or 'skin architecture'. Otto's work has become known to a world audience because of the structures he designed for the Olympic games held in Munich in 1972.

R Body ' Under Tension ' *Architectural review* 134 (801) November 1963 324-334.

P Cook *Experimental architecture* (Studio Vista, 1970) p 51.

G Minke ' Tensile Structures ' *Architectural design* 38 (4) April 1968 179-182.

362 TENTH STREET TOUCH (after East Tenth Street, New York): A phrase used by Clement Greenberg to describe a characteristic of Abstract Expressionist paintings of the 1950's: the frayed out ripples, streaks and specks of paint left by a loaded brush or stroke of the palette knife.

363 THIS IS TOMORROW (TIT): An influential exhibition, designed by twelve teams consisting of architects, sculptors, painters and photographers, held at the Whitechapel Gallery, London in 1956. Each team created an environmental unit in an attempt to synthesise the different arts. English Constructivist artists such as Anthony Hill and Victor Pasmore participated and also ex-members of the *Independent Group*: Eduardo Paolozzi, Richard Hamilton, John McHale and others. Some displays were composed of images drawn from popular culture and the exhibition included Hamilton's seminal collage 'Just what is it that makes today's homes so different, so appealing?'. This is Tomorrow is chiefly remembered as a landmark in the development of English *Pop Art*.

L Alloway 'The Development of British Pop '—essay in—*Pop Art* by L R Lippard and others (Thames & Hudson, 1966) 26-67.

364 TOWNSCAPE: A campaign mounted by the 'Architectural review' in the immediate post-war years for improved planning of the urban environment, especially concerned with the need to reduce the quantity of street furniture and to improve its disposition. Recent writers on architecture dismiss the Townscape philosophy as picturesque and claim that in concerning itself with the surface appearance of towns it dealt only with the symptoms of urban blight not the root causes.

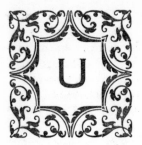

365 ULM: Because of its cumbersome title, 'The Hoch-schule für Gestaltung', this influential German college of design was referred to throughout the design world as 'Ulm', after the town where it was located. The idea for a design school to continue the principles of the Bauhaus was first suggested in 1948 and the school opened in 1955. Its first director was the Swiss Concrete artist Max Bill, who also designed its buildings. In 1956, after policy disputes, Bill was replaced by the Argentine painter Tomas Maldonado. Ulm was noted for its rational approach to design education and its emphasis on scientific and mathematical techniques: Reyner Banham described it as a 'cool training ground for a technocratic élite'. Ulm was closed by the German government in 1968.

D D Egbert *Social radicalism and the arts: Western Europe* (Duckworth, 1970) 700-705.

R Hamilton ' Ulm ' *Design* (126) June 1959 53-57.

366 ULTIMATE PAINTING: The American artist Ad Reinhardt claimed that the paintings he produced between 1960 and his death in 1967 were the 'ultimate abstract paintings '. They consisted of a series of almost identical canvases, square in format (60" × 60"), divided into nine squares and painted in slightly varying shades of grey or black. Reinhardt believed that the possibilities of abstract painting were finite and that his late works represented the culminating point of the easel painting tradition, beyond which it was impossible to proceed.

See also Invisible Painting.

B Rose ' The Black Paintings '—essay in—*Ad Reinhardt: Black Paintings 1951-1967* (catalogue) (NY, Marlborough Gallery, 1970) 16-22.

367 UNDERGROUND ART: This expression refers to art created during the late 1960's by relatively unknown or amateur artists associated with the development of anti-establishment culture, variously described as 'the Underground', 'Counter Culture', 'the Alternative Society', 'the Youth Culture'.

Such art usually consists of graphics such as posters, cartoons, illustrations and magazine layouts which are featured in Underground press publications such as 'Oz', 'Ink', 'Friendz', 'It', etc. Poster artists frequently exploit *Op Art* effects and simulate the drug delirium of *Psychedelic Art*; magazine illustrators draw on the same sources and are also influenced by French Symbolist painting, Art Nouveau and Surrealism. Underground graphics are often called 'freaky' because they delight in nasty, grotesque and pornographic subject content; obscenity and violence are employed for radical political and social reasons. New printing processes—offset lithography and the IBM type setting machine—enable layout designers to create unusual effects by overprinting and by the superimposition of several colours.

Underground artists who have become known to the overground world include Michael English, Martin Sharp, Mike McInnerrey and Mal Dean. Many Underground artists, especially in the United States, imitate the comic strip narrative form; Robert Crumb, Ron Cobb, Victor Moscoso and S Clay Wilson have all become internationally famous for their humour and graphic skill.

Underground art can be criticised on the grounds of technical crudity and eclecticism but it does have an uninhibited, raw and direct character that provides a welcome contrast to the austerity of *Minimal Art* and *Conceptual Art*.

See also Alternative Architecture, Visionary Art.

T Albright 'Cartoon visions on Muni walls' *Rolling stone* (95) November 11 1971 p 10.

G Keen and M La Rue—editors—*Underground graphics* (Academy, 1970).

368 URBAN GUERRILLA ARCHITECTURE: A demand by HIM—Herbert Ilya Meyer—for direct political action in architecture to solve housing problems in cities by the use of all available land and waste and surplus materials.

H I Meyer 'Viewpoint: thoughts on Urban Guerrilla Architecture ...' *AAQ* 4 (1) January/March 1972 58-59.

369 USCO (Us Company): An American artists collective, founded in 1963 by Steve Durkee, Gerd Stern and Michael Callahan, located in an abandoned church at Garnerville, New York. Members of USCO include poets, film makers, engineers and artists; the composition of the group continually changes. USCO is committed to the multi-media approach to art, and has produced *Kinetic Art* environments, *Happenings* (called ' Be Ins ') and a multimedia discotheque. Recently they established, in conjunction with a number of behavioural scientists from Harvard University, an organisation called the ' Intermedia Systems Corporation '.

See also Inter-Media.

R Kostelanetz *The Theatre of Mixed Means* (Pitman, 1970) 243-271.

R E L Masters and others *Psychedelic Art* (Weidenfeld and Nicolson, 1968).

370 UTOPIAN ARCHITECTURE (also called Fantastic Architecture, Visionary Architecture): The constraints of everyday architecture are legion—the needs of clients, budgets, materials, building and planning regulations, etc. Therefore it is not surprising that many architects produce designs, in the form of drawings or models, for Utopian projects that transcend mundane limitations; see for example Conceptual Architecture, Absolute Architecture, Imaginary Architecture, Aerial Architecture, Chemical Architecture, Megastructures. Projects such as these are unlikely ever to be constructed, at least in the foreseeable future, although occasionally some Utopian projects are realised on a small scale, temporary basis at international expositions.

The book ' Fantastic Architecture ', first published in Germany in 1960, provides a corrective to the partial view of modern architecture as a logical and rational development by illustrating the strange forms of Antonio Gaudi, the primitive structures of Ferdinand Cheval and Simone Rodilla, and the expressionistic elements in modern architecture. It identifies Bruno Taut, Hermann Finsterlin and Paul Scheerbart as the main fantasy architects and the 1920's as the chief era of such dreaming. Frank Lloyd Wright also produced extreme designs, such as his mile high office tower, and Buckminster Fuller devised a plan to enclose the whole earth in a spherical, geodesic structure.

To dream of Utopian solutions enables architects to develop technology, materials and methods far beyond their current limits, and their conclusions may possibly help to precipitate change. However, as Peter Cook points out, the Utopian label can be a disadvantage: ' timid pragmatists can dismiss any experiment or any new concept as "utopian", and thereby remove it from the discussion of practical issues '. It can also be argued that vast Utopian schemes are a sign of megalomania in the architectural profession: having always seen themselves as ' universal men ', architects tend to believe they know best regardless of the real needs of the people.

U Conrads & H G Sprlich *Fantastic Architecture* (Architectural Press, 1968).

P Cook *Experimental architecture* (Studio Vista, 1970) p 28.

M Nicoletti ' Flash Gordon and the twentieth century utopia ' *Architectural review* 140 (834) August 1966 87-91.

' Opinion: Visionary architecture at the Museum of Modern Art, New York ' *Architectural design* 31 (5) May 1961 181-182.

W Vostell & D Higgins *Fantastic Architecture* (NY, Something Else Press, 1969).

371 UTOPIE GROUP: A French experimental architectural group formed in 1967, concerned with the social utility of architecture, the notion of expendability and the use of pneumatic structures. The members of Utopie are J Aubert, J P Jungmann, A Stinco and H Tonka.

J Aubert and others ' Utopie ' *Architectural design* 38 (6) June 1968 p 255.

' La Pneumatique ' *Architectural design* 38 (6) June 1968 273-277.

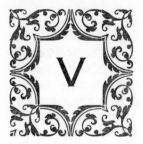

V

372 VAKUME: An acronym standing for 'Visual Audio-Kinetic Unit: Multiples and Environments', a British multi-media workshop group making use of combinations of light, sound, colour and movement to create relaxation/dream/meditation environments. Members include Patrick Carpenter, Brian Browning, June Jackson and Linda Jones.

J Scott 'Art: Vakume 6' *New scientist* January 27 1972 227-228.

373 VERWISCHUNG: A German word meaning 'to obliterate', 'to efface'. Wolf Vostell, an artist associated with the avant garde group *Fluxus,* uses Verwischung to describe a *Destructive Art* technique.

See also Décollage.

374 VIDEO ART also called TV Art): The Latin word 'video', meaning 'I see', was used in the United States during the 1950's to refer to television. Technological developments in the field of television hardware in the second half of the 1960's have made it possible for private individuals, in this context fine artists, to afford portable video equipment: a camera linked to a video tape recording machine (images are stored on magnetic tape) plus a television monitor screen. This system enables tape cassettes to be produced and sold for showing on television sets in the home. These tapes can be marketed in the same way as gramophone records and sound tape recordings. The significance of video tape is that it breaks the monopoly of television previously held by large broadcasting companies. Enthusiasts in the United States have founded a magazine called 'Radical software' to publicise the revolutionary potential of video.

The video system has been described as the 'mirror machine' or 'seeing yourself on TV' because, by training the camera on oneself it is possible to watch oneself on the television monitor. This characteristic of video allows precise artistic control. Once something has been recorded it can be instantly played back and if unsatisfactory the tape can be wiped clean and the item re-recorded. Many artists have become intrigued by the possibilities of video: Nam June Paik, Keith Sonnier, William Wegman, Klaus Rinke, Joseph Beuys, Stana Vasulka, Bruce Nauman, Andy Warhol, Les Levine and Stan Vanderbeek. A number of these artists are concerned with *Performance Art, Process Art* and *Body Art,* forms that are transitory by nature. Thus videotape enables such activities to be recorded for presentation in museums and galleries or on commercial broadcasting stations. Tapes can also be sold to private collectors; in Germany Gerry Schum has established a 'Videogalerie' to market tapes.

Douglas Davis, in an analysis of the qualities of Video, claims 'vibrant nervous colour' as one new asset. He also believes that 'at its aesthetic core video is art dematerialised'.

See Conceptual Art.

D Davis 'Video Obscura' *Artforum* 10 (8) April 1972 64-71.

J S Margolies ' TV—the next medium' *Art in America* 57 (5) September/October 1969 48-55.

G Youngblood *Expanded cinema* (NY, Dutton, 1970) 257-344.

375 **VISIONARY ART:** According to Thomas Albright the mystical, symbolic, and religious undercurrents of early *Psychedelic Art* in San Francisco have developed into a new movement which he calls 'Visionary Art'. The paintings and drawings of the new movement are characterised by the use of vivid colours, by a graphic sensibility, and emphasis on subject content. Its sources are Surrealism, oriental religions (Zen, Yoga, Sufism), the occult, and the drug experience. Albright identifies at least a dozen artists as belonging to the Visionary Art movement but none has yet achieved international recognition.

T Albright ' Visuals ' Part I *Rolling stone* (88) August 5 1971 34-35.

T Albright ' Visuals ' Part II *Rolling stone* (89) August 19 1971 34-37.

T Albright ' Visuals ' Part III *Rolling stone* (91) September 16 1971 40-42.

376 VISUAL COMMUNICATION: In recent years many colleges of art and design in Great Britain and Europe have introduced courses concerned with Visual Communication, covering such topics as advertising, television, photograhy, films, comics, illustrated magazines, and typography, in addition to the traditional disciplines of drawing, painting and lettering. As the editors of 'Art without boundaries' point out, the term ' Visual Communication ' is sometimes used as a substitute for ' Graphic Design ' (which in turn was coined to replace ' Commercial Art ').

H E Ehmer—editor—*Visuelle Kommunikation* (Cologne, Dumont, 1972).

G Wood & others—editors—*Art without boundaries 1950-1970* (Thames & Hudson, 1972).

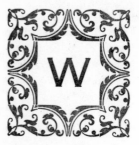

377 WASHINGTON COLOUR SCHOOL:

Two Washington painters noted for their emphatic use of colour—Morris Louis and Kenneth Noland—achieved international recognition in the late 1950's and as a result drew attention to Washington DC as an art centre. The colour school tradition established by Noland and Louis was continued by several other Washington artists: Gene Davis, Tom Downing, Howard Mehring and Paul Reed. Their canvases are usually extremely large, totally abstract and immaculately painted. However, not all critics have succumbed to their charm, some finding them ' gutless ' and describing them as ' cosmetic abstractions '.

See also Stain Painting, Colour-Field Painting, Hard-Edge Painting.

L J Ahlander ' The emerging art of Washington ' *Art international* 6(9) November 25 1962 30-33.

E Stevens ' The Washington Color Painters ' *Arts magazine* November 1965 30-33.

378 WEST COAST SCHOOL (also called the Pacific School): The major art centres of the United

States are located on the Eastern and Western seaboards of the continent. Since 1945 many artists have settled in the West Coast or have become internationally known because of movements originating there. Art has flourished in San Francisco, in Los Angeles, and to a lesser extent in Seattle. Periodically art critics publish articles posing the question ' is there a West Coast School?' (the answer is usually ' no but . . .').

The most important West Coast artists and movements are as follows: Mark Tobey and Morris Graves (two artists who lived in Seattle and were influenced by Oriental Art—the East has close contacts with the Western states of the USA); *Bay Area Figuration; Hard-Edge Painting; Pop Art* (represented by the artists Mel Ramos, Wayne

Thiebaud and Ed Ruscha); Edward Kienholz (the creator of *Tableau* who moved to Los Angeles in 1953 and produced many of his best assemblages there).

In recent years Los Angeles has overtaken San Francisco as the leading art centre and is the home of the *Finish Fetish* cult. Los Angeles art epitomises the virtues of the West Coast ' School ': variety, vitality, an openness to new ideas, experimentation and eccentricity, craftsmanship, freedom from too much emphasis on the past, a tolerance towards disparate styles and extreme aesthetic ideas.

See also The Los Angeles Fine Art Squad, Los Angeles Provos, Custom Painting, Funk Art, Psychedelic Art, Visionary Art.

' California 70 ' *Arts magazine* 44(8) Summer 1970.

Eleven Los Angeles artists (Hayward Gallery, 1971).

BIBLIOGRAPHICAL NOTE

The 1970 edition of LOMA—*Literature on Modern Art* (Lund Humphries, 1972)—an annual bibliography compiled by Alexander Davis, lists approximately 5,000 items: exhibition catalogues, periodical articles and books. As LOMA covers the period from Impressionism to the present day, at least half these items, at a rough estimate, relate to art before 1945 and thus fall outside the scope of this glossary. However, if one assumes a figure of 2,000 items per year for twenty seven years the total literature on art since 1945 amounts to 54,000 items; since LOMA does not cover architecture several thousand more should be added (needless to say I have not read anywhere near this total). In view of this mass of literature, it is not possible to provide a complete bibliography. Articles and books consulted in the preparation of this glossary are listed beneath each entry; these references are selective and for further information readers are advised to search 'Art Index ', LOMA (first issued in 1969) and for architecture the ' RIBA Annual Index of Periodical Articles '. Many entries on art are also to be found in the ' British Humanities Index '. Unfortunately the subject headings are different from index to index, but those in LOMA are, in most cases, the same as in this glossary.

Whenever possible I have listed the major artists associated with each art movement and readers should find it a comparatively simple task to trace further details about named individuals via the many monographs on artists, biographical dictionaries of artists and library catalogues.

In view of the above remarks, the following bibliography is limited to books and selected articles that provide general or international surveys of the post-war period.

ART

H H Arnason *A history of modern art* (Thames & Hudson, 1969).

M Brion & others *Art since 1945* (Thames & Hudson, 1958).

W Grohmann—editor—*Art of our time: painting and sculture throughout the world* (Thames & Hudson, 1966).

W Haftmann & others *Abstract art since 1945* (Thames & Hudson 1971).

J P Hodin & others *Figurative art since 1945* (Thames & Hudson, 1971).

U Kultermann *The new painting* (Pall Mall, 1969).

U Kultermann *The new sculpture* (Pall Mall, 1968).

U Kultermann *Art-Events and Happenings* (Mathews Miller Dunbar, 1971).

E Lucie-Smith *Movements in art since 1945* (Thames & Hudson, 1969).

A Pelligrini *New tendencies in art* (NY, Crown, 1966).

N Ponente *Modern painting: contemporary trends* (Geneva, Skira, 1960).

M Ragon *Vingt cinq ans d'art vivant . . .* (Paris, Casterman, 1969).

H Rosenberg *The de-definition of art: Action Art to Pop to Earthworks* (Secker & Warburg, 1972).

G Woods & others—editors—*Art without boundaries 1950-70* (Thames & Hudson, 1972).

ARCHITECTURE AND DESIGN

'Anniversary issue: a visual record of 21 years, 1949-1970' *Design* (253) January 1970.

R Banham ' Design by choice, 1951-1961: an alphabetical chronicle of landmarks and influences' *Architectural review* 130(773) July 1961 43-48.

R Banham ' Revenge of the picturesque: English architectural polemics 1945-1965'—essay in—*Concerning architecture* edited by John Summerson (Allen Lane, The Penguin Press, 1968).

L Benevolo *History of modern architecture* 2 vols (Routledge, 1971).

J Burns *Arthropods: new design futures* (NY, Praeger, 1972).
P Cook *Experimental architecture* (Studio Vista, 1970).
J Dahinden *Urban structures for the future* (Pall Mall, 1972).
A Ferebee *A history of design from the Victorian era* . . . (NY, Van Nostrand Reinhold, 1970).
A Jackson *The politics of architecture* . . . (Architectural Press, 1970).
J Jacobus *Twentieth century architecture: the middle years 1940-65* (Thames & Hudson, 1966).
C Jencks *Architecture 2000: predictions and methods* (Studio Vista, 1971).
J Joedicke *Architecture since 1945* (Pall Mall, 1969).
F MacCarthy *All things bright and beautiful* . . . (Allen & Unwin, 1972).
W Pehnt—editor—*Encyclopedia of modern architecture* (Thames & Hudson, 1963).

GLOSSARIES

J N Barron *Language of painting: an informal dictionary* (NY, World Publishing Co, 1967).
' Dizionario dei nuovi termini d'arte ' *Casa vogue* (14) May/June 1972 122-123.
M de Molina *Terminos de arte contemporaneo* (Columbia, Bienal de Arte Coltejer III, 1972).
Phaidon dictionary of twentieth-century art (Phaidon, 1973).

INDEX

This index contains names of artists, critics and institutions, titles of exhibitions, and subjects. Numbers refer to the alphabetical entries not to pages. Numbers in italics indicate a main entry in the glossary.